Door to
in 81 Days

Roger Gill

Seven Arches
Publishing

Published in 2019
By Seven Arches Publishing
The Flat, New Inn Farm Beckley, Oxford, OX3 9TY
www.sevenarchespublishing.co.uk

A catalogue record for this book is available from the British Library.

The author gained permission for identification from all those people who
could be recognised by his descriptions or were named. He took care to represent places and organisations accurately.

Cover design and typesetting by Alan McGlynn.

Printed in Great Britain.

ISBN 978-0-9935985-6-2

For Kate, Laura, Alice and Max

Good reading

Roger

England

1: News at Ten

I am a European with one foot in the Pennines and the other in the Apennines.

Every summer since 2007, we have driven from Hebden Bridge in England to our small holiday town house in Santa Vittoria in Matenano, Italy. More than 2000ft up in the Sibillini Mountains, in a region known as Le Marche – between the Apennine Mountains of central Italy and the Adriatic Sea – this remarkable town keeps a lookout over the whole region.

Fortunately, Santa Vittoria has not yet been too close to the epicentre of a strong earthquake despite being in a region where people are always afraid, always ready for the worst. The magnificent beauty of the town and its surroundings counterbalances what terror awaits. This place really is an example of the 'bel paese.' For six weeks, every year in the summer, we drive from an apartment in a millstone-grit converted dye works, in a former fustian mill town in England's Calder Valley, to the sand-coloured palazzos, cobbled streets and cool colonnades of middle Italy.

When looking for something to read on one of these journeys, I discovered a paperback on my bookshelves that had somehow remained hidden, unread, for years. 'A Time of Gifts' by Patrick Leigh Fermor (PLF) is the autobiographical account of his walk from London to Constantinople in 1933, at the age of 18. He eventually wrote two more books about his travels along this route. All three books, I discovered, are gems for the armchair traveller.

One night, with that well-thumbed book flopped open on my knee, I was watching the ITV News at Ten. Its rousing title music was accompanied by a spectacular aerial image of Western Europe at night-time with its city lights on full beam, shining out of a dark green background. Glancing at the television screen, my eye scanned a diagonal line from the UK to the foot of Italy. Immediately, I imagined PLF walking across that baize landscape, turning left near Stuttgart and following the River Danube past Budapest. It would be laughable, I said out loud, that anyone of my age and physical condition could take on a challenge such as that. Anyway, whatever I might have been dreaming about, my life was about to suffer an earthquake of its own.

2: Three Stents

On Thursday 19 August 2010, at the age of 63, my heart was on the verge of packing up.

Walking 100 yards without stopping several times was impossible. It was difficult for me to do the most basic of things like walk to the pub. That day, we were going to celebrate my daughter's A Level results. On the way along the canal side, I needed to sit down, to catch my breath, on lock gates, walls or benches before we could toast her success.

This faltering had been building up slowly over the summer holiday, while we were in Italy. First my shoulders ached when walking on the hills, and then I began to need a rest before walking home after a meal. I consulted my doctor from abroad and was told to take it easy and book an appointment for when I returned to England.

By the time the A Level results hit the mat I was feeling defeated; my wife and daughter looked on, nervously.

The person who had taken part in London marathons, a long-distance sponsored cycling event from Saint Petersburg to Moscow, and the European South Downs 80-Mile Cross Country Challenge seemed like someone else, masquerading as me. Had I really completed them in the years between 1983 and 1998?

I was lucky not to have a heart attack in the interim. On 19 October

2010, I was lying on an operating table with the surgeon probing around in my heart in an attempt to free a right artery blocked by plaque. He told me, sounding like a drain specialist, that he would spend up to an hour trying to unblock it. If that did not work he would go straight to open-heart surgery to make a bypass. He said that the theatre was double-booked for both procedures, should they be necessary. For that, I signed on the dotted line.

From that moment on, my life was in the hands of an incredibly skilful surgeon who was going to wiggle a wire, which had been inserted into an artery in my groin, to help my blood flow normally again. With only a grainy black and white image on the screen to act as a guide, he edged, by the millimetre, towards the blockage before he began to prod.

I could see the whole procedure on the screen beside the operating table. The seconds were ticking away. Incredibly, he breached the blockage in less than two minutes. As the probe came out the other side, I saw the blood flood through my heart in a massive gush. What was, until a moment before, a rivulet the breadth of a needle now ran like a torrent.

I felt a surge of energy after having been saved. The image of an unstoppable deluge filled my mind. I decided, from that moment on, that I was going to respond to life with the same kind of gush. I imagined the endless possibilities of a life of action. I had a momentary conviction, a sublime feeling, that I could do anything or go anywhere.

Having used the thin thread of wire to pass two stents up to the now unblocked artery, the surgeon said: 'I could put another one in if you like; I'm guessing that you don't want to come back in a year's time to have the third inserted?' Any irrational worries about feeling like a clunky transformer vanished instantly, as I nodded and mouthed my tearful permission.

3: William Albert Gill and the Plan

Unwittingly, my father had started all this in motion in 1950. William Albert Gill died when I was three and three quarters. I have no real recollection of him, just some disjointed memories told to me or scattered around in photographs, the books and magazines he read, and artefacts such as his hand-carved scout's woggle. He died at the age of 41 of, as my Mum told me, 'a weak heart' caused by a severe bout of pneumonia.

An adventurer at heart, he led a Rover Scout Troup in Lambeth, London, with the occasional rural bivouacking weekend thrown in and, according to the story passed down to me, on one of these camps a young man had forgotten his groundsheet. William lent him his. He slept that night on the bare, wet ground and caught pneumonia.

Now I know – because this was part of the ongoing chat with the surgeon as he prodded – that both my father and I suffered from hereditary heart disease and the pneumonia link was just part of a diversionary story because in 1950 very little could be done for anyone with an unrelenting build-up of plaque in the arteries.

In fact, as I was told in a tone that was meant to generalise the blow: 'heart disease is one of the more common gifts a father can pass onto his son.' In my case, it was a poisoned chalice from a man I was just beginning to know. I remember that, at the time, kindly neighbours told me not to worry because 'your Dad has gone to live with Jesus.' As a boy of three, that news gave me an instant dislike of the man called Jesus. I wanted my Dad with me, not waltzing off to live with someone else.

From 2010, thanks to our joint history of an active life reduced to limping between places to perch for breath, the man who had left me alone at the age of three, and whom I never forgave for giving up his groundsheet, became a real person in my mind, not just an absent parent. Finally, I reconciled myself to the fact that he had no choice in leaving me. He became my soul mate and my inspiration for making his unfulfilled dreams of adventure a reality.

It is impossible for me to pinpoint the exact day when I actually announced to myself that I was going to walk from my front door in England to my front door in Italy. It just popped up as a fully formed idea. I would follow Patrick's route to the Black Forest and then branch out on my own over the Alps into Italy. When I finally voiced it out loud, Kate, my wife declared: 'I always suspected it, but this proves that you are mad.' But straight afterwards we just laughed nervously in amazed confusion at the prospect.

4: A Reprieve

'An Adventure in Arabia' by W.B. Seabrook (published 1927) is part of my Dad's heritage: one of William's books that fascinated me from an early age. This is Seabrook's account of his travels, in 1924, among Bedouins, Druses, Whirling Dervishes and Yezidee Devil Worshipers. How could a teenager like William, born in 1909, from one of the very poorest parts of Lambeth in London, with such a strong taste for adventure, not be drawn to read such a book?

Increasingly, as I grew up, it grabbed me too. Now I know, through Internet searches, that Seabrook was a far more complex character than William ever imagined. Seabrook experimented in witchcraft and voodoo, coupled with a tendency towards sadism and alcoholism. A later book of his called, 'The Magic Island' is credited with introducing the idea of zombies into popular culture.

Instead of being an armchair adventurer, dreaming of Arabia, I was going to do something bolder and more real to give thanks for being alive: not following in the short-lived footsteps of my father. He could be my soul's companion, but I was going to lead the way for both of us.

Who knows how many grandfathers, great grandfathers and great, greats going back generations in my family had suffered the same fate: had their dreams been shattered or cut short by faulty hearts? I would never know but, beyond William, I imagined a whole host of family members who would want to join me in some big adventure.

As I lay in my hospital bed recovering from the stent operation, holding a pad firmly into my groin to stop the blood seeping out from the probe's hole, I felt too tearful to even think about the adventure. While lying there, I spent my time texting everyone I could think of to say that I had survived and welling up every time I heard the whoosh of the text leaving my phone.

It took me a few days to walk any distance because the wound needed to heal completely, but within a couple of weeks I was walking and jogging again. When I went back to see the surgeon for a three-month check-up, he discharged me. He said: 'you are one of the lucky ones. You could have died at any stage before the operation but now the stents appear to be working well.'

I asked how I would know whether they were continuing to work and if there were limits on my physical exertions? I was told to tune into what my body was telling me. If I felt that I was losing momentum or had any unusual pains, I needed to get them checked. If not, I was free to do anything I wanted to do.

I received this news with a mixture of elation and foreboding: elation because I wanted to waste no time in planning an adventure and foreboding because becoming aware of what my body was telling me was a terrifying prospect. I began to worry, irrationally, that at any moment the stents would become dislodged and float around or that they might just clog up.

I was worried that I would get sucked into monitoring my body with the same kind of despondent intensity with which, as a 'latchkey kid', I had listened to the ticking of the mantelpiece clock while waiting for my Mum to come home from work.

Calming down from these negative feelings, I vowed always to eat a sensible diet and take regular exercise. I kept telling myself that if I could listen to my body without getting paranoid, I could do anything. I still had to work for six more years but that would give me time to get fit, and save, for what I wanted to do once I retired.

5: Training for 1200 miles

My dream of doing something on a grand scale like Patrick Leigh Fermor never deserted me, but how could I think of a long journey like that unless I had tested my abilities on a shorter route? So, I planned to walk the Pennine Way, one of the first modern, long-distance footpaths in England, which winds its way from Edale, near Sheffield, to Kirk Yetholm, in Scotland just one mile from the English border.

Officially opened in April 1965, it is a mere 275 miles in length, but I discovered it is one of the hardest UK walks imaginable. With its unpredictable weather conditions, peat bogs and bleak hilltops, it can sap your strength in ways I never thought possible. Brilliant training for what I envisaged would be the bogs and bleak hilltops of retirement.

In September 2014, it took me 17 days to finish the Pennine Way, just a year before I was to retire the following July. When you reach the Border Hotel in Kirk Yetholm they give you a certificate and a free pint of beer. It was while I savoured the beer that I finally felt able to allow my mind to plan an even more demanding adventure.

On 5 July 2015, two days after I retired, we drove to Italy to explore the route that I might take. We only stopped briefly in major places so as not to spoil the actual event, but it was enough to know that Switzerland was out of the question because of the cost of cafes and accommodation. I would board an overnight ferry at Hull, which would take me to the Hook of Holland right where Patrick had landed. My continental journey would start from there; ignoring the fact that PLF caught the train to Rotterdam and began his walk from the city centre.

A chimney sweep helped me to make the final choice about my way over the Alps.

Between Ulm and Augsburg, in early 1934, Patrick met a sweep at the start of his journeyman year. This involved walking from place to place, getting a wide variety of work experience in order to finish his apprenticeship. It was a tradition in Germany for various apprentices to undertake a journeyman year to broaden their experiences. Firms conducting the same trade in Germany and neighbouring countries were obliged to give work to these itinerants. This particular sweep had chosen to walk from Germany to Florence over the Alps via the ancient city of Trento in Italy. He and Patrick struck up a friendship and for days, after waving goodbye to each other, Patrick wondered whether he had chosen the correct destination. Would Florence have been a better bet? Obviously for him, Constantinople beckoned more strongly.

So, I planned that after crossing the Black Forest, I would head for Trento in Italy having walked over the Austrian Alps. I estimated that if I left at the end of April, I would get to Austria sometime in June when the sun would have melted the snow.

Everyone I spoke to picked up these sketchy ideas about dates. The most common question that I encountered was: 'When are you leaving and when do you hope to arrive at your destination?' It was as if people could not feel comfortable with discussing my project unless they could see the limits of it. They needed some dates: a boundary for their imagination to work within. My project was born with a birthday of 21 April accompanied by a predicted end of 10 July. It had been given a life.

On my 69th Birthday, on 11 February 2016, I began a 10-week programme of fitness training published by The British Heart Foundation. It was designed as a preparation for a multi-day hike. They omitted to define just how many days were implied by the term 'multi-day', but the plan excited me, so I made it my schedule. Following this, I walked, swam and ran my way through the next 70 days – getting fitter by the week. With four days to go, on 17 April, I walked 20 miles in one day for the first time. Then I exercised gently on the run-up to the leaving day.

That all sounds quite scheduled, but inside I was churning with anxiety about the enormous challenge upon which I was about to embark: I was terrified, but in an imperceptible way. A serene swan but paddling frantically beneath the surface – very hard to live with as my mood changed with every cloud of misgiving that floated over me. Lucky really that I could pack and re-pack my rucksack, program my satellite navigation system, lay out my complete kit of Rohan walking clothes and brand new Salewa boots, pose for photographs for the Yorkshire Post, and print off and post my proxy vote form for the EU Referendum – all of which kept me busy in the last few days.

Kate, and my daughters Alice and Laura plus Alice's partner Max all helped to keep me sane, on track and well-focused by making me concentrate on the breakfast leaving party planned for 8am on 21 April, and the funds coming in for the two charities – suggested by Alice and Laura – for which I had decided to walk: The British Kidney Patients' Association and Creating Adventures for Adults with Complex Learning Difficulties.

6: Muggers

Max climbed up the inside of chimneys for a living. There is certainly nothing Victorian about that. Beyond being Alice's partner and a very well qualified rope-access specialist, he helps to keep the nation's lights on by making sure that the power station chimneys are free of soot and nesting birds. That is when he is not on oil rigs making every-thing safe for the workers there.

I had this improbable, but romantic, notion that he might pop his head out of one of these chimneys near Leeds at the top of the M1 and would be able to see me walking past on my way to Hull.

When his workmates heard that I intended to walk from our apart-ment in Hebden Bridge in West Yorkshire to our small holiday house in Santa Vittoria, in Italy, they sniggered, saying that it would be a miracle for me to get to Hull without being mugged. They believed that only the intrepid or foolhardy would attempt such a trek owing to the urban cutpurses and vagabonds that abound in that neck of the woods.

So, when I turned, unharmed, into the precinct of the Hull Ferry Port, I breathed a sigh of relief to know that I had defied their gloom-laden predictions and won a bet that was never placed. I gazed into the distance, hoping to catch a glimpse of the ferry that would take me to The Hook of Holland. It was there, like a cardboard cut-out on the horizon.

I was thinking simultaneously about my throbbingly sore blisters, the forlorn-looking families who I had just seen coming out of Hull Prison after Sunday visiting and that, having already covered the first 89 miles, I would not see England again until the end of August, a whole season away.

Then I caught sight of a gang of teenage boys who seemed to ma-terialise straight out of a documentary about urban youth and the loss of innocence. Their leader, with a long crowbar, was attempting to prise open a massive padlock. The others were standing around, with open mouths. Dressed in regulation grey, stained tracksuit bottoms, they looked up in a flash like a herd of startled wildebeests as I arrived on their patch.

The chances of a walker disturbing them must have been quite slim. Even I was mesmerised by the steady stream of cars speeding past containing people who would not have taken time to observe this grazing herd as they headed towards the passport barrier and loading ramps.

They circled me – in silence to begin with – and I started to feel that my winning bet with the cooling-tower boys was going up in a puff of smoke. Then the one wielding the crowbar said in a slightly aggressive and mocking tone: 'Where are you going?'

'To Italy,' I replied, feeling that I was teleported back to my first day at a state boarding school when I was grilled by older boys about who I was and could only answer in snatches between croaks from my breaking voice.

'Yes, but how are you getting there?' Another of the gang quizzed as they all took a step closer.

'Walking.' I said, 'I'm walking to Italy from Hebden Bridge, near Halifax.'

'Nah, you can't be,' a couple of the herd chorused, looking round for a parked car or bus or anything that fitted their view that I was lying. 'How are you going to do that?'

What I said next could easily have inflamed the encounter because I realised in that instant that it sounded like I was stating the blindingly obvious only to mock their dumb disbelief.

'Well, you see these feet?' I was beginning to feel that if I didn't get moving soon they might snap out of their zombie-like stares and relieve me of my phone and money.

'When I get off the ferry in Holland I am going to put one foot in front of the other and keep doing that until I get there.'

It suddenly dawned on me that this simple set of actions summed up the whole enterprise, but for them it seemed nothing more that the ramblings of a crazy old man.

They started to back away and the crowbar kid rallied them in their slightly bewildered retreat by saying: 'Nah, leave him he's mad.'

In a second, they were marching towards the main road showing me the back of their fatigues while I turned and headed towards the looming ferry that was to deposit me in Holland, my second country, the next morning. Never had I felt so glad to be declared crazy.

With my mobile phone and money still in my possession, I was back on course although I hadn't a clue how I was going to survive with multiple blisters on the soles of my feet that were making my exit from Britain feel more like a medieval penance than an intrepid hike across Europe.

7: Leaving Home

This was the end of the fourth day and the leaving breakfast party on the canal side in Hebden Bridge was still flickering in my memory as I plodded towards the ferry, my cabin and sleep. A band of friends had come to wish me well, take photographs and eat bacon sandwiches in the emerging sunshine of a late April morning in the Calder Valley.

Kate gave me a tearful kiss to a ribald shout of 'steady on there!' Immediately a bluff Yorkshire response rolled along the towpath: 'Well she might never see him again,' which momentarily stunned me and the well-wishers into a reflection of the enormity of the undertaking being celebrated.

Having waved goodbye, posed for photographs by the lock and trotted over the bridge out of sight, the dignity of my departure got lost in the early morning mist over the canal. Disorientated, I had to rush back to my family and friends – who were already getting on with their lives without me – to collect my packed lunch. As I set out for the second time, I looked really homespun and not the rugged explorer of my dreams. I had a heavy rucksack perched high on my back but was compromised by carrying a low-grade plastic shopping bag containing my sandwiches in my non-walking-pole hand.

Leaving aside the sandwich incident, the camaraderie and tenderness of the farewell, the promise from the rising sun, and the stabbing emotions of leaving home would be the litmus papers with which I could compare every new experience in the next three months.

Having just escaped the clutches of a local band of dervishes, my own rather grey-flannelled version of a Seabrook escapade, I walked up the gangway into The Pride of Hull, proud to be the only pedestrian on board and headed for my cabin for a snooze before dinner.

The plan of a sleep was rather short-lived owing to the constant bombardment of helpful announcements from a ceiling speaker telling me about such things as the opening time of the shops and the cast list of the cabaret evening to come. My cabin had a porthole with a view of the cars still queuing to board across to my walking route from the main road, with the wildebeests just tucked out of sight.

I found myself in the throes of reflection, tempted to abandon ship and head for home or perhaps plough on and see how far I could get. Could I claim that I had given it a good shot and that, for someone my age, midway into Germany to somewhere like Cologne, was in fact a success?

The trouble was that my peardrop-sized blisters on the heels of both feet had reduced my walking style to an awkward shuffle, despite all my roadside treatments of Second Skin and plasters. I walked with a gait more suited to a pyjama-clad patient allowed out of bed for the first time after an operation and attempting to get to the toilet without calling the nurse.

I gingerly made my way up to the duty free shop and begged for an empty cardboard box that I squirreled back to my cabin as fast as I could and there I cut out two insoles for my very lightweight slippers. The kind of shoes which have rubberized nail heads under your feet to provide a massage as you walk along, but in my case they were aggravating my blisters with a vengeance – it was as if two playground bullies were pummelling my feet to get me to agree to steal a flickknife for them.

Sometime later, dressed in limited civvies of a tee shirt, warm top, feather-light trousers and really awful socks that rode under my heel every three strides, causing me to stop continually to hitch them up, I hobbled to Starbucks with my cardboard innersoles curbing my misery to treat myself to a pie and chips chased down with a cappuccino. While I ate, I gazed out at the smooth lines of a darkening coastline broken occasionally by the towers and chimneys of a distant oil refinery.

As I was shuffling back to my room I heard my name called out from behind me: 'Roger – is that you?' I whipped round to see a most cheerful looking man with a full red beard talking into his mobile and grinning at me. For a moment, I thought he was addressing another Roger further down the corridor, but then I heard him say to his caller that he had found me and that he was ringing off presumably so that he could get to me before I disappeared into the bowels of the ship.

Confused, I momentarily forgot my blisters and waited in anticipation for this mysterious encounter to unfold. It transpired that this man was Damian and that his partner worked as a teaching assistant at a school in Rochdale that I had visited as a consultant and she had found out that he and I might be on the same ferry that night. Having been told of my journey, he was instructed to look out for an intrepid retiree, with a hitherto red beard, fast fading to grey, who looked like he might be off on a long walk. Not easy really with only about 1300 people on board.

As we were ensconced in the bar alongside his team of factory sprinkler fitters, I learned that he was just about to give up his somewhat forlorn hunt when he spotted me emerging from Starbucks. The phone call was to check on my description before the final pounce. Drinking a very welcome couple of pints of lager with him, I got my first taste of uninhibited congratulations from a stranger. I was bowled over by his admiration for my journey, but worried in equal measure by talk of the mileage and the many setbacks that I might encounter. Damian made me feel courageous. His pints and hugs of congratulation were salves for my worries, but deep down in my darkest moments, I lacked faith in my eventual success. I felt as if I was outside the gates of hell waiting for them to open. Without knowing it then, these gates were to creak open many more times in the coming weeks.

8: On the Way to Hull

The voices from the ceiling began at about 6am in the morning with helpful instructions about breakfast and disembarkation. I had plenty of time between eating croissants and queuing with the cyclists and coach party trippers to think about my experiences in England before I slipped almost unheralded into Holland at 8:30am on 25 April.

The flotsam of my journey so far was in the forefront of my mind. I wondered how long these memories would linger before new deposits washed over them on the shore. Apart from trying to conquer issues to do with my feet and rucksack straps, it was the unpredictable nature of encounters along the way that caused my mind to race.

While I had walked through Leeds, along the canal, on the first day, I had come across the 'Say Hi' zone where pedestrians are encouraged to disentangle themselves from their headphones and actually greet their fellow travellers. I loved this idea now that I was spending many hours a day passing people along the way. I vowed to do this as a matter of course and in the proper language of the place where I was. I would begin this when I had reached The Hook of Holland. I started immediately and with some success, despite still being constantly ignored by most of the earphone brigade.

Some people try to blank out your presence, especially those at bus stops – they are the worst offenders of all. I discovered that if you walk past any bus stop and there is more than one person queuing, the chances of getting any response was nil; everyone tries to look into the distance as if expecting the bus to materialise even on an empty road or pretend to be thinking about matters of deep philosophy. They have no idea how much a simple nod means to someone who might be walking for eight hours that day without the opportunity for a real conversation.

In England, I had been walking for two days when I saw my second river. Unlike the first, the Calder, which is right outside my front door and very famous for its propensity for flooding the local town, this one was elusive and I came upon it by surprise. I was walking through the outskirts of Selby past the eerily quiet Rank, Hovis and McDougal factory, it being a Saturday and operating with minimal staff. Around me were piles of pallets and an empty lorry park. The path ran below a high grass banking as if above me was a train line or a canal. At the end of a few weed-tangled fields and some scrub meadowland I turned a corner near Turnham Hall and saw the River Ouse for the first time.

I shuddered with delight; not because a name in a geography textbook had come alive, but because its hazy silver skin and the way it snaked through the green fields touched my need for company. In some unspoken way I felt it was a sign of friendship.

In the promising sunshine of that cold spring morning, I had the first inklings of what tribes of wanderers in Europe, long before the Romans, might have felt like when they reached a riverbank and knew that to follow it meant the promise of the sea and beyond. I felt as if I was becoming connected with the landscape in a way that I had never had time to experience before.

I was still thinking of this when I came across the magnificent Minster in Howden beside which I slumped to eat my packed lunch provided by the previous night's B&B. The cheese and tomato sandwiches had become divinely warm in my rucksack pocket and the two fillings had merged together forming a blissful marriage within a blanket of white bread. This was only my third day away from home but lunch on the road was never so good.

The Minster is officially called a 'Safe Ruin' because while at a glance it looks intact, it was left greatly distressed in 1548 by Henry VIII's henchmen who, having destroyed the monasteries, then set about to batter the collegiate churches. With my warm sandwich demolished, I promised myself that I must keep on moving so as not to become a safe ruin – I only had a day and half left before the ferry from Hull sailed without me.

On the fourth day I discovered the Yorkshire Wolds. They had to be crossed before I could drop down into Hull. For a while I was away from the semi-industrial, urban landscape of Leeds and Selby and the noisy and litter-strewn A63. Now I was surrounded by rich farmland peppered with the crumping sounds from 12 bore shotguns – probably automatically operated to scare away the pigeons. The weather was promising as I climbed steep lanes edged with fields covered in the light green patina of their first crop of the season.

After I dropped down to below the biting windy tops of the Wolds and saw the Humber Bridge in the distance, I came upon what I first thought was the most achingly beautiful sight of the journey so far. One that made me forget my blisters immediately. To my left, beyond the low gnarled hedges that lined up beside the road, high up above a field, fluttered a bird that I took to be a kestrel. It bobbed and tussled against the wind to keep its height in a way that showed its majestic strength.

The way it stayed still by moving its boomerang-shaped wings while turning its head from side to side to search for prey filled me with wonder. I kept thinking that I was the only person alive who could experience this moment.

The hawk knew nothing of my existence but I had clocked his: I felt in a privileged place. Just then, and in a field beyond this one, I saw another hawk, its mate, perhaps, lifting its body in a similar heft against the wind. Two hawk hunters in one go. I was becoming so enthralled that it felt wrong to be absorbed. My blisters throbbed with me standing still, so I edged down the road, trying to keep a clear sight of the birds.

Then suddenly my world was turned upside down, and I looked around me expecting gales of laughter to knock me over. These hawks were kites! They were tethered to the ground by very thin metal poles that could only be seen from a certain angle. Bird scarers – the like I had never seen before – which had tricked me into feeling elation at a private showing of the natural world. 'OK,' I thought as I went on my way. 'I've been tricked, this was a mistake, and I must be on my guard in future. On this walk, I must see things for what they are; not what they appear to be.' Talking to myself about this humbling incident, and my attempts at forgiveness, consumed the time it took to get to the outskirts of Hull.

I began to compose a list of test indicators to prove whether you have reached the edge of town or city. In England you start to see front gardens with lots of small pebbles instead of grass. It makes the front of the house look like a cemetery. Often people try to get a car on top of the pebbles as well as household items ready for the tip. Then, invariably tattoo shops spring up. I have to declare a liking for these. Not that I have a tattoo yet, but I did call into several along my way and always found the people who ran them to be sympathetic, kind, generous and helpful. Next, people of both genders start to have wildly dyed hair and there are more take-away shops than restaurants.

The Netherlands

1: Herons and Hagelstenen

Eventually, the daydreaming about the beginnings of my 1200-mile journey was abandoned because I was jolted back into the present by a ceiling command to walk ashore via a nearby walkway.

Suddenly, without a fanfare, I was on a stretch of concrete in The Netherlands. I watched cars navigate around the slip roads under the watchful eyes of the custom officials, just as I had done, as a driver, on several occasions over the last few years. I was just adjusting my straps and getting out my laminated map for the day (cut into a strip of 13cm so that it, like all the others for the whole journey, would slip conveniently into my trouser pocket) when I caught sight of three white transit vans parked up.

The fitters from the bar last night were checking their loads and preparing for their trip to a factory in Rotterdam in need of sprinklers, when I was met with a chorus of: 'Hey Damian, there's that bloke who's walking to Italy.' 'Good luck mate.' 'Go on son.' 'Hope you make it Roger.' With that, Damian emerged from the back of one van and gave me a massive wave. In seconds all they could see was my rucksack and my walking pole held high. I was on my way. Putting one foot in front of the other as any other crazy man would do.

The lowlands ahead of me were miraculously flat. The landscape had been conjured out of the sea, beginning in the 10th-century, by technology that was way ahead of its time. Huge dykes had been built to keep the sea back; about half of the land at that time was under the sea, while graceful windmills, which litter the landscape, were erected eventually to pump any unwanted water back out to sea again.

I walked for an hour along the Moezelweg cycle track, which is laid into a wide stretch of grass running between the landing stages for commercial shipping and the motorway floating high up on enormous banking, on my way towards Rotterdam. Herons with massive wings filled the sky, circling round at low levels before perching on groynes, like statues, waiting for fish, while a family of Greylag geese, with flashing orange beaks, waddled across the grass towards the slopes of the motorway causing me to question, aloud, (I became fond of talking to the animals that I came across as sometimes they were my only companions for the day) whether it was a little too early and precarious to teach the goslings the danger of motorway traffic.

My solitary conversation was drowned out by extremely loud music coming from a Land Rover parked nearby. An engineer for Essent NV was working at a small sub-station but what struck me most was the tune blasting from his cab. It was: 'I've Got The Power' (1990) by Snap. I could feel the electricity of the music pulsing through my body. It immediately summed up my feeling of striding out into the unknown.

I gazed in awe at my feet as they crunched into the sandy grass that was laced with countless pieces of smashed seashells. The tiny pinpricks of colour produced by the shells made me feel like I was a moving subject in a pointillist painting. Walking along this ancient, exposed seabed, I was surrounded by the trappings of today's technology – modern wind turbines with huge white blades and silvery petro-chemical plants whose chimneys regularly belched jets of fire into the grey, ice-laden sky.

Patting the side of my trousers forlornly, I discovered, as it began to rain, that my 13cm map for the day must have fallen out of my pocket somewhere back along the Moezelweg – probably as I was jogging up and down to, 'I've Got The Power.' The number of times that I had said 'Goedemorgen' to cyclists going the other way had given me a sense of moving forward so the thought of going back to look for a map was out of the question. I decided to rely solely on Google

Maps on my phone, which was a big mistake. Actually, it was my third mistake. My first was those disastrous rubber shoes with the fakir-style innersole of rubberized nails and then, secondly, there were the kestrel kites. It dawned on me, slowly, that if the rubber shoes were the stone inside a snowball and each subsequent mistake was another layer of snow, the snowball was inevitably going to be of monstrous proportions by the end of the journey.

I was heading for a ferry at Rozenburg that would take me across to the small town of Maassluis and the voice on my mobile told me to turn right and then head for a bridge over the first canal. Simple. I was only a few metres along what looked like a narrow cycle track going over the bridge in the pouring rain when I saw a flashing blue light ahead of me. As I approached the police car, with its back door open, a fierce looking policeman shouted at me to: 'Get in!' in a tone of voice that might otherwise have been used to force a reluctant and aggressive bull into the back of a cattle truck.

As soon as I had bundled my rucksack and myself into the back seat we took off at speed. I was interviewed in staccato fashion as to my reasons for walking on such a busy road, where I was going and where was my passport. I must have passed the interview because both policemen seemed to calm down, especially when they heard of my destination and my reasons for walking (neatly summarized by a few words about charity fundraising and retirement). In an instant, I promised myself to learn this capsule of information in Dutch, German and Italian so that my next scrapes could be more speedily expedited.

By the time they dropped me at the ferry landing they were almost inclined to sponsor me but warned me in a stern, but friendly, fashion to keep away from busy roads in order to reach my destination in one piece. Wise words, even though I felt like a schoolboy who had just survived a ticking-off from the headteacher and badly needed to see some mates to tell them how brave I had been in the face of authority. Actually, I was wobbling like a blancmange the whole of the time on the ferry ride to Maassluis.

I grew very fond of these short water crossings that cropped up regularly. Now, I was on a car ferry, painted battleship grey, edging its way across pewter coloured water under a leaden sky: a symphony of grey to still my thumping heart. I decided to take a break at the next possible café, wherever it was, to recover and work out on my phone what route to Rotterdam would keep me furthest from the busy roads.

The Eetcafe De Kroon on the Haven canal in Maassluis was a perfect place to regain my composure. The maritime-themed walls were dotted with boards of knots and pictures of barges with old-fashioned sails. While a flashing jukebox offered the widest choice of music I had ever seen. I ate my Dutch-style cheese on toast and drank my coffee to the latest Bulgarian pop songs, which I had chosen from a selection that also included music from Greece, India, Italy, Poland, Romania and Russia. Cultural references on jukeboxes in England are rather limited by comparison, I was sad to admit. I spoke sporadically to the very pleasant Indonesian women who served me as she gave me snippets of her twenty or so years in the Netherlands and some much-needed advice about getting to Rotterdam on foot and not in a police car.

Sitting alone in this Eetcafe for a calorie-building second breakfast or perhaps an early lunch, I sharply remembered another reason for me being there. PLF had arrived at The Hook of Holland on 10 December 1933 and then journeyed by train to Rotterdam from where he took 13 months to walk into what we now call Istanbul.

So far, I was nearly five days up on PLF and fast approaching his starting point. Here I was, 51 years older than him, attempting to follow his route and keep roughly to his timetable with the first 78 pages (neatly razor-bladed off and bound with a strip of elastoplast) of the first book in his trilogy, 'A Time of Gifts' to guide me. Luckily, a writer called Nick Hunt had repeated the entire journey in 2011, so I also had the first 66 pages of his book, 'Walking the Woods and the Water' as a companion. Of course, I would only have these two authors ringing round my head, while skirting the banks of the River Rhine, until I reached the Black Forest after which they went east along the River Danube while I would branch out on my own down to Lake Constance and the over the Austrian Alps to Italy. Even as I said this to myself, I could not believe it would happen.

In the afternoon before I reached the centre of Rotterdam I

followed the direction of the River Lek – walking against its flow – that runs through Rotterdam and out to the sea. Its takes water from the Rivers Rhine (flowing by Arnhem) and the Waal (flowing by Nijmegen): friends of mine for many days to come. My route on the Broekpolderweg was a little way inland from the river, at the bottom of the banking beside the noisy A20 motorway. Not that I saw much of anything because some sudden and explosive torrents of hailstones caused me to retreat into my wet weather clothes like a tortoise in its shell. From a narrow slit onto the world, I could just make out coots and moorhens nesting in the little canals beside the polder surrounded by fields as far as the church spires on the horizon, and the odd cyclist who tacked past leaning into a wall of wind and hail in front of them.

A man in a small car, who I assumed had been fishing before the weather changed, stopped and offered me a lift. I replied rather lamely, hoping he could understand English:

'Thank you but I have to walk because I am being sponsored and this SPOT device, which was flashing every few seconds, on my ruck-sack would show my friends at home that I was moving too fast to be walking. They would think that I was cheating.'

He nodded and seemed to understand and I followed up with: 'What do you call these white pieces of ice in Dutch?'

He replied that they were called 'Hagelstenen,' which when he pronounced it, with a rumbling guttural first half and a hard stress on the 'stenen' at the end, my first word in Dutch sounded remarkably like the aggressive, stinging, frozen bullets that they were.

I spent the rest of the afternoon plodding along polders between the vast fields of grass for cattle and early sprouts of wheat now that the sugar beet season was well and truly finished. As I got nearer to Rotterdam, built up areas appeared as if part of a mirage. While I was walking among fields my mind opened out to fill the space around me but as soon as I came near to civilization I came down to earth very quickly, absorbing the many competing and conflicting senses that bombarded me like ghost particles.

I was intrigued at some of the street names like Thomas À Kemp-isstraat. Echoes from A Level history reverberated in my head and with the aid of my O2 mobile roaming deal I was able to satisfy my curiosity about Thomas à Kempis while still walking along the pavement. He was a 15th-century church canon who wrote what was to become the most translated religious book after the Bible: 'The Imitation of Christ.'

I almost bumped into a lamppost while I was reading some of the most famous quotes from his book, especially after my recent encounter with the wind and stones of ice. One that stayed with me at least until I reached the very centre of Rotterdam was: 'As long as you live, you will be subject to change, whether you will it or not – now glad, now sorrowful; now pleased, now displeased; now devout, now undevout; now vigorous, now slothful; now gloomy, now merry. But a wise man, who is well taught in spiritual labour, stands unshaken in all such things, and heeds little what he feels, or from what side the wind of instability blows.'

I was soaked to the skin, a bright pink rash – all over my ankles and legs – was itching and my blisters pulsed with pain. I decided that I could not 'stand unshaken' any longer: it was time for a beer. I found a café only about 7 miles from the city and dived in. It felt like fate was beckoning me, when in the toilet, I read a poster for a forthcoming Blues Festival at which one of the star turns was to be Mr. Boogie Woogie and The Blisters. I stood drinking my beer too scared to sit down in case I never stood up again.

I began to love the by now customary conversation, rather like a well-choreographed minuet (this time with the barman), which usually began with: 'Where are you going?' I then took pleasure in the look of mystified amazement that filled their faces when I told them that I was walking from England to the middle of Italy. Followed by 'What ... walking?' After which they used their fingers in a way to mimic a puppet walking just to make sure we were talking about the same activity. Then there was a brief moment when they seemed to be inwardly guessing my age and level of fitness before breaking the ice of their incredulity by asking: 'what will you do when you get there? Walk back to England again?' This courtly dance interlude invariably ended with a coda of laughter leaving me space to plan a polite but hasty exit or at least change the subject.

From then on, all I could think about that day was getting to my

Airbnb in Rotterdam. During the last hour before arrival, I realised that I would have to add to my list of indicators concerning the approach to a city: an avenue of Money Transfer Shops appeared like palm trees running down to an oasis. This city was certainly multicultural because people could send funds to places like Tunisia; Bangladesh; Brazil; Columbia; Peru; Morocco; Senegal; Ghana; Uganda; and The Congo.

2: The Mayflower not the Speedwell

I met Dittrich, my host for the night, outside a café near his apartment, as arranged. After rushing from work as an investment banker to welcome me to his apartment, he guided me, shielded from the downpour under his city-gent's umbrella, to a fabulously appointed room with a magnificent view. We entertained ourselves with the usual minuet. But he wanted to linger more than anyone else to date on the enormity of the challenge and the bravery that was necessary. I began to feel rejuvenated after the exhausting day by his supportive questions – he certainly lived up to his Twitter tag of 'Passion is everything.'

I enjoyed hearing about him and his family. I started off in a new direction by asking: 'How long have you lived in this apartment with such a fantastic view?' From where we were standing, we looked down on the Hofplein, which is an octagonal fountain surrounded by tramlines. Not far is the church in which a Leiden Separatist branch of The Pilgrim Fathers worshipped before, on 22 July in 1620, they sailed away in the Speedwell to Southampton to meet up with, and sail alongside, the Mayflower from Plymouth to Cape Cod. Unfortunately, the Speedwell was leaking badly by the time she cleared Land's End and had to turn back leaving the Mayflower to eventually make the journey alone. She arrived at Cape Cod on 11 November 1620 having left Plymouth in early September.

From that moment, I resolved to be a Mayflower rather than like the leaky Speedwell. My resolve was cemented by Dittrich's enthusiasm and The Pilgrim Fathers' determination.

Dittrich pointed out an All You Can Eat Japanese Buffet Restaurant to which I could stagger later. He told me that the apartment really belonged to his parents who lived in Curaçao and that he had his own house near to the Erasmus Bridge. I revelled in the idea that, all before dinner and having walked more than 20 miles that day for the privilege, I was learning, by way of a welcome to Rotterdam, about The Dutch West Indies, the famous blue-coloured alcohol named after his parents' island, the exodus to America by Christian separatists, and – as he went on to relate – the World War Two bombs that wiped out most of the city centre in May 1940.

Had I arrived on 13 May 1940, or any day before that, I would have seen, as Nick Hunt describes: 'buildings of orangey brick with plaster curlicues, peculiar gabled rooftops with pretty patterns of red and white tiles, resembling almonds set in a cake.' At five in the morning on 10 December 1933, PLF 'wandered about these silent lanes in exultation. The beetling storeys were nearly joined overhead; then the eaves drew away from each other and frozen canals threaded their way through a succession of humped backed bridges. Snow was piling up on the shoulders of a statue of Erasmus.'

There would also have been, before May 1940, the whole gamut of early 20th-century flats, houses, factories and warehouses, for this was a major port and industrial hub with a skyline of cranes, steaming chimneys and windmills. People would have been going about their daily lives on foot, by bicycle, on trams, in horse-drawn wagons, on stream-driven barges and by bus. But the German army had arrived days before by seaplanes, dinghies and parachutes aiming to capture the bridges and bring Rotterdam to its knees. The city was to capitulate as part of Hitler's plan to overrun the Netherlands by threatening major cities, one at a time, with extinction.

In this case, after a few days of fighting in the streets, the Dutch agreed to surrender in acceptance of the German demands. Tragically, it was too late for the commanders to warn off the pilots of the bombers who were planning to arrive at 1.20pm on 14 May 1940. Even the German soldiers in the streets panicked when they heard the shriek of the planes' engines approaching the city. Red flares were launched, into the sky, in an effort to warn off the pilots but not before some bombs had been dropped causing billows of smoke that prevented about 60 more planes from seeing the flares. That afternoon these 60 bombers obliterated the entire centre of the city.

This was why I was now gazing out at boulevards – American in proportion – lined with shiny skyscrapers interspersed occasionally by much older, renovated, brick and grey slate tiled buildings like the City Hall. Beyond my proposed Japanese feeding station for tonight lay the statue of Erasmus, which strangely escaped even a scratch from the bombing that killed about 900 people, destroyed 25,000 buildings and made 80,000 people homeless.

Fired up by Dittrich's stories, I walked ever so gingerly to demolish my sushi banquet and then went to bed early in preparation for my walk the next day to Dordrecht and meeting up with my wife, Kate, on her birthday.

3: Swoops and Curlicues

The following morning, I walked out of Rotterdam in a jaunty mood. I had been worried about how people in Europe might relate to me since to them I might be a Brexiteer who wanted nothing more than to sail away from the mainland in a metaphorical Speedwell. But chatting to Dittrich about his ideas from an international banker's perspective, I was reassured that people at home would see the fiscal folly of leaving just now and even if the referendum was in favour of leaving, the government might well overrule it given the precarious state it would cause during the longed for financial recovering that we were all seeking. Apart from believing that my proxy vote to Remain would help win the day, my feelings of optimism also waxed because my blisters were becoming bearable.

By 10am the sky conspired to take the edge off my elation. It was gloriously blue in parts but grey cumulus clouds gathered to threaten unwanted rain for my entry into Dordrecht. Sharp beams of sunlight left a sheen on any remnants of the early morning rain causing the huge mosque and the three irregular towers of the ultra-modern De Rotterdam building on either side of the River Nieuwe Maas to glisten invitingly.

As for Kate, I felt slightly guilty for having made so much of the leaving ceremony when we would be together again so soon after, but not enough to prevent me looking forward to the next three days of much-needed camaraderie. We planned to spend King's Day (27

April) wandering round Dordrecht soaking up the atmosphere of this very special celebration in Holland and then walk together to Gorinchem and afterwards on to Tiel before Kate left for her flight back to Manchester.

After crossing the bridge and making my way out of the city, I was accosted by a man who ran shouting and gesticulating wildly across a busy main road to get my attention. It became obvious from his appearance that a seagull had defiled his coat quite liberally. I was lost for words especially since my only Dutch vocabulary centred on hailstones. Cold and icy this was not. The hot, liquid mess was edging down his sleeve as he came within feet of me. 'Geluk, Geluk,' he repeated with the maniacal look of a 16th-century religious zealot who had seen a sign in the sky.

'Oh, I am so sorry for you,' I empathised, 'You just can't trust these awful birds to leave you alone these days, I blame Hitchcock.' I gambled on him not understanding me, in the heat of the moment, but hopefully feeling soothed by my tone. Later, a few 100 metres down the road, I realised that I had totally misjudged the situation.

He was probably ecstatically happy at receiving this benediction from the sky. Now I knew two Dutch words, the most recent meaning 'Good luck.' And what is more, I marvelled at how, with only the English Channel between us, a happening such as this could be received in such diametrically opposed ways. If in England, my sleeve had been coated like this on my way to work I would have vented my entire repertoire of swear words on the escaping bird while pathetically trying to grab it from the sky in a vain attempt to demand some sort of natural recompense and justice.

After that the slog of the day began. In a few minutes, I was passing the Feijenoord N.V. football stadium. I considered the fact that I never really knew what city it was in. So much for my knowledge of football. I had planned a route through Ridderkerk to follow the way of my 'two guides,' as I called PFL and Nick Hunt and I loved the sounds of the roads they had chosen: Ijsselmondse Randweg; Rijksstraatweg; Langeweg; and Rotterdamseweg. The last of which was chosen to lead me straight to the ferry that would take me across to Dordrecht. Just as the names held a kind of other magic for me, so did the houses that I saw on my way.

Soon I was walking in the countryside with tiny canals, affluent-looking houses and fenceless gardens sloping down to the road. It became a kind of domestic, velvet grass and tree-lined idyll. I felt elated but wondered why, because after all it was an unfamiliar landscape: people lived here, sure enough, but it was somewhat alien because the architecture of the houses drew on references that did not resonate with me. I had seen similar buildings on previous trips to Amsterdam and Delft. But now I was passing homes with time to ponder, I had plenty of time to indulge my reflections when usually they would get submerged under the flood of everyday.

I grew up in a mock Tudor semi-detached house with black wooden planks embedded in white plasterwork. It was on a new estate built on open farmland, outside London, in the mid-1930s. When I was young, I had no idea about the Tudors and the architectural references that influenced my daily life. They just soaked into my existence. Elsewhere, growing up, I remember seeing Saxon churches, Norman castles, Georgian houses, Victorian redbrick villas and 1930s seaside houses with metal window frames that curved in a way that seemed so at odds with the small leaded angular windows we had at home. Later in the 1960s and 70s concrete became fashionable as an architectural finish.

On leaving our sixth form, while I trained to be a teacher, a friend had already got a job as a sub-editor on a London-based magazine dedicated to promoting the artistic use of concrete in buildings. He pointed out some prime examples in our schooner-of-sherry drinking jaunts 'up west' on our Honda 50s. We saw how the evolving South-bank Centre, beside the River Thames, flourished using innovative building methods and modern concrete finishes in this time of the so-called swinging sixties. Looking back on it all, I am not sure many historians would associate this ground-breaking era with schooners of sherry.

I realised then that we probably all walk around with minds filled subconsciously with snapshots from the buildings we see on a daily basis, have seen in the past or inhabited at one time. These pictures, tucked somewhere away in our brains, must, I thought, give us a sense of belonging and security.

The astonishing but simple difference in the Netherlands were the windows either side of the front door. They were enormous. Far bigger than you would imagine given the size of rest of the building. Perhaps they signified wealth or importance. Either way they worked. I was grabbed by their magnificence. However, the owners, having established a sense of grandeur, then felt they had to conceal what they were doing inside from the passers by outside, which is why the windowsill inside was often dominated by a huge vase that contained fresh or dried flowers of noble proportions and various other ornaments designed to limit the view.

Outside many of these houses, close to the front door and these windows, owners invariably grew a tree with spreading branches trained on posts and heavy-duty wires. These trees towered like crucifixes in a sea of pebbles. It was too early in the year for much leaf growth but I imagine that in full summer the goings on inside the houses were modestly obscured by foliage. Thinking about this and other features such as brightly painted weatherboarding, steep roofs and their ornately shaped gables in the form of steps, bells and necks, I felt my boundaries being stretched.

I thought that I might grow to love these over-sized windows, these baroque steps, swoops and curlicues that flourished around me. I could live here. But then my feelings of elation were slightly constricted by a sense of foreboding that behind the leafy crucifixes a life of quiet desperation could be acted out and no-one would know. Marriages could grow stale and solidify behind the enormous vases in a perfectly civilized and ordered manner, in which an escaped divorcee could say 'I was quietly dying there.'

Then I saw in front of me what looked like a hill. This could not be true. I marvelled that I had not seen a hill since the Yorkshire Wolds. And of course it wasn't. It was just, I found out, a steeply sided road bridge over the A16. From the top, I caught a glimpse of Dordrecht Groot Kerk with its prominent bell tower, fronted by four enormous clock faces. It was still a few miles off but I felt energized to be on the verge of meeting Kate and having a day off.

As planned, I trudged along the Rotterdamseweg to reach the

boarding point for the ferry to take me across to Dordrecht. This being a relatively short day of walking, just over 15 miles (I would never have thought of saying that a few weeks previously) and being a little early for meeting Kate, I decided to look for a café to rest in before crossing over to the island.

4: Cucu and the Moluks

It turned out that I was standing outside the perfect spot. It was an Indonesian Restaurant called Cucu, which from inside gave me a good view of the landing stage and, on the far bank of the River Maas, a row of houses, restaurants and warehouses overshadowed by the Grote Kerk. With its dark red bricks, tall narrow windows and huge clock faces, the church possessed a faintly industrial aura laced with a degree of spiritual penance provided by a delicate spire on the far side, reminiscent of a thorn plucked from Jesus' crown. Had the starched 18th-century protestants of Dordrecht been lined up outside their magnificent place of worship, I imagine that an organised, industrious, punctual and purged congregation would have welcomed me.

On my side of the river, in Zwijndrecht, I was a world away from this organised and efficient Christian ethic. In the restaurant, on this bank of the Maas, they would be celebrating Eid in a couple of months' time. A strikingly beautiful woman by the name of Leila Hamer-van Oorschot welcomed me like a traveller in need of care, calm and simple food: 'Would you like to put your rucksack down there and sit at that table, where you can keep an eye on the ferries, and let me bring you a tasting-plate of our really authentic Indonesian food?'

I was her only customer for lunch, it being 3:05pm, so all the while she was busying around getting my food, she regaled me with stories of her family, why the place was called Cucu and, with the hint of a tear in her eye, why she was keeping family history alive through the food that she served. Cucu is Moluccan for grandchildren and, in this case, the grandchildren of Grandma Neila Pattisahusiwa were honouring her life, as the wife of a soldier in the Royal Dutch Indian Army and a much-loved mother of eight children, by creating this haven of gastronomy and welcome.

The restaurant had walls the colour of a cloudless blue sky as dusk approaches, wooden tables with a beautifully smooth surface that needed no cloth and low-slung basket lights, all of which made one feel close to a warm ocean even though, in Zwijndrecht, the cold North Sea was all that was on offer. Hung on the walls were pictures of islanders in lush surroundings tending crops, carrying heavy loads on their heads or standing over mountains of vibrantly coloured fruit and vegetables.

I had no idea of the significance of the word 'Moluks' but, as I discovered, I was not alone in this ignorance. The Dutch, it seems, keep a low profile when talking about their role in the East Indies, especially after World War Two when Indonesia was fighting for its independence and the Moluccan Islands wanted to be free of Dutch imperialism.

As I listened, it slowly dawned on me that this feeling of being at home was Leila's greatest achievement. She spoke quietly but from deep in her soul about her grandparents' arrival from the Moluccan islands and I got the impression that they had been stranded here, bereft of the life illustrated on the walls. So, it was Leila's life's ambition to keep alive the traditions of her family's original homeland so that the next generation – her daughter and her grandchild – should know their true heritage and cherish the idea of belonging somewhere.

I was piecing together a jigsaw of sadness and hope. Later, I looked up how Grandma Neila came to be in the Netherlands. When the Dutch could no longer support the Moluccan cause for self-determination against the fledgling Republican Army of Indonesia, and facing a lack of international support, the Dutch government organised a hasty withdrawal for all the soldiers and their families so that they could be discharged in the Netherlands rather than on an island chosen by the Republic. These soldiers had to make a choice of whether to join the Indonesian Army or leave their homeland and sail to Holland, uncertain of what kind of life lay ahead. They left behind the South Moluccan Republic whose existence was not recognised by Indonesia and which, to this day, has never been given the status that its people wanted.

In 1951 Neila and her hastily demobbed husband found themselves in a former Nazi concentration camp – Camp Vught – on Dutch soil, without hope, comfort and citizenship. They belonged nowhere. Neila made a home amongst the ghostly echoes lingering around the camp: she created a garden and kept chickens. Over time, she and her husband had eight children some of whom bore their own children. These grandchildren would become the Cucu running the restaurant when it opened in 2014.

The Moluks fought a long, hard, and sometimes violent, battle for recognition and Dutch citizenship, but it was the Neila style of resilience that, for this family, won through in the end. My taster plate of colourful, spicy lunch took on a symbolic value, signifying the yearning for the warmth of home, family and belonging, which can be recreated in another place by a strong family that values faith, tradition and fortitude.

Many of the people who had asked me about the reasons for my walk had assumed it was some kind of pilgrimage, which in a sense it was because I was following the footsteps of PFL for at least some of the way. However, I began to realise that my stopping points were my Stations of the Cross. These had to grow out of my own experiences that made a difference to me. As I boarded the ferry to make the crossing to see Kate, for the first time in a week, I realised that I had discovered my first pilgrim's waypoint: an oasis of victory in the form of a restaurant dedicated to Neila's resilience in the face of adversity.

When, in December 1933, PFL made this ferry crossing it was already dark. He saw that 'a multitude of anchored barges loaded with timber formed a flimsy extension of the quays and rocked from end to end when bow waves from passing vessels stirred them.'

Nowadays, the barges are much larger; they lack sails and are probably too long to moor alongside the ferry terminal. All I saw were a couple of ferries ready for different crossings and a row of parked cars: a view that lacked all semblance of the romance conjured up by the 1933 scene.

On disembarking, I quickly found the route to our meeting point because we had both been here before, it often being our first or last port of call when travelling to and from Italy by car. PFL had fallen asleep in a waterside bar and been led upstairs, like a sleepwalker, to an attic bedroom that sported prominently a picture of Queen Wilhelmina. A room for which, in the morning, the landlady would refuse any payment because the walk had tired out this handsome 18-year-old. Wistfully, I wondered if (using different criteria, of course), I would qualify for a free room or, come to that, a free anything?

As I passed the Grote Kerk a peel of bells welcomed me, playing a tune rather like the music of a hurdy-gurdy fed with those Braille-like embossed pieces of card. I only had to turn the corner into Grotekerksbuurt to meet Kate and find the B&B, next to our friend Felice's Atelier Studio.

We first met Felice on a previous trip when, stepping into her studio, we were taken, among other things, by her elegant, hand-made scarves for men made from recycled materials with unusual patterns and textures.

5: Kings' Day

Miraculously, Kate turned into the same street a little further up at exactly the time that I passed the tail end of the church. There we were (one having walked from home, six days ago, and the other flown into Amsterdam a few hours ago) like giggly teenagers lost for words. We hugged with all the romance that wet anoraks can afford, then rang the doorbell of the Blom aan de Gracht, me not caring at that point about its Dutch translation with connotations of flowers by the canal: the flowers for Kate's birthday tomorrow that sadly I had failed to buy along the way.

Soon we were sitting on the edge of our bed and Kate caught a glimpse of my badly blistered feet. She quickly realised that I had not been exaggerating during our nightly FaceTime sessions. In the evenings, I was still not able to walk (in my lightweight rubbers shoes) at more than a snail's pace. So Kate had bought a packed tea that we could enjoy without leaving the room. Bliss. Unromantically, our first night together, after nearly a week apart, was given over to tending to sore feet, washing socks, eating propped up on pillows and rearranging rucksacks. That and a few beers in a nearby bar was the zenith of our reunion.

King's Day dawned in drizzle. A cold wind raced along the canal outside our room. We began the celebrations by having our breakfast in the bakers across the road. They serve a medley of bio yogurt, granola, breads, croissants, coffee and jams: truly from farm to fork. From the window of Nobel's Brood, we could see tables and stalls being erected for the traditional household flea markets – no tax required for sales on the royal birthday – white plumes on the band members' orange-trimmed helmets that were being fluffed up, and the result of wardrobes having been raided for orange clothes or accessories, which would create a whoosh of national fervour to keep people's 'Dutchness' topped up for a whole year.

Our entire day passed in a blur of self-indulgence. I began to feel very guilty about not walking 20 miles. Successfully concealing this guilt, Kate and I sauntered around town making plenty of stops to have hot chocolate, eat a hearty lunch and listen to the marching bands. Ragged bits of blue sky sometimes appeared beyond the clouds. The inevitable showers could not dampen the spirits of revellers. At least there were no hagelstenen.

Outside her Atelier Shop with her table of antique bits and bobs, Felice had persuaded a roving group of singers with ukuleles to sing Happy Birthday to Kate in Dutch. The look of enjoyment and appreciation on Kate's face was in stark contrast to the rather worried look that appeared when she remembered that for the next two days she would be accompanying me over a distance of about 40 miles.

To make up for the lack of flowers, I had booked dinner at a fish restaurant called De Stroper - The Poacher in Afrikaans. It was only a short stagger along the Grotekerksbuurt, which runs beside the Wijnhaven canal.

Over dinner, we talked nonstop about my experiences. Kate's powers of listening, empathy and concentration were tested to their limits as I went into verbal overdrive like someone who was out on parole or had suddenly been rescued from a shipwrecked island.

During the evening, we asked the waitress and restaurant owner what King's Day was designed to celebrate. Apparently, the origins of this tradition began when Queen Wilhelmina (the one who watched over PFL in his attic) was a five-year-old princess. Prinsessedag was first held on 31 August in 1885. When she became a queen, at the age of 10 in 1890, it changed its name to Koninginnedag (Queen's Day).

This apple-faced, blond girl of five whom, as the photographic portraits show, kept her rounded bloom – but not her blond hair – throughout her reign, presided over the House of Orange until 1948 (when I was one year old) at which point her daughter Juliana became queen and the celebrations moved to her birthday on 30 April.

It was Juliana's daughter Beatrix who, in 1980, chose to process the festivities around different Dutch towns each year instead of the parade being only in front of the Soestdijk Palace near Utrecht.

So the royal family came to the Dutch people. But there were the occasional horrific consequences. In 2009, the royal family was attacked while they were in an open-top bus travelling through the town of Apeldoorn. A man called Karst Tates, who for some reason had a hatred of some or all of the royal family, drove his Suzuki Swift at the bus, but missed it causing the death of seven people in the crowd. Tates died later that day of the injuries caused by the crash. Queen Beatrix was adamant that the visits by the royal family would continue, but further celebrations for that year were cancelled. Luckily for Dordrecht it got its turn on 27 April in 2015 when the present King (Beatrix's son) and his family made their visit on his Koningsdag.

The next day, we began our walk in the rain. Coming from Yorkshire we might, in April, have been more surprised by fair weather. So, with waterproof trousers and fully zipped up jackets, we set off to begin a friendship with huge rivers that would, for me, last until the Adriatic.

From the moment I had seen the Ouse, only a few days before, I knew that I was strangely drawn to the idea of trekking alongside great rivers such as the Waal, Rhine, Inn, Po and Brenta.

The Rhine and the Danube are the main arteries of Europe. Once they were the boundaries of The Roman Empire. Now they carry our commercial lifeblood. Barges ferry millions of tonnes of goods per year from major cities like Basel and Cologne to ports such as Rotterdam. It is big business.

Slowing down in the final stages of its long journey from the Swiss Alps, the Rhine splits into three tributaries. After Nijmegen, in its last 50 miles, the old river cannot cope alone anymore and has to share its load. Kate and I were spending two days walking the Waal, which is one of these tributaries.

Watching the barges stopped us thinking about our feet, the continual rain and a chill wind. At lunchtime, we sat on a riverside bench to eat hard-boiled eggs, bread and fruit. Like children, with a brand new I Spy Book, we took a great delight in spotting the different flags being flown; marvelling at the cars on board and trying to guess what cargoes were being transported.

Simply astounding was the length of the vessels. Some powered cabins can push up to three vessels that are, in total, about 200 metres in length. Others are shorter, often capable of sailing on the open sea. On the barges that carry stacks of containers, the captain's deck is perched high above the load, making it look like a stork's nest on top of a chimney.

In this way, we passed Sliedrecht and Giessendam without feeling the pain.

At Boven-Hardinxveld we came across some spectacular engineering. Maintenance firms for barges and river cruisers, which would soon be carrying hordes of tourists towards places like the castles and vineyards of the Middle Rhine, have devised massive winching systems for getting the vessels out of the water for servicing or repairs.

An undercarriage on rails runs down into the water. Once the huge supports are engaged under the hull, a tall crane, on a platform high above colossal lookout towers, begins to pull the hulk out of the water up a network of rails. It is then chocked securely so that work can begin.

We were transfixed. At home in Hebden Bridge, the dry dock for small barges, on the Rochdale Canal, is interesting, but here the sheer size of the enterprise almost made us gasp.

Sometimes, we were forced to walk inland. The blanket of grey clouds and the continual mizzle made the fields look forlorn. So far, I had not come across many wooded places in the Netherlands and today was no exception. This was not surprising since there are fewer trees here than in almost any other European countries. Thin trees such as birch, line the straight, flat and seemingly endless narrow roads that run besides dykes. Then there are stunted, pollarded willows dotted around in fields. They stand like chess pieces across boards of land that have been successfully rescued from the sea. Obviously, pollarding is useful in providing supple branches for making things. We also wondered whether their roots were vitally useful in sucking up unwanted water from what could become waterlogged land. They might even help to knit together the predominantly sandy soil.

Even though this was very early days in my adventure, I was beginning to identify a phenomenon that I named 'The Phantom of The Last Five Miles.' It seemed that whatever length of walk the day held, the last five miles were the hardest. My mind became more like jelly. Thoughts became confused. The capacity to speak impaired. Spirits flagged badly. I might have blamed myself alone for this had not Kate suffered the same fate as we were approaching Gorinchem.

Having chatted ceaselessly together along the way, she fell silent in the final five miles. Any attempt on my part to ignite a conversation was met with a grunted reply, which roughly translated as: 'Leave me alone – I have got to do this on my own.'

So there we were, shattered. She chipping away at the invisible wall in front of us, and me staring stolidly at her rain-coated rucksack along the tarmac cycle paths. Lush green banks of grass on either side of us bulged with wild, yellow flowers. A colour that gave hope in contrast to the battleship grey of the sky, which promised yet more rain.

6: Nuff Respect and Goodbye

PFL spent the night in a police cell in Gorinchem. Apparently, in the 1930s, if there were spare cells a student traveller could sleep in one – a kind of pre-war couchsurfing arrangement.

By contrast, we were staying care of Airbnb and were pleased to meet Mina, our host, and get unpacked in our self-catering guesthouse in a small side street within striking distance of the main thoroughfare. Within a very short time we had gone from communing deeply with 'The Phantom of the Last Five Miles' to making a cup of tea in our own kitchen and planning our banquet of falafel and salad. The house was called Bij De Tijd, which translates as 'At The Time'. Whatever that actually meant, we certainly appreciated the respite that this timely bijou hideaway afforded.

After preparing our meal, we set off to find Mina's recommended bar for a drink. It was my routine to arrive somewhere, tend to feet and aching limbs, wash, change, find a bar, have a meal and retire. It was unusual for me to be still compos mentis by half past nine. After today's walk, I noticed that Kate fell in line with this timetable with no objection. It was customary to have a random conversation before turning in and tonight was no exception. We spoke to two Glaswegians, apparently builders, who had made Holland their home more than 20 years ago. We were particularly fascinated with their take on the similarity between the Scots and the Dutch language. For example, the word 'ken' when meaning 'understand' seems to be used similarly in both languages, but there were many more examples forthcoming – so many that our eyes began to droop and we made a polite exit in favour of falafels and bed.

If the distance from Dordrecht to Gorinchem was slightly less than 20 miles, the one to Tiel was going to be longer to maintain the daily average. That is why we were up, breakfasted and out on the road by 7am on 29 April. This was to be Kate's final day with me until I reached the Black Forest in Germany many weeks hence.

With such a flat terrain people could be excused for thinking that walking through Holland would be boring. Nothing could be further from the truth – unless it was raining all of the time, when the cold wind insisted in hitting you in the face and the only place for respite was a bus shelter.

Towards lunchtime we had to veer away from the river and walk through some forlorn-looking housing estates. Today we had promised ourselves to stop at a café along the route and have a sit-down lunch, but nothing appeared. Instead, we drank water in a bus shelter and shivered.

Our route along the Steenweg took us to a bridge over the motorway. On it a small boy and his mother gazed at the lorries speeding below us. The silver exhaust pipes, which stood vertically beside the ornate driver's cabs, glistened in the fine spray that spewed from the vehicles in front.

What made the sight even more special was the boy's delight at the different toots and whistles that the wagons made in contrast to the monotone klaxons on British motorways. Here, in our eyrie, on the bridge, high above the traffic, the bird noises and other trills kept us spellbound – as they did our much younger fellow spotter. For a moment we forgot the dreary day.

By mid-afternoon, somewhere between the Zandstraat and the end of the Pipersestraat we realised that it was a great mistake, my fourth, to rely on dreams of coming across a welcoming café. The calories consumed while walking 20 miles could not be replenished by hope alone. So at the top of a small incline, as if in a mirage, we spotted a mobile café. Suddenly, we were happy and almost skipped into its small car park. In the space of a few minutes we were sitting on stools with our fingers diving into plastic trays topped full of chips. Dutch chips dipped in mayonnaise.

As we surfaced from our calorie rush, we saw that we had been joined by a group of workmen who had come for their own fat-fried fix. Their order was more complicated than ours. Watching them made us study, more carefully, the cabinet that contained the entire menu. Arranged in neat piles were what looked like an array of children's play food – plastic items, which children pretend to cook in their playhouse kitchens and offer to unsuspecting adults along with a cup of tea. Plastic tea cups with nothing in them, of course.

There were sausages of different lengths and thicknesses, from saveloys to thin frankfurters; square breaded items that could be processed chicken or pork; and round yellow discs of unimaginable filling. The colour-range of the food was quite limited on a spectrum from bright orange to a dull flesh hue.

The family that owned the café deep-fried the orders eagerly, turning the play food into scalding hot delicacies that satisfied every customer's pent-up cravings for stodgy, fatty food. They were artists in their own right. Creative with cholesterol. One could feel arteries clogging up even while gazing at the bags being ferried back to the car park.

Not long after, fortified by the chips, we were striding through the outskirts of Tiel. We were in a satellite estate called Passewaay, when a driver stopped his delivery van and offered us a lift. He said kindly, 'I have seen you both five times today, while I have been delivering. Would you like a lift somewhere?'

I gave my prepared speech about not being able to take a lift, but we felt the warm glow of acceptance from random people for what we were doing. This glow kept us going along the side of the canal that led to near the centre of town. After crossing a bridge and weaving our way through side streets we eventually arrived at Tiel station in time for Kate to catch her train back to Amsterdam.

There on the station, also waiting for the train to Amsterdam, via Utrecht, was a young man, whom I discovered was called Aristoteles Mendes. He was a black rapper from Amsterdam with dreams of world fame someday. We swapped stories. My energy and resolve flooded back as our different worlds collided. His hopes and dreams inspired me and he was kind enough to say: 'Nuff respect' about my adventures, which I took to be a real accolade. Feeling buoyed up and validated, I said a fond farewell to Kate for a month or so until we were to meet again at Sigmaringen, in the Black Forest.

7: Noddy and Big Ears

Sitting on a cold metal bench watching the train become a pinprick in the distance, I travelled quickly from elation to desolation. Luckily, I was learning to conquer these swings of emotion by burying myself in detail and planning. So I looked up the way to my B&B, investigated where I could eat that night and mapped my route for the morning.

The next morning, 30 April, felt like the start of a new chapter. I was to be alone until Heidelberg, in Germany, when I would see Alice and Max. The sky was a sheet of grey but the lack of rain gave me hope. So far, I had walked 170 miles but it still felt like part of the beginning. In my mind I always reverted to images of departure and saying goodbye: measuring everything by how far I had come. Destinations and distances ahead seemed too frightening to dwell on or even comprehend.

Searching for a sandwich shop first thing in the morning became a ritual that blocked out the negative thoughts about what lay ahead.

I grew to love the bread in Holland and Germany. My favourite rolls were granary coated with seeds of all kinds like pumpkin, sesame and flax. This type of lunch turned out to be my main treat of the day. The harsh conditions always seemed more bearable when I remembered the lunch, which I had stashed away in my rucksack.

Just outside the bakery in the square in Tiel stands a statue of Flipje. To Dutch children he is as famous as Noddy is in the UK. Flipje is made of interlocking raspberries because he was originally the mascot of a jam factory in Tiel called De Betuwe.

I was reminded that this area is famous for its orchards bearing apples, plums, pears and cherries. Kate and I had walked beside many of them the day before. Massive dogs resembling Rhodesian ridgebacks (also known in South Africa as Van Rooyen's lion dogs for their ability to fight off said lions) guarded very long greenhouses. These were serviced by a fleet of forklift trucks, trailers and tankers. I concluded, from the presence of the dogs, that the theft of fruit must have been making the growers very jittery or, horrifyingly, that there were lions roaming the length of the Waal.

Harmsen van der Beek, a Dutch commercial artist, created Flipje in 1935. Beek (as he signed himself) had an eventful life. He became famous in Holland for his drawings of Flipje's adventures. His wife wrote the stories in rhyming couplets rather like the way the stories of 'Rupert the Bear' were written.

By the end of the 1940s his reputation was such that the London publishers Sampson Low approached him to illustrate the stories of their new character called Noddy. They hoped that Enid Blyton could develop Noddy into a rival for Mickey Mouse. Rival or not, Noddy was a fantastic success for Blyton and Beek. In 1953 Beek tried to persuade the jam company to let him release the Flipje books into the UK market. Unfortunately for him and us, they refused. He immediately resigned from De Betuwe and six days later he died suddenly. Fortunately for Blyton there were other talented Dutch illustrators who could keep Noddy driving his taxi around Toytown, while being harassed by Mr. Plod.

As I walked towards the ferry that would take me across the river from Tiel and towards Nijmegen, I wondered whether the jam people ever regretted not letting Flipje go to the UK. Their fame, and that of Tiel itself, might have spread (sic) even further.

I stopped worrying about De Betuwe's limited horizons and Beek's untimely death as I tried to remember all of Noddy's friends. Sadly, I could only get as far as Big-Ears, Mr. Plod, Bumpy Dog and Miss Prim the teacher. Particularly Miss Prim who had reminded me of all the starchy teachers I had had in my infant and junior schools.

When I got to the landing, the first ferry of the morning was idling and ready to go. The Waal was wide enough at this point for the trees on the other side to resemble the fringe on the mouth of a flycatcher plant. They waved slightly in the early morning breeze and beckoned me in. The view was sliced in two as one of those 200-metre barges slipped by silently on the other side of the river heading towards Cologne or Basel.

The way ahead for me, towards Nijmegen, was to be mainly paths and narrow roads through farmland. I warmed to the journey especially since the sun showed itself in snatches.

There seemed to be plenty of time before the ferry departure as the pilot was out of his cabin and chatting to the ticket man. This gave me a moment to read the information board beside the gangway. A story unfolded of the river floods in 1995, which caused death and havoc in the whole of northern Europe. A global warming catastrophe in a time when many people seemed unaware of the phenomenon.

To my shame, I did not remember this disaster at all. The morning after the first floods the local news reported that: 'A quarter of a million people were fleeing their homes in the Netherlands last night as rivers swollen by rain threatened to burst through the dykes. Mocking centuries of human endeavour, the rising torrents bore down on defences along the Rhine, the Waal and the Maas, forcing the evacuation of vast swathes of the Dutch countryside. Communities became ghost towns as tens of thousands packed their possessions on to cars, tractors, trucks and bicycles and joined crawling traffic on roads leading out of the polders.'

People were given two days to get out of their homes but those in Tiel were told to move immediately. They were bundled into buses and taken to evacuation centres. In all, about 100,000 people in Holland had to be looked after in temporary accommodation. This was the region's worst natural disaster for 40 years: the great rivers of Europe discharging destruction in Biblical proportions.

As the ferry cast off from the jetty, I looked over to Tiel's city walls abutting the river. There were markers attached to the brickwork that showed graphically how much higher the water was in 1995. I was shocked.

Suddenly, my thoughts of friendly rivers with a calm, purposeful disposition, which were somehow guiding my way to Italy like benign beacons, sank to the bottom of the Waal. By the time we landed, on the Warmel side, I had shed any romantic thoughts about the environment through which I was walking. It was, I realised, all part of the journey. I was slowly becoming at one with my surroundings. Knowing it for its raw unharnessed magnificence.

As I surfaced from the long uphill slope rising away from the river, I set off in the direction of the town of Warmel, hoping to later find some more rural stretches to prevent a walking diet of houses, shops and factories. Cutting across my route at right angles was a long crocodile of walkers looking as if they were in a power-walking event. Many of them had two sticks and were striding out with a Nordic Walker's gait.

I was beginning to forget what day it was, but after checking it was Saturday, I decided that this must be the Warmel Walking Club out in force. After a few miles the crocodile had looped around and was coming my way. This gave me a chance to latch onto Miriam and her father and find out what was going on.

In fact they were from all over the region and this was a 40km course designed to give them practice for the world's largest walking event, which takes place every year in Nijmegen. They call it 'The Vierdaagse,' which is Dutch for 'The Four Days' or alternatively 'The Peace and Freedom Marches.' This was a very special year for the walk because it was its 100th anniversary. It started in 1909 but there were years during the wars when it did not take place. It is a four-day event in which an entrant walks 30, 40 or 50 km a day depending on their age or category. Each year, starting on 3 July, more than 40,000 people, from 46 counties, take to the road. This event attracts the same number of participants as the London Marathon.

Miriam told me more. The finish, she said, 'is a very emotional affair.' Members of the public, who support the walkers, give them glad-
ioli flowers, which have symbolised victory since Roman times. Even
the Nijmegen road through which the walkers pass to reach the finish
is renamed Via Gladiola while the marches are taking place.

I was slightly out of breath while listening to Miriam because her
basic pace was faster than mine, but I was intending to cover this sort
of distance for about three months so speed was not quite so important
– at least that was what I told myself. I tried to encourage Miriam by
saying 'I will think of you and your father on 3 July when hopefully I
will be somewhere in a seaside town down the Adriatic coast line.'
Did I imagine it, I wondered, or did she increase the pace slightly, at
that point, out of walkers' spite for my unintended bumptiousness?

In keeping with my custom of asking everyone about the impending EU referendum, Miriam explained, 'I have not heard much about
it but, I guess, it will come on the TV on the day and I might see something about it then.' No European Union fervour about Brexit there
then.

When our paths diverged, I waved goodbye, wishing them 'good
luck at Nijmegen.' Then I turned into a long, straight avenue of tall,
thin trees and tramped along Liesterstraat running parallel with the
Waal. In the distance, was the town of Beneden-Leeuwen.

8: The Barking of Small Dogs

Once again, in this beguilingly flat country, I was drawn to these birch
tree, yellow flower lined, narrow roads. They either sucked me gloriously into the future, or drained the life from my legs, leaving me at a
wobbly standstill, depending on the time of day and my mental state.
Clumps of soon-to-be-flowering irises grew in the ditches, their tall
sculptured leaves braced against the wind.

Occasionally, I was startled by the sound of a clapperboard behind
me. Out of the blue, a lapwing juddered overhead and landed in a waterlogged field. Making less noise, large white storks circled gracefully
until they lowered their undercarriages onto fringes beside the dykes.

After the Ridgebacks, I was continually on the lookout for dogs, particularly large ones. In the distance, I saw what I thought to be a group of people standing around a car with its hatchback open. Beside them were about three small ponies. As I got closer and straining my eyes, I realised that these ponies might be enormous dogs. On seeing me, one of the people loaded two of the dogs into the car, leaving another loose in the road.

By this time, I was coaxing myself along, promising an extra beer that night if I managed to survive the day. Soon I was within calling distance, so I shouted: 'Is your dog OK with strangers?' With the typical laugh and shrug of the shoulders of many dog owners who don't acknowledge the fear of mere mortals, the man called out, 'Yes, it's fine. He won't hurt you.'

Slightly relieved, I was fascinated both by the enormous black and white dog, and a miniature brown and cream coloured goat, which the man was feeding from a bottle.

The farmer, who I later found out was called Willy van Heck, told me that his dog was not interested in me at all. 'He is meeting two possible mates. They have been put in the car because we only allow a short greeting the first time – to see if they like each other.'

I breathed a sigh of relief and asked: 'Why does the breed look so familiar to me?'

Willy replied that 'I guess everyone has seen a Landseer painting. Well this breed is named after him because he brought some over from Newfoundland to add a feeling of stature and nobility in his paintings of rich folk.'

I grew to feel at ease standing in the middle of the lane next to one of the biggest dogs that I had ever seen. Partly because Willy and his wife Tonny were so welcoming and keen to share tales of their animals. After the two 'girls' had been driven away by their owner, Willy and Tonny invited me in for coffee and cakes. Their farmhouse was a large building set just off the road surrounded by trees; flanked by out-houses for their animals. I thought momentarily about the time I might lose in sitting down for coffee, but in seconds I was entering their kitchen with thoughts of Nijmegen on hold for half-an-hour.

Being a novice at pet owning (I have only ever had part-ownership in a budgerigar, a goldfish - won at the fair - and a cat called Spam named after a sketch in Monty Python), I settled down to hear about the menagerie that lived on the farm. They had Landseers for breeding, a small mob of Jack Russells, a dozen cats, and – from various countries in the Dutch colonies – rare-breed, miniature sheep (I had thought they were goats, earlier) and a herd of cattle.

The kitchen was warm and inviting but the bedding and baskets scattered around, and the prize certificates on the walls indicated that this was truly a farm run on shared ownership lines: humans and animals.

What struck me the most was the role played by the Jack Russells. I was probably the last person alive to find this out, but while the colossal dogs sleep in the shed the Jack Russells keep watch for possible intruders. Then, when something sets them off they run around barking so as to wake up the slumbering giants.

Out of the blue, while Tonny was telling me this piece of animal law, I summoned up an image of Nigel Farage barking away about the hordes of immigrants queuing on the poster behind him. In doing so, he was successfully waking up the sleeping dogs of racism, xenophobia and nationalism. Willy snapped me out of my daydream by offering me another cake, which I took, but only to tidy up the plate.

It was hard to leave this cosy farmhouse, but with stiffening legs and too much self-inflicted cake inside me I felt the need to make up for lost time. I had accommodation booked for one night hence with a guy called Peter through the Couchsurfing App, but tonight my target was to reach a cheap hotel on the outskirts of Nijmegen in time to wash myself, and all of my walking clothes, before the nightly ritual of beer and bed.

Nijmegen is a fulcrum of historical interest. From the time that the Romans settled there, on a hill above the Waal, to the accidental destruction of its ancient centre by 'friendly' bombs dropped by the Americans – it has drawn visitors from across the world. Not forgetting, for a moment, the thousands of walkers who come to join Miriam and her father for four days in July.

I was following PFL's route studiously, and, like him, this was to be my last night in Holland before crossing into Germany. I soon realised that, over the centuries, the city's close proximity to Germany is what has given it such a high degree of importance.

When PLF reached Nijmegen it was dark by the time he got to the quays. He recalled: 'Then for the first time for days, I found myself walking up a slant and down again. Lanes of steps climbed from the crowding ships along the waterfront; between the lamplight and the dark, tall towers and zigzag facades impended... I had supper and after filling in my journal I searched the waterfront for a sailors' doss-house and ended up in a room over a blacksmith's.'

When I arrived on the city bypass, about an hour's walk from the centre, I found my hotel, which was part of an economy chain unknown in the UK. Even if I had tried to find Patrick's doss-house or blacksmith's, I would have been unlucky because he arrived in 1933 and in 1936 they built the famous bridge across the Waal, which effectively plunged the Lower Town, by the quays, into economic decline and eventual dereliction. Even before the bombing in 1944.

9: The Blue Hand

I had planned a day off while in Nijmegen to look around and absorb the atmosphere. It also gave me a chance to check up on my physical shape. My blisters were healing up nicely, there were no black toenails so far, and knees and hip joints were without undue pain. Before packing up at the bypass hotel, I awarded myself seven out of ten given that my shoulders were feeling continually strained by the weight of the rucksack and my pear-drop sized blisters still had some fluid left in them before becoming just a patchwork of pink skin under my heels. Every day, I put jelly-lined tubular shields on my toes and they seemed to be protecting me from damage. These and the various creams and foot rubs were keeping me going.

As far as the rest of my body was concerned, I checked that while walking. I was becoming adept at assessing every twinge and ache, and letting myself know if it was safe to move on or whether I needed a break. Heartbeats and breathing also came under constant scrutiny. Any hint of an irregular heartbeat or a blockage in the blood flow and I could legitimately wave the white flag.

Before I left home, many people had told me a similar story: 'I would love to be going with you (actually I hadn't invited them) but

I could never do anything like that because my knees (hips, back, or legs in general) play up. I bet you'll suffer somewhere along the way.' Kindly, they avoided adding, '…at your age.' This was why I kept a running commentary on those seemingly vulnerable parts. I couldn't bear to come home early and be told, 'There, I told you so.'

Today being Sunday I planned a walk into the old part of the city. My friend Felice from Dordrecht was driving over to meet me to show me around and wish me good luck as I left the Netherlands. We met right next to the main square, close to the City Hall, in the oldest pub in Holland called De Blaauwe Hand.

The barman told me 'This pub, which opened in 1542, used to be next door to the Laeckenhal (Cloth Hall) where material for clothing was dyed. Workers used to come in for a drink with blue coloured hands. So its name evolved.' Simple really.

Felice and I toured the Grote Markt and I posed for a photo beside the famous statue of Mariken – the young girl who arrived in the city with an empty shopping basket but a spirit full of hopes, who then met the devil in disguise (handsome young man, of course) and spent seven years living a life of depravity (in Antwerp), but was finally re-deemed after spending seven years in a convent with iron rings around her neck. This story has been performed as a miracle play, but equally I thought there could be cynical tourists who might spot an underlying symbolic similarity between Mariken's story of woe and university life in the UK with its resulting student-loan iron rings round the neck, especially if there had been an Erasmus year of de-pravity in Antwerp as part of the course.

We spent most of our time together looking at the site on which, in about 10BC, the Romans built the 'Oppidum Batavorum', a kind of administrative centre from which the Romans and the local tribe of Batavians ruled the entire region.

We listened carefully to the extremely knowledgeable guide as he told us about the slaughter of three Roman legions (about 20,000 men) by Germanic tribes in a forest nearby. Later, we learned about the gruesome retributions meted out on these tribes.

But the idea that struck me the most, beyond all this slaughter and mayhem, was that Roman soldiers marched about 32km a day on their way across.what we now call Europe. Here I was hoofing towards their homeland (at least for the soldiers who came from Italy) at the same distance per day. No better way to put one in touch with historical characters, I mused.

The rest of the guide's talk became a blur to me, as I dwelt on the 32km. I heard but did not fully absorb the fact that, long after the Romans had gone, Charlemagne built a fortress-cum-palace here. Many centuries later, when it was pulled down in 1796, the angry citizens of Nijmegen persuaded the authorities to spare two chapels.

I came back down to earth when I realised that Felice and I were standing in one of these chapels. I now understood why I had seen a magnificent statue of The Holy Roman Emperor, Charlemagne (King Charles the Great) on horseback in the centre of a roundabout on the outskirts of the city. The horse was rearing and ready to gallop in the direction of the German border. Just where I was going tomorrow.

Before that I had to find my bed, or rather my 'couch' for the night. I said goodbye to Felice, who had been so welcoming to us in Dordrecht, and set off to meet Peter. I had, albeit briefly, already met him that day. On my way in from the bypass, I had stood outside his apartment block just to log its situation when a young man of his description cycled up to me. We had quickly ascertained whom we were and that I would be back in the late afternoon. Privately, I felt that he was surprised by my age, but if he felt that our age gap was going to be a challenge in terms of conversation, not even a flicker of hesitation betrayed it.

He was almost an archetypal tall Dutchman with a bike. On the other hand, from his perspective, I was probably the archetypal old English man, recently retired, feverishly ticking off things on his bucket list. We struck up an instant rapport. His whole life had been upturned since I had booked my stay. Changes in job, accommodation and long-term relationship had happened in quick succession. He seemed quietly dazed by it all. I tried to listen and understand. I was feeling my way because I was not sure, in practice, of all the niceties of this kind of arrangement for free accommodation.

There might be 10 million Couchsurfers around the world, and a whole app's worth of information to read, but that did nothing to help on my first outing in terms of how to relate to my host. How long to sit and chat? When to offer to take them for a meal. How to find out what the sleeping arrangements were. Gradually, I learned to take it easy, relax and let it all unfold.

I offered to take him out for a meal and he chose a fast food Asian Noodle Bar. I was very happy with that: it was close and cheap. Since this was Peter's first hosting, he suggested that afterwards we went to a pub and meet up with a more experienced host for a drink. I was pleasantly amused to find myself, yet again that day, in De Blaauwe Hand – this time drinking beer with two very affable Couchsurfing hosts. They quizzed me at length about my walk and, in return, I heard about Michael's surfing adventures in America. They were kind enough to say, at the end of the evening, that our conversation had been easy flowing and that my age never entered their minds. I concluded that lying must get easier after three strong Dutch beers.

Bed was a makeshift affair in the living room. I had cushions on the floor over which I laid my own sleeping bag. There among the stereo system, a propped-up guitar, book shelves and the contents of my rucksack spread around, I slept contentedly assured that I had got the hang of Couchsurfing even though it was quite exhausting in terms of listening, accounting for oneself and staying up beyond my 9pm deadline. Just before I dozed off I checked my phone to discover that I had it all to do again tomorrow night in Goch, Germany, with another host, called Chris.

10: Dana T Mudd

The next morning was already warm with blue sky blossoming overhead as I walked up the Kronenburgersingle in the direction of the Keizer Karelplein, the roundabout on which Charlemagne gallops that would lead eventually to the forest between Holland and Germany.

King Charles had only been in situ since 1962, before that (I learned from reading the very informative boards along my route) the area had been the scene of the Battle of Nijmegen on 17-20 September 1944, fought mainly between the American paratroopers of the 82nd Airborne Division and the German SS. Panzer Division Frundsberg, which had previously been fighting on the eastern front.

I waved goodbye to Charlemagne, promising that I would find out much more about his life while walking through his domain. After all, some historians have called him the Father of Europe. My route took me up the Groesbeekseweg, an uphill climb through thick forest on each side. This was my first hard uphill stretch after walking in Holland for a whole week.

At the small town of Groesbeek I sat and relaxed at an outside table belonging to a café in the main square. The sun was strong and for the first time I delved in my rucksack for the sun cream. After paying for my coffee and roll for lunch, I was persuaded by an old man, who judging by his age could just have been a wartime boy, to read all the boards containing fascinating but harrowing details of the battles fought nearby as part of Operation Market Garden.

One huge blown-up photograph was of the street in which I stood. Visually, I was transported back to 17 September 1944 when an American glider pilot called Dana T. Mudd had just landed his glider safely. He was standing with a parachutist called Sergeant Albert Rowe from the 505 Parachute Infantry Regiment and an unnamed paratrooper. All three were described as being from the 82 Airborne Division, but were obviously doing different jobs.

Mudd's glider was one of the first 22 of 200 gliders, which had been used to bring in men, jeeps, trailers and guns. I warmed to him especially because I had been in the Air Training Corps at school and learned to fly a glider. Being a glider pilot, he was not trained to fight. He was assigned to bring in his load and await further orders. Sergeant Rowe looks suspiciously at the camera, the unnamed soldier is smiling and Pilot Mudd, the only one without a rifle, is looking bemused with his mouth open. Three days later Dana Mudd and the other pilots were ordered to fight with the 505 (including Sergeant Rowe) to strengthen the battle force.

One day later Dana Mudd was killed in the nearby town of Uden.

Our guide in Nijmegen told us that he was a boy when the troops landed. His house was commandeered. His family had to sleep in the cellar so that the soldiers could be on the ground floor ready at a moment's notice. Thousands of allied soldiers were waiting to cross the bridge over the Rhine and push onto Berlin. Only they could not capture the bridge at Arnhem and the mission failed. He told us that this was the largest airborne landing ever and that the gliders had flown 300 miles from bases in England.

All this made me lament Pilot Mudd even more. His glider was a colossal canvas-covered metal-framed bird with space for soldiers and cargo on its plywood floor. The cockpit was a bulbous contraption in which the pilot and co-pilot steered the 'flying coffin', as the men called them, at about 70 mph after cutting loose from the tug plane. These men wore a badge on their tunics with a 'G', which stood for Glider, but they knew in their hearts that it really stood for Guts, as they had no weapons, no parachute and no protection against enemy fire.

After staring in silence at the photograph for several minutes, I turned to walk away. The noise in my ears was of soldiers shouting, the frantic flap of parachutes, the massive thud of gliders as their wheels buckled and they bellied on the grass. Afterwards, that was overlain by the repeated sound of gunfire and the awful scream of exploding grenades. The picture that kept flashing before my eyes was of Dana Mudd lying dead in the streets of Uden, a long way from home, unprepared for fighting, still looking bemused and with his mouth open.

In the harsh sunlight, on the way out of Groesbeek looking for the German border, I was navigating through tears. Shortly afterwards, I took a side road towards the forest. A team of builders were working on a house and I asked the way.

'Yes' the supervisor said, 'you keep going, and when the road becomes a track – you are in Germany.'

Another worker called out, 'where are you going?' When I had delivered my rehearsed speech, he visibly warmed to me. 'The Dutch love Italy as well', he said. I imagined that he could see the mountain villages and medieval cobbled streets. When I tried to wheedle out of him why they liked Italy so much, he replied without a smile: 'It's because it's cheap and we don't like spending too much.' So much, I thought, for a romantic view of life.

Germany

1: From Syria in Crocs

As the track appeared, I saw a cottage on my left and to my right a bench on the grass verge. My Satnav showed that my blue dot had just stepped into Germany, but I had seen no sign. So I walked back and looked again. Nothing.

Just then an old man on a bike came towards me from Germany. Actually, he was my age, at least, and I made a mental note to stop saying to myself 'an old man' about people of my age.

'Excuse me,' I said politely, 'Are we in Germany here?'

'Yes we are,' he was wonderfully matter of fact. 'Are you lost?' He wanted to know.

'No. It's just that I saw no sign of a border.' His look of amazement made me feel that I should have just kept my head down and not started this conversation.

'There are no borders anymore. In Europe, we are all one people. It's been like that for years and years.' He kept his head high and cycled on with a superior look that made me wither inside.

I thought, 'Thank goodness I am entering a forest where I can hide my stupidity: where I will not meet anyone else who might expose yet another international faux pas.'

As I walked the Groesbeeker Weg, trees gave way to farmland to the east. In the garden of one farmhouse was a large working model of a Dutch windmill reinforcing the idea that I had never crossed the border in a borderless Europe. Quickly, I reached the centre of the tranquil German village of Grafwegen, which comprised houses and farms set around a road junction overshadowed by a dense looking forest spreading south.

I was about to turn into Grafwegener Strasse, which led to my intended path through the forest, when I caught a glimpse of three women dressed in black hijabs flanked by three men in jeans and jumpers, as well as several children who were about to clamber all over the climbing frames that were scattered across the village play area.

We stood and looked at each other. They seemed fascinated by my appearance as a walker who looked as if he was destined for distant places. Equally, I was surprised, perhaps wrongly, about seeing a Muslim family so soon into Germany, particularly in such a relatively remote place.

Smiling and nodding, it quickly became apparent that we were not going to be able to speak with each other. But by miming and the odd word in English and German, I learned, in snatches, that they were from Syria, they had escaped lots of explosions, they had walked for 15 days and that the children were calmer now. All that with only Crocs on their feet.

The rest was guesswork on my part. There must have been long train journeys involved. The community, I assumed had given them the village hall to call home. There must be food and support available as the children seemed fit and energetic. Smiles all round showed that life was kind to them now. Whatever the future held for them, I left with a feeling of hope that this extended family had made it to safety and that the village had taken them in.

I had a flashback to September 2015 when, as we had seen on television in the UK, hundreds of Germans had clapped Syrian refugees off the trains at Munich after their tortuous journey to freedom. I knew there would be backlashes, a criminal element might surface and countless other problems would crop up, but this family's delight at being safe sustained me, that day, in my walk through the forest.

For most of the afternoon, I was completely alone. The track was straight and so was everything else about this manufactured forest of fir trees. The sun shone at such an angle as to dapple my view between the trees and make shadows across my feet. To break up the symmetry, the forest floor was a tangle of brambles and saplings. I walked for hours, it seemed, without seeing more than a few cyclists and the odd pedestrian that crossed my path at right angles. With so much time spent scanning the path by my feet, I was beginning to notice some radical differences in the countries through which I passed. In England, woodlice beset my footfall, in Holland (especially after the rains) I had to dodge thin slugs the size of bootlaces and now in Germany I had to avoid shiny, blue-black beetles surrounded by miniature orange and white butterflies. I was delighted to be climbing up the mini-beast ladder of evolution; glad to have left the lowly woodlice behind and moved on to brightly coloured butterflies.

Patrick Leigh Fermor, walking in December, remembering only 'woods and snow and sparse villages in the dim Westphalian landscape and pale sunbeams dulled by clouds.' As he arrived in Goch, he was confronted by National Socialist flags and shops selling things like Hitler Youth blouses for Hitler Maidens. My entry was far less dramatic.

I wandered into the main square and found a café in which to sit and wait for Chris, my Couchsurfer host, while having a beer after my 19.7mile walk. Chris worked for BMW in the technical support department; so I was not surprised when he drove up to the square in a large, rather antique-looking BMW. He whisked me out of town (promising to drop me back in the same spot in the morning to maintain the integrity of my route) to his house in a quiet suburb. His large frame was ideally suited to the enormous BMW motorbike – in a state of being put together again, ready for an imminent tour abroad – that I had to negotiate around to get into his kitchen from the back entrance.

Chris's house was a bachelor's paradise. There were projects on all exposed surfaces, begun and left unfinished – bits of motorbike engine, piles of papers and even a model train track in the loft. He certainly seemed like one of those leather-clad guys who roam in groups on the P&O Ferries, at which men like me stare enviously. A Satan's Slave, or something similar, that in a cohort ride noisily round Europe wafting a cloud of confidence behind them, strangely, and in inverse proportion, covering lesser male onlookers with droplets of chagrin, wherever they go.

Chris was welcoming, kind and chatty. He suggested that, as I wanted to buy him a meal out, we went to an All You Can Eat – Mongolian restaurant. We had a great time looking through the containers full of possible delicacies, lifting lids and cooing over the range of meats and fish that could be fried or griddled in front of you. We filled our plates high. By the time we rolled back to Chris's place I felt that I might one day qualify to be a slave for Satan if gluttony was an essential requirement.

A veritable fountain of interesting information flowed from Chris during my stay with him. He loved being German and was proud of his country but alongside that he felt truly European. There seemed a real sense of psyche unity between him and other Europeans. On a family level, he had inherited his love of all things practical from his father who had been a prominent electrician in the area. His father had been responsible for all the electrical work on a nearby nuclear power station – one that had been decommissioned before it even opened. Apparently, when news spread about the disaster at Chernobyl, the German politicians, bowing to public protests, decided to shelve their plans for this new nuclear plant on the banks of the Rhine, near Düsseldorf. So, after being bought by a rich German industrial magnate, the Schneller Bruter power plant became a fully-fledged amusement park instead. Now people enjoy themselves on the 40 rides never thinking about Uranium, fallout or nuclear waste. Since then, the Germans have well and truly caught the decommissioning bug because, as Chris told me, their plan is to do away with all nuclear plants by 2022.

2: Shin Splints, Liniment and Dripping

It was hard to say goodbye to Chris the next morning. He had been so thoughtful about my walk, particularly since he had hosted Nick Hunt when that writer was following in PLF's footsteps a few years before me. He knew the score. It dawned on me, when walking away from Chris's BMW in Goch's main square on my Day 13 that I had slept in the same bed as Nick. Hoping that his skills at writing might have rubbed off, I also began to worry that I might have picked up something else; namely his shin splints.

Nick had developed leg pains even before he got to Tiel, so when he left Goch his treatment was to bind his legs with makeshift puttees; so tight that his calves swelled up and he was forced to loosen the bandaging every so often until it was comfortable enough to walk on. I knew all about this sort of problem owing to marathon running in the '80s. I genuinely thought that my training for this adventure using the British Heart Foundation plan for long distance walking would have ensured that I was not vulnerable to shin splints, but no such luck.

My right leg got progressively more painful as I walked from Goch to the small town of Weeze. Thankfully, a gang of grass cutters were out with a JCB, a flatbed truck and several foot soldiers with strimmers. The verge between the cycle track and the main road was deep in incredibly soft cuttings, on which I walked in ecstasy. Hard surfaces were taking their toll and I had to think quickly. A panic-struck Google of the NHS website informed me that I should take a rest of two weeks with my leg up as often as possible. Wise information, no doubt, but I could not follow it and keep to my self-imposed arrival date of 10 July. I banked on trimming my distance for one day and hoped that would ease the pain enough for me to make up for lost miles later on.

I cancelled my booking for accommodation at Kerken that night and altered my route to a B&B Pension in Twisteden, which was a more manageable distance in my condition – only 10 miles instead of 20. I felt relieved immediately with my plan and was even positive enough to look up and wave at the Ryanair flights thundering over my head on their final approach to Weeze airport. Full, no doubt, of visitors to Düsseldorf which was only a short bus ride away for them, but two days walking for me.

The sun was bright and the blue sky the colour of a blackbird's egg. I had plenty of time to see what was around me, as my pace slowed and I spent less time pouring over maps. I noticed that colourful maypole-type garlands were appearing along the way, in trees, on flagpoles and even festooned on the handles of bicycles.

A young woman, who had just delivered her child to a play group, told me that: 'On the first day in May, around here, people put up these garlands to ensure that crops will grow well and there will be a good harvest later in the year.'

What was enthralling about this custom was that it was so widely observed. Mostly, the offerings comprised an evergreen wreath laced with blue, yellow and white ribbons, hung on a decorated pole. The pole was often topped off with a budded branch that was also laced with similar ribbons. These blue and white streamers fluttered in the breeze in vibration with the shades of the sky and clouds behind them. I soaked in their pagan spirit. These upright poles were in stark contrast to the flat ploughed fields around me that reached out to the horizon. The line along the bottom of the sky was broken in places by a different kind of supplication: a thorn-shaped church spire.

A stone crucifixion scene, which heralded the community's dedication to other unseen forces, stood guard at the entry to each village. But it was the villagers' entreaty to the fertility gods that intrigued me the most. My close proximity to the new shoots of wheat, the trenched up rows of white asparagus and the wide expanses of strawberry plants gave me a kind of pre-Christian bond with the soil, the new growth and food on the table with which the cold stone could not compete.

Occasionally, where the soil was dug below the humus line, I saw that Holland's sandy sub-strata persisted here. Only this time there were no seashells to decorate the surface. There, below my feet was a direct link with my footfall over the last nine days. The glaciers, from the last ice age, had receded millennia ago, and eventually the land had been drained for agriculture. Now people, however unconsciously, still felt the need to commune with the same gods that the first human settlers worshipped. They prayed to gods who once lived beyond the clouds. People's ribbons now still flutter in the same direction.

Just to bring me back to earth, I saw a scattering of woodlice on the first pavements of Twisteden. Gone were the shiny beetles surrounded by butterflies. The creatures at my feet personified my ailments. However, these negative thoughts were completely dispelled when I arrived at Pension Peters, just off the high street. I had been slightly nervous about turning up early, but I was met by kindness, understanding and a soft bed on which to sleep for the rest of the afternoon. What is more, my landlady gave me a tube of German horse liniment for my shin splints. She said that it worked on her horses without fail, so I was convinced. My plan was to sleep, coat myself in the liniment and stagger to the Italian restaurant that I had noticed on my way into town – without jumping any fences on the way.

The Italian restaurant served food that was far from being truly Italian – the cannelloni was straight out of the freezer and the meat was cooked to an Italian recipe only by virtue of the parsley sprinkled over it. The packet sauce that coated everything was well stirred, if I was trying to be kind. However, the wonderful German wheat beer washed it down without me having to think too much about it.

My main preoccupation was to get to bed and sleep my leg problems away. This plan worked until about three in the morning when I woke suddenly only to find that the pain lingered ominously. I spent the next hour rubbing more horse liniment into it and taking even more tablets. I wondered whether binding my leg would help and eventually found an elasticised bandage at the bottom of my rucksack that gave some much-needed support.

By the time I was on my way, after breakfast, in the direction of Düsseldorf, I was so trussed up, lubed up and drugged up that I felt confident to carry on. I was giving myself a second chance. Any sign of weakness in having to sit down for too long on the way and I would have to admit temporary defeat. Fortunately, the weather was divine. The wide expanse of farmland oozed the smell of manure. This infused my experience but did not spoil it. The vast green swathes of spring wheat, patches of yellow rape dotted about and borders of dark green woodland lifted me. They spread out before a sky that was peppered with small white cumulus clouds joined together by the exhaust-scratchings of jets heading out of Weeze or into Düsseldorf.

I was planning to walk as far as I could that day and find accommodation when I could go no further. I walked gingerly for the whole day. I stopped to eat my packed lunch prepared by my horse-whispering landlady, but also, in the mid-afternoon, I pulled up at a roadside cafe/bar where I ate a plate of Spargel covered in Hollandaise sauce. This two-lunch day was a reward for walking while severely hobbled.

It was high season for Spargel or white asparagus which is solidly part of the German culture at this time of the year. The frequent roadside stalls selling Spargel sell mountains of this delicious vegetable, when they are not selling copious punnets of succulent strawberries.

When I had covered 21 miles, I knew it was time to hold up the white flag. I was in an outer suburb of Krefeld called Hüls and I asked a group of people if they could recommend a cheap, friendly place to stay with a local-food menu. Without hesitation one of them chimed in with, 'go to the Hotel Gasthaus Kling about 100m from here. You will be happy there.' Within 10 minutes, I was lying on my bed wondering how I had managed the distance from Twisteden. Probably because it was absolutely flat and the weather was kind. I fell asleep soon after.

I had booked a table for dinner and after entering the dining room I was glad I had. It was a small snug room with dark-wood panels. There were pictures of old Hüls on the walls. I learned, by wandering around before my starter arrived, that the town was once famed for its manufacture of damask and velvet. This was a weaving town with a reputation for high quality material. Coming from Hebden Bridge with its reputation for fustian, I warmed to it immediately. The very word 'damask' gave it a sense of magic, for me. This cloth might have been the subject of tales told along the Silk Road from China to Europe. I learned that the material's name comes from the word Damascus, a city that has long lost its magical aura since it sank into the morass of civil war.

Larger groups consisting mainly of couples of about my age surrounded my solitary table for one. They were noisily enjoying the home cooking. Huge plates of meat and potatoes were brought out from the kitchens along with litres of beer from the bar. People were wolfing down platefuls of Spargel. After my second lunch of the day, I knew exactly why.

My starter was a local specialty served in a small bowl with bread soldiers. It was dripping topped with crunchy granules of pork crackling. The waiter was surprised that I knew what I was eating but once tasted, it could never be forgotten. My mum used to spread it thickly on slices of white bread for us as a mid-week treat after the fat from the Sunday joint had been cooled so that the jelly separated from the fat. A sprinkle of salt was all that was needed to make a meal of it. I had not tasted this gastronomic delight for about 60 years.

Trusting that one more try at dripping after so many years would not do any permanent damage to my arteries, I dipped in my bread and was transported back to my childhood, along on a silk road of different kind. After this, the pork schnitzel, potatoes and beer were merely a very good sideshow.

I slept soundly except that in the middle of the night I sat up, awakened by some intermittent scratching beneath my TV cabinet. Fearing that I would have to become The Pied Piper of Hüls, I thought of other ways to rid my room of this intruder. After coughing and bouncing up and down on my bed to no avail, I threw two shoes, in quick succession, at the cabinet. Either my visitor settled down for the night or it scurried off to another room. Whatever happened, I slept deeply from then on.

3: A Beer on Father's Day

At breakfast, I bumped into a woman who was to make me forget my painful leg for a few hours. She was here from Holland with her husband but he was not staying with her. He was an inpatient at the local hospital, which had a great reputation for its treatment of cancer. His doctor in Holland had arranged for a local diagnosis and after that he was able to choose a hospital for the follow-up course of treatment. He chose this one in Germany. She always came with him and they made the Gasthaus Kling their home from home. She was one of these people who spread a kind of radiance whenever they speak. Her warm, winning but self-effacing manner endeared her to me immediately. I was so mesmerised that I forgot to ask her name.

We spoke of my walk, the state of Europe and Germany's welcome of the Syrian refugees. By her gentle comments and questions, she boosted the sense of purpose about my journey so well that I forget my shins until well into the morning. Her support for the refugees was unequivocal. Whatever the problems that might come afterwards, Germany – in her opinion – had acted from the highest moral ground. It was as if she shone with the values that could not be budged by the barking of small dogs. I left feeling levitated by this chance encounter over breakfast.

In all that passion for what was happening around her, I thought it strange that she knew little about the whole Brexit affair. I wondered afterwards whether we possessed too high an opinion of our own importance in the minds of other Europeans? Perhaps the 'Great' that the Brexiteers wanted to put back into Britain was not the correct 'Great.' The phrase, 'Outwardly Great rather than Inwardly Great' kept rattling around in my mind as I navigated my way towards Düsseldorf.

In crossing the town of Krefeld, I wondered why there were, on every corner it seemed, gangs of young men drinking copious amounts of beer so early in the day. I plucked up the courage to ask a small group, who replied almost in unison 'It's Father's Day. This is what we do.' After a surreptitious Google, out of sight, I confirmed their explanation. Apparently, while originally you had to be a father to celebrate on this day, it has become more like a National Day for Men, generally. One custom is for groups of men to buy a barrel of beer and pull it behind them on a trolley while they perambulate round the countryside getting more and more drunk.

Having read that, I was therefore not so surprised when I came across such a trolley being pulled ahead of me on a country lane. There they were – five men and a dog. They took it in turns to pull one of those push chairs, which can be fixed to a bicycle. It had a tent on top, in this case to keep the sun off the beer.

My ambivalence about this whole performance was abandoned in favour of solid opposition when I saw what they were taking turn at doing. One by one, they peeled off towards the verge beside the road. In one hand they held a phone (looking at the screen rather than talking to someone) and in the other their manhood, while urinating into the field. When they all got going again, I never heard any conversation between members of this Father's Day group because whatever was on their screens was more engaging. The only time that they acknowledged one another was when bending down to replenish their plastic glasses. And so they drank the barrel dry.

During the afternoon, I kept mainly to country lanes, footpaths and the edges of fields. Eventually, I turned the corner of a long hedgerow and saw, like a long lost friend, the River Rhine. Suddenly, there was life along the riverbank, and it was far more varied than the groups of boozy men who had grabbed my attention so far that day. I turned right along the smooth tarmac cycle tracks and large grassy verges. The tracks seemed to lead all the way to Düsseldorf, which sparkled in the distant sunlight on the other side of the river some miles away. It was like entering a party that was in full swing after walking along a quiet side street to get to the front door.

The Rhine flowed steadily towards the sea to my left while hordes of people enjoyed some sort of sport on the wide grassy riverbank. Overhead, I saw the underside of huge planes preparing to land at the city's main airport. I wove my way between cyclists, roller skaters, skateboarders, joggers, Nordic walkers, recumbent bikers, blade skaters and small groups of water-bound people pulling on their wet suits.

Just before I stepped from the grass underfoot to the pavement, I spotted the best cycle sighting of my walk. An enterprising company had customised a fleet of ordinary bikes to resemble Harley Davidson motorcycles. The tourist easy-riders, many with long beards and tattoos, dressed in checked shirts and bandanas, followed a tour guide who was pointing out the city's sights from the saddle of a Harley to beat all Harleys. My host Chris back in Goch might have looked down on these wanabee bikers, but I felt a strong kinship welling up inside me. Satan's Slaves on push bikes! Much nearer to my capabilities, I thought.

At one point, I became a sight on the Harley tour. The guide, who looked like a young Mick Jagger, pointed my hat out to the group as an unusual object of great interest for tourists. (My wide-brimmed hat was made out of recycled lorry tarpaulins from Brazil. I had put it on because the sun was so hot that afternoon.) The group all cheered. I gave a royal wave as they peddled past.

After the rockers on pushbikes, pedestrians became more frequent as I approached the wide bridge that spanned the Rhine. I teamed up with a very smart, tall woman, and her equally willowy, blond daughter who looked about 18. They told me that they disliked but tolerated the drunkenness on Father's Day. However, they stayed away from the city centre because it could become very rowdy. I wished that I had known that before I booked my Airbnb room in an apartment, above a restaurant, in the Altstadt (Old Town).

They enlightened me about the beautiful gardens that ran down to the water's edge from the road along which we were now walking. These plots were in the same tradition as allotments in Britain. Apart from the expected vegetable plots, many of these had fairly sizeable cabins, BBQ areas, playgrounds and sun bathing platforms as well. Apparently, they could be bought or rented. Sometimes families kept them for generations. All the while we were talking, we watched families enjoying these gardens under a cloudless sky. At home, allotment owners sometimes use their plot as an escape from family life, but here everyone was enjoying outdoor life: family and friends together.

An avenue of severely pollarded trees flanked our entrance into the city proper. The river was wide and busy with container barges: just another typical business day on the Rhine.

I thought of Father's Day at home in England when I would get two cards, and something like a pink tee shirt and a book token. In the evening, on such a day, I might even have a pint of beer if the mood took me. But when I turned into the Altstadt, I was met by a tidal wave of cheering, guffawing, football-chanting and rabble-rousing men. They were standing outside bars all the way up the cobbled street in front of me. With my rather ragged Catweazle appearance, I felt decidedly ill at ease and out of place.

The very orderly, commercial scene on the Rhine had turned quickly into a swashbuckling, chaotic, raucous nightmare in the space of a few 100 metres.

My room – when I located it above an Italian restaurant just beyond the Bier Kellers – was within earshot of the revelry, but its comfortable bed with a middle-eastern type quilt, shelves of books, choice pictures on the walls and little pencil sketches dotted around made me feel relaxed immediately. After leading a solitary existence for many days, it was pleasant to lie on the bed and listen to the snatches of conversation as tourists passed below my window. It was soporific.

Upon wakening, as twilight deepened, I descended to the street in search of food. Steering clear of the Italian place on my doorstep, I moved a few yards away and discovered, for the first time, the magnificence of a German restaurant that brews its own beer – a Brauerei. This one was called Zum Schiffchen and was established in 1628. The owners seemed dedicated to preserving an old-fashioned atmosphere with dark wood, stained glass, heraldic motifs, suits of armour, waiters with long blue aprons, mahogany tables with benches, foaming tankards and piled-high plates of roasted meat.

I entered into the spirit with no prompting. Soon I was sipping a large glass of dark beer, which was, I discovered, a famous Altbier from Düsseldorf. It is a kind of brown ale brewed by using warm top-fermenting yeast. To build up my strength, I ate a good-sized plate of liver dumplings, mashed potatoes and sauerkraut followed by apple strudel and vanilla sauce.

All around me, I heard the clink of cutlery, the hum of good-humoured talk and the thud of glasses as they were laid to rest on mahogany. Unless you place your hand, or a beer mat, over your glass the waiters assume that you want a top up. I witnessed many new beers arriving and tongues loosening all the more.

Leaving before my glass could be replenished, I was in bed in less than 15 minutes. I scoured the pages of PLF's razor-bladed book to find a reference to this city. I wanted to see what I might have missed. In 1933, he had walked an hour past the Altstadt and bedded down in a workhouse: 'I rang a bell and a bearded Franciscan monk in clogs unbarred the door and led the way to a dormitory…' At least I had a room to myself and was wrapped in a quilt. But I could not feel totally self-satisfied because of the constant throb coming from my right shin. Promising myself a liberal coating of horse liniment before setting off in the morning, I fell asleep despite the fact that Father's Day was still going strong in the background.

4: Catweazle in Chemical City

As the day dawned, I left early because the distance to Cologne was about 24 miles, which I estimated would take me about 10 hours including stops to apply more horse liniment. By 7am I was finishing my cappuccino and brioche, and packing my seeded triangular sandwich into my rucksack. For the first hour at least, I had to walk through the suburbs of Düsseldorf.

At one stage, under an enormous flyover, on the concrete apron of a vast roundabout, I met a West African woman from Togo. In a mottled conversation consisting of English, German and French (her mother tongue), I established that she had been living on this roundabout for 13 years. Space blankets, chairs and large bottles of water, which she appeared to have ferried there in a supermarket trolley, surrounded her. I wanted to give her money but she refused, saying: 'No, it's alright mister. I am fine. I make a living.' She pointed to the bottles of water, which I guessed she sold to passing motorists who pulled up at the roundabout. I left her, totally bemused about her life and how she managed. Most of all, I wondered how living in the middle of a busy road intersection could be sustainable over one month, let alone 13 years. She became embedded in my mind as a symbol of resilience, which was to nourish me in times of doubt and weakness over the weeks ahead. Another pilgrim's waypoint.

The straight line between the cathedral at Cologne and Düsseldorf was not very long, but the River Rhine swerved in wide curves at this stage in its course. Leaving me little option than to take a more circuitous route. So, sometimes I was walking along the riverbank while at others I was deep in countryside among flower-strewn meadows and newly ploughed farmland. There were lots of people about. Walkers and cyclists mainly. Apart from yesterday being Father's Day, it was also Ascension Day in Germany, which is why many people had taken another day off today, to see them through to the weekend.

There was a real holiday mood in the cafes at which I stopped. Drinking coffee at 11am, after nearly four hours on the road, I was sitting surrounded by people of my own age who had arrived from the houses opposite, mob-handed with their Zimmer frames. They were smartly dressed for the occasion in that the men wore jackets and ties, and many of the women had on pleated skirts and sensible shoes. They had come for coffee, showing all the signs of enjoying a comfortable life in retirement: chatting to friends and eating large slices of cake. Seemingly, without a care in the world. I wondered why so many of them needed Zimmer frames. They looked like a walking-aid convention rather than a typical coffee group of the third-age.

We obviously did not have much in common. In the end, a smile and a nod at each other, was all we could manage. Needless to say there was also a suppressed sense of suspicion on both sides. I queried the need for so many Zimmers and they probably wondered where this old guy could be going dressed like that and wearing those tired-looking walking boots... It seemed that the distance between us was far, far greater than from there to the cathedral.

During the late afternoon my Google maps showed me a riverside path that would lead me, in about two miles to a cheap hotel at which I intended to stay for two nights. This would give me a free day to explore Cologne.

I arrived at the Rhine and began to look for the correct path going south. According to my map there was a huge blank area of land beside the river, which I took to be fields. What I was actually confronted by was, I found out later, the largest chemical plant in Europe (Chempark in Leverkusen) through which there appeared to be no chance of walking. Vowing never to trust my phone maps again, I quickly worked out my options.

Either I could persuade the guard on the gate to let me walk on the road between the various buildings, which would lead me directly to the main road close to my hotel. Or I could take the road right around the Chempark, which would add a few more miles to my already long trek for that day. Since I was thoroughly worn out already and depressed by not finding a riverside path, I stiffened my sinews and headed for the red and white striped barrier.

Ahead of me was a factory site larger than a small town. There were tall office blocks, factories with chimneys and space-age buildings with elaborate external pipe work that made them look like Le Corbusier meets Star Wars. There was a throb and hum arising from the plant, adding an extra aura of mystery, which made me imagine the chemicals of the future that were being brewed there.

I slipped in between the end of a barrier pole and the stand at which a driver could press for assistance, and walked tall towards the sentry box. Quick as a flash, the guard on duty raced out and stood squarely in front of me blocking out the view.

'Where do you think you're going?' He said in an even more aggressive voice than the police in Holland. In all fairness, I was not like their normal suited visitor. What on earth, he might have thought, would Catweazle be doing strolling through this chemical city?

'Please can you help me? I am a British traveller who is walking to Italy and you are not on my map. Would it be OK to walk through your site to save me a few miles?'

I said all this in a polite, semi-pleading tone, hoping to appeal to his softer, more feminine, side.

Bemused and stony-faced, he called for assistance. Another guard came to his aid and between them they virtually frog marched me through a pedestrian turnstile and deposited me on the road outside. They entered into no explanation or conversation of any kind.

Confused and belittled, I took my other option, which involved walking around the whole site. As I moved off, I wondered whether they took me to be a spy or bomber with a rucksack full of Semtex. Or perhaps just an eccentric, self-important Brit who thought that Europe owed him special concessions? A bit of a Boris or a Nigel, perhaps. Who knows?

Tired and in very low spirits, I traipsed on towards my bed hoping to catch a glimpse of the twin spires of Cologne cathedral on the other side of the river. I felt in need of the solace that this celestial pointing would give me.

While I was walking, I looked up the Bayer company whose sign on a tubular walkway over the road, at one point, read: Science for a Better Life. They were a major stakeholder in the chemical city. I was fascinated to learn that their best-known product was Aspirin. I was not so impressed to find out that they invented the name 'heroin' and that they marketed it as a cough mixture, a substitute for morphine-based cough suppressants, before 1910. They can also add the first

widely used antibiotics and birth control pills to their list of achievements. Since they purchased the renowned (or infamous) firm called
Monsanto in 2016, Bayer has become a world leader in the field of ge-
netically modified crops. It began to dawn on me why the barriers of
entry were so forcibly drawn. Who would want a ragged-trousered
wanderer, with a knapsack full of goodness knows what, in close
proximity to the epicentre of genetic modification?

My low spirits had sunk to pavement level by the time I reached
Roggendorfstraße, and Hotel Friends, in the area of Cologne called
Flittard, between Leverkusen and Stammheim. I was some miles away
from the centre of the city but from my bedroom window I could see,
on the horizon, the twin-spires.

Between us it was thickly wooded in parts, and the Rhine created
a natural boundary, but there above all other buildings rose the spires
of Cologne cathedral, like the upended roots of a wisdom tooth or the
fork in a snake's tongue. I could not quite understand why I was so
fascinated by the sight. It was partly due to having the next day off in
order to say that I had walked into Cologne from England, and because it gave me a spiritual focal point to contemplate rather than Zimmer frames and woodlice.

That evening, my mood vacillated from ecstatic to morose and
back again. I had been away from home for 16 days and still had about
66 to go. I had walked 288 miles, so far with about 1000 ahead of me.
My blisters were healing but my shin badly needed a restful day tomorrow. The smallest thing was likely to deflate my positivity. The
last five-mile syndrome was getting more pronounced in the late af-
ternoons especially when chemical cities got in the way. Was this the
point at which I could bow out and say that I had tried my best?
Would Cologne be seen as a good place to turn back? I needed to sleep
on it – this pilgrims' negative waypoint.

5: A Carer for Chloe

How wonderful to wake up and remember that I was free for the day.
In a better mood than yesterday, I planned my sightseeing over breakfast. I had to catch a bus to the train station at Leverkusen. A train
would then take me to the city centre. By about 10.30am I was waiting

on the deserted station platform for my train.

The silence was broken by the squealing noises of Chloe in her wheelchair. As a disabled adult, wheelchair-bound and only capable of saying some words, she was cared for and pushed by the wonderful Elsa. I found out their names after we became friends that day.

Chloe and I bonded straight away. It did not matter that my German was limited. We were all waiting for the train and that was all that mattered to Chloe. She grew increasingly anxious when the train did not arrive on time. Looking down the line worriedly, we both imagined the disappointment of not seeing Cologne that day.

When it became obvious that the train had been cancelled, Elsa came up with a clever plan. If I was willing to be Chloe's carer, until we got to Cologne, she could use her Over 60s Travel Card and I could use the carer's version. The plan was to catch a bus to another station and then we could take a direct train to the centre on another line. I would be helping out, so would travel for free.

My caring endeavour did not start very well. I began to wish Chloe had a motorised chair when I tried to steer her down the steep ramps to the street level where we waited for the bus. Then I manoeuvred the heavy wheelchair, and the even heavier Chloe, onto the bus with much huffing and puffing. But the rewarding side kicked in when Chloe announced to everyone on the bus that I was helping her today, by squealing enthusiastically while pointing at me. I smiled and nodded, playing it cool, as if to say: 'It's nothing.'

Chloe could count the bus stops, so I learned some basic German that morning on the way to the U-Bahn. Later, safely on the train, we noticed how crowded with tourists it was becoming. In medieval times, Cologne and its cathedral was one of the most popular destinations for pilgrims in Europe; it still was by the look of it.

When we got off the train at Cologne, we were faced with a throng of tourists. Chloe had no intention of being impeded so she started shrieking intermittently at the top of her voice as if to say: 'Make way there, we want to come through.' The crowd parted like the waves of the Red Sea. In no time at all, Chloe, Elsa and Moses were in the station lift rising up to the main concourse of the Dom Hbf station. Taking only a moment to grab a leaflet about the cathedral, we were sucked out of the station by the warm air and brilliant sunshine.

Once in the fresh air, I bent to shake Chloe's hand to say goodbye and, with a mixture of sadness and relief, gave back the Carer's Travel Card to Elsa. She thanked me for helping and wished me good luck on my travels, or at least that is what I thought she said. As they wheeled off to the shops to our right, I swivelled round to get my first proper view of the cathedral. In no time at all, I had morphed from a trainee carer to a hopeful pilgrim without even getting changed in a phone box.

I was looking directly at the tallest Gothic building in the world. I admitted to myself that I was still a bit shaky on architectural terms such as 'Gothic' even though I had read up on them time and time again. But in one glance, I abandoned any sense of ignorance and just soaked in the aura of this magnificent building. Built on the site of a Roman Temple and having taken 632 years to complete, this epic place of worship had withstood 14 bombs in World War Two and the ignominy of being belittled by The Washington Monument and The Eiffel Tower in 1884: they took away its status as the tallest building in the world. It certainly had stamina.

The original 13th-century stonemasons, who began the carving of this creation, were such highly valued craftsmen that they were to spend the rest of their lives building cathedrals in places like Strasbourg, Prague and Metz. The clergy had convinced medieval people that a cathedral was an earthly representation of heaven, so every part of it had to be perfect. Quite a demanding criterion with which stonemasons could be held to account, I whimsied as an ex-inspector of schools.

Feeling myself coming down to earth again from a sublime, solitary moment of wonder, I caught sight of the tourists gathered on the steps at the base of the station-facing side of the cathedral. They looked like ants trying to figure out how to circumnavigate a massive obstruction that had just appeared in their way.

I thought perhaps I should go inside and explore the place where pilgrims had come for centuries to be near the skulls and bones of the Three Wise Men, but when I arrived a service was in progress. Milling about in the crowd, which was ready to pounce as soon as the singing stopped, I felt uncomfortable with the continual talking, videoing and photography, so I slipped away to find a chemist in which to buy a new toothbrush and some more painkillers.

Looking back at the front of the cathedral, as I headed to the shops, I wondered if other pilgrims, in the past, had arrived after weeks of walking, and been suddenly repulsed by the crowds all around them. Even the cathedral seemed mystified. The two towers, which I had eyed so longingly from afar, now gave the impression (standing guard on either side of the main entrance) of a pair of shrugging shoulders: confused in stony silence.

On leaving the chemist shop, and remembering that I was a tourist as well as a pilgrim today, I had the choice of a ride on a 'chuffer train' around the city, a tour on a talking red bus or being whisked away, on high, by a cable car. I chose none of these, but instead opted for lunch in the only riverside tavern left standing after the war. It was just the kind of establishment that PLF might have visited in 1933. He had fallen in with some sailors with whom he eventually hitched a two-day ride to Koblenz on a river barge. I guessed that shin splints might have plagued him as well and that he needed to rest, or was it, I wondered, perhaps a lengthy way to sober up after imbibing too heavily in the tavern?

Steering carefully around a pack of noisy football supporters outside, I slipped into the Haxenhaus zum Rheingarten that lay in the shadow of the cathedral and facing the Rhine footpath. I was fascinated to find out that beer had been served there since 1231. This was 17 years before the stonemasons even arrived to begin laying the foundations up the road. At least they had somewhere nearby for lunch.

It was very quiet inside, as everybody else was enjoying the sun in the tavern's gardens that ran down to the river. I stood at the bar refusing to emulate PLF who, keen to impress his newfound sailor friends, had ordered beer, but only as a chaser for the spirit shots he was downing. The ghosts from his book had never felt closer than now, as I stood in this world of dark wood, waiting to order a small local beer and half a metre of sausage with sauerkraut. Sausages were served by the metre or half-metre and I was being reserved, it being lunchtime. In the evening, I would have been sorely tempted by the huge knuckles of pork, sheathed in knobbly, criss-crossed crackling, which were being dispatched to several tables nearby.

As I ate and drank, I read about the legend of the Heinzelmännchen von Köln. Apparently, long ago, the townsfolk of Cologne had become thoroughly lazy. They were supported in their sloth by a pack of elves that finished all the jobs people had started during the day. In the end, the wife of a local tailor taught the lazy citizens a lesson. One night, she scattered a sackload of dried peas so liberally around the town that each and every one of the elves slipped over and injured themselves badly. They were last seen heading for the River Rhine to escape the town, never to return. Some woodcarvings near the door of the tavern told the story of the elves and how, thanks to the tailor's wife, the townsfolk of Cologne became as hard working as they undoubtedly are today.

Before I caught the train back to my hotel, I spent the rest of the afternoon of my pilgrimage wandering along the riverbank looking at the relaxed office workers and holidaymakers, wondering if I, unlike them, would be able to summon up the energy to walk to Bonn tomorrow. After all, this was my day for contemplation. Would I give up gracefully, having come so far, or find the strength to soldier on?

As usual, when surrounded by crowds of people, I felt exceptionally lonely. I took a selfie with my back to the cathedral just to be like everyone else. With that, my pilgrimage was done: it was time to go.

I woke up several times in the night assessing the degree of pain from my shin and the weight of my resolve. Gut instinct told me that I would carry on, but the voices in my head kept saying things like, 'Well you gave it your best shot. For a man like you, you did brilliantly – you have nothing to be ashamed about...'

By the time I was eating croissants and drinking a double-shot cappuccino, I had managed to subdue the voices. I knew that the events of yesterday had somehow influenced me in deciding to keep going, but I could not quite put my finger on which one in particular.

Was it Chloe's strident determination to part the waves and get to the shops at all costs? Was it the inspirational moment when I gazed on the work of countless stonemasons over 632 years? Was it the tailor's wife who rescued the townsfolk from lives of inactivity? Was it my nightly FaceTime chat with Kate, which always buoyed me up after a hard day? In truth, it was probably a mixture of all of these – a composite pilgrim's waypoint.

6: Italy comes to Bonn

Today my destination was Bonn, the old capital of West Germany before the wall came down and everything was moved to Berlin. As if matching the event of three days before for the men, today was Mothering Sunday. The streets in Cologne were strangely quiet as I walked through the city on the eastside of the Rhine after an early breakfast. I saw some dutiful sons and daughters, emerging from florists with bunches of brightly coloured flowers, but that was about all.

On and on, I passed streets of unopened shops, tree-lined avenues of smart houses, apartment blocks and offices – all silent. With so little happening, I had time to think about the tailor's wife, thinking she might be the answer to my conundrum. Her role in the story intrigued me. Was she the archetypal mother who clears away all the barriers in life so that her children can become decent adults? Possibly. Especially since I was taken with how the story synchronised with it being Mothering Sunday. But I then veered towards another interpretation. Was the tailor's wife – me? If I gave up on my adventure, would I be like the citizens of Cologne: opting for an easy life; letting others, in the guise of elves, do everything for me. I would always be living my life through others: reading their travel books and not writing my own. Somewhere, from inside, thanks to this pilgrim's waypoint, I had awakened the strength of my resolve; resisted the temptation to always rely on elves. My inner tailor's wife, with her bag of dried peas, had brought me back to life. I needed to do this every day: take responsibility, not rely on the elfin community.

No sooner had I realised, for myself, the meaning of the Heinzelmännchen von Köln than I came down to the banks of the Rhine again. Within seconds, I sat down on a riverside bench: unceremoniously rolled up my trousers, and took off my boots and socks. I was eager to rub liniment into my shin, tend any remaining blisters and tighten my bindings. I was back. Back in full swing.

Lost in self-absorption, it was only later I realised that a couple of cyclists perched at the other end of my bench had moved gingerly away to another seat so as to give me more space or, more likely, to hide their disgust at the sight of my dilapidated feet and medical ministrations.

At mid-morning, I sat alone in a waterside café having a well-earned coffee, while listening to Acker Bilk's greatest hit: Stranger on The Shore. I could not get over how, in mainland Europe, British music legends were celebrated on a daily basis. The flowering of our famous musicians is glorious, but when they begin to fade we ignore them disgracefully in favour of the next bright attraction. But here, Acker's records are played regularly in almost every café. More topically, and to prove my point: Damien Rice, Mike and The Mechanics and Massive Attack were all set to perform in Cologne or Bonn, as advertised on huge posters along my route.

As I left the café, a large Mothering Sunday party arrived for the consumption of frothy coffee and giant slices of cake, which, I noticed on many other occasions, is a favourite German pastime. I slipped past them, not wanting to spoil their celebrations with the unendearing, and yet still powerful, odour of liniment.

Later, with about 10 miles to go before I reached Bonn; I began to sense a change in the scenery. In the distance, on the horizon, I caught a snatched sighting of some hefty hills. I checked on the map and found that these were the Siebengebirge hills. Like Arthur's Seat in Edinburgh, they are the cooled remains of molten volcanic rock that bulged up, millions of years ago, through a split in the earth's surface. Apart from the long hill out of Groesbeek in Holland, my last contact with uplands the size of this was when I crossed the Yorkshire Wolds. Having called on my best self to keep me going, I now felt that I was rewarded with a new sense of adventure caused by the impending change of landscape. What I had read about at home was soon to reveal itself: The Middle Rhine, where the river flowed through steep valleys covered in grape vines, beckoned.

My afternoon was spent meandering along wide grassy strips beside the river. Bonn, on the other side, was poking its head above the trees. At last, on the final approach I had to cross over on the Mondorf to Graurheindorf Ferry and make my way along Milchgasserweg towards the main station. I was going to meet Domenico.

This young man has grandparents who live in Santa Vittoria in Matenano (my destination) and every year he spends part of his summer holiday with them. We had bumped into each other at the Bar Centrale, run by the wonderful Bruna, Diego and Kevin, in the summer of 2015 after he had finished his first degree in mathematics at Padua. He heard about my intended walk and that I might possibly pass through Bonn. Since he was then about to move there to study for his Masters in pure mathematics, he pledged that there would always be a bed for me there, if I wanted it.

So in the late afternoon of Day 18, after a tiring 24 miles, I stood outside Bonn's main station looking for a young man who, I remembered, vaguely, resembled Bob Dylan on the front of his 1963 second album 'Freewheelin.' I felt slightly nervous about the evening ahead. I knew precious little about advanced mathematics, only a few facts about Beethoven (the most famous son of Bonn) and had only read superficially about Max Planck (Domenico's student accommodation was next to The Max Planck Institute for Radio Astronomy). I struggled to understand anything about Quantum Physics beyond the idea that it was totally different to Classical Physics and that many brilliant minds had tried, and generally failed so far, to find if and how the two might fit together in one grand theory. Perhaps String Theory was the answer but that idea was too hard to think about after such a long day. I worried that I was going to be totally out of my depth, especially if his friends from Italy and Poland were as, or even more, brainy.

Within minutes of meeting my host for the night, all of my worries had disappeared. Domenico and I were sitting in the city's main square drinking beer and gazing at a magnificent statue of Beethoven. We talked about music, the mathematics of topology, and his passion for poetry. I swapped tales of, and examples from, Ted Hughes for his on Giacomo Leopardi, one of Italy's most famous poets. I could not have felt more at home.

That evening Domenico and his university friends had planned a special meal. Everyone was bringing a dish with a general theme of Italy or Poland. These twenty-something young men and women, mostly from different parts of Italy with only a couple from Poland, had sought out the Bonn delis selling the most authentic Italian and Polish produce. They also had regular food parcels sent to them from loving Mamas who were determined that their fledglings would not starve for the want of home delights.

They had transformed the common room in their block by pushing all the armchairs back and making a large dining table out of those usually set up for solitary study.

It was tempting for me to know that I was about to taste the best prosciutto from Parma, sweet tomatoes from Sicily, Polish beer and ham, and frittata made from local eggs and Italian vegetables. All served with wraps and salad. Afterwards, cake was lovingly offered from stashes probably kept hidden in individual bedrooms and, to finish, freshly brewed espresso coffee (the best I had tasted since leaving home), was brought upstairs from someone's bedroom hotplate.

The meal was magical because, in the candlelight, this group of young friends perched on the edge of the next steps in their life, with exams over, spoke of their memories of being together, the past and what lay ahead. They asked me many questions about my adventures. It seemed as if my journey prompted talk about what they wanted to do with their lives.

We revelled in the food and the talk. At times, the conversation turned in the direction of the potentially inflammable topic of which region of Italy produced, for example, the best prosciutto or tomatoes. But the flames never got going, despite the usual waving of arms that could so easily have fanned them. At the end of the meal, I glowed with exhaustion and they shone with promise. They were ready to keep drinking and chatting, while I slipped away to bed. It turned out that for a wandering visitor, at this university, not knowing enough about mathematics or physics was no drawback at all.

I did not even feel the need to inject into the conversation my pre-prepared facts about Beethoven. My favourites in reserve were about him dipping his head in a bucket of cold water before he composed anything, and that if someone in the audience talked during a performance, he stopped, packed up and left immediately.

In the morning, I left them sleeping while I set off, after a welcome shot of strong coffee, to cover the 21 miles to Bad Hönningen. There were, I realised while tiptoeing through the hushed streets of the Bonn university district on a Monday morning, certainly still advantages to being a student in that no-man's land after exams.

7: Dragon's Blood and Chocolate Boxes

Until I reached the car ferry just south of Oberwinter, I planned to keep to the Roman side of the river. In doing so, I saw my first German castle on the Rhine near Bad Godesberg. It was a bit of an anti-climax because instead of Rapunzel towers and arched windows, it was shaped like a children's sandcastle with a flag stuck in the top. It had a commanding view of the hills opposite but, in keeping with Sod's Law, it was closed on Mondays. Not daunted, I spotted a Haribo factory and spent an hour talking to myself, on and off, about life in the castle; in the type of high-pitched child's voice so appealingly demonstrated by the adults in the UK advert. Out of deference to passersby, I stopped my ramblings momentarily until they had disappeared. More importantly, I did not want to be locked up, as a crazed vagrant, so early on my journey down the Rhine.

I was not walking in PLF's footsteps today because he would have still been hunkering down or sobering up on a barge loaded with cement going toward Karlsruhe. Being on the west bank of the Rhine was a pleasure but I realised, too late, that I had missed being close to what could have been another pilgrim's waypoint. It was the legendary Dragon's Rock, on the east side, at which Siegfried was reputed to have slain a dragon and sealed his own fate in the process. I had missed it because, way over on the other bank, I had been so absorbed in talking to myself, like a child. Typical.

While eating my lunch on a riverside bench after taking the car ferry, I read the famous story of Siegfried taken from an epic poem called: The Song of the Nibelungs. Like all great tales, I immediately felt it had been written with me in mind. It also contained some unusual devises such as an invisibility cloak. I wondered where I had read that before?

After killing the dragon, Siegfried rubs himself all over with dragon's blood to make himself invincible. But a small leaf, from a nearby linden tree, falls on his shoulder. This creates a patch of skin not covered by the blood. A vulnerable spot. Much later in the saga, Hagen drives a spear into this spot, on Siegfried's shoulder: killing him while he was drinking water from a river.

My muscles were beginning to seize up. If I stayed to read the full story, I knew that I would not get to Bad Hönningen by dusk. Equally, I knew that Siegfried's attempts to become invincible, the dragon's blood; the patch of skin and the spear would all linger in my mind for a very long time.

The change in scenery, which I had first experienced on the approach to Bonn, seemed even stronger now. Houses looked a little more alpine here; grand, affluent chateaux were perched on the high wooded hills. I was expecting to see lederhosen being worn at any moment. At precisely 1.24pm, I saw my first grapevine. That sealed it. I had passed from the beer-drinking north to the wine-drinking middle of Germany.

I could not wait to do some tasting, especially if it was served in a glass with a green stem. As a child, I had thought that type of glass the ultimate in sophistication.

Soon after, I walked through an archway at the base of a tall tower into a village called Erpel. I just stood and gazed at the quaint gabled houses with towers attached to their sides, the inns that looked as if they had been welcoming travellers for centuries, and the clusters of tourists who were eating cake and drinking wine. A group of pensioners, some with Zimmer frames, asked me what I was doing. After telling them, one man with a walking frame mused: 'It's all relative though. If you get to Italy: that would be an achievement. If I get back to my car after this cake: that would be an even greater achievement.' We all laughed. I went into the café to ask if they could fill up my water bottles: everyone was so keen to help.

A bar room sergeant major had said to me, in an inn just before Düsseldorf, over a lunchtime beer, that I should 'be prepared for the Middle Rhine. It is too much like a chocolate box, too padded, and too comfortable: too unreal – like a Disney film set. The real Germany is right here. If you can – don't go there.'

I have to admit that certain places on this stretch of the Rhine felt a bit like being in a film set. I imagined that I was about to move from scene to scene until I reached Mannheim. After which I had to branch off up the River Neckar to arrive at Heidelberg: where I was going to meet Alice and Max (he of the cooling towers).

With the sergeant major's warning ringing my ears, I was always on the lookout for things and events that did not conform to his apocalyptic vision of hell for the real Germans. I found some in Bad Hönningen.

I stayed at a guesthouse occupied mainly by workmen dressed in blue-serge bib and braces, away from home for a few days. We were lucky enough to be hosted by a wonderfully motherly woman who took us all under her wing. At breakfast the next day, she piled our plates high. Then in a nurturing way, like a lioness raising her cubs, she showed us how to fill up some paper bags with things for our lunch: rolls, ham, cheese, eggs and fruit. We could take as much as we wanted. My fellow guests tucked their next meal down the front of their bibs, like marsupials, while I made my rucksack even heavier.

As I walked away from this as yet out-of-season spa town, I was sure that the kindness and generosity that I experienced at breakfast would never appear in a tourist video promotion. Siegfried and his dragon's blood would always bask in the limelight.

8: Nursing Homes and Naked Women

My route from Bad Hönningen to Koblenz, on 10 May – Day 20, took me deeper into the real Germany beneath the top layer of the chocolate box. I am sure that the sergeant major had not ventured this far.

By 7.36am, I had seen a vision of my future self. I was passing a house with a large front garden, in a small lane, slightly away from the Rhine. There sitting on a bench was a life-sized model of a stout, solid looking old chap, reading a book. He had a tuft of white hair above his forehead, but was bald elsewhere except for a further fringe of white hair, at the back, falling down to his collar line. He was dressed in a light blue lounge jacket and knee-length black trousers tucked around thick, woolly socks. He wore comfy black slippers, the type one needs for a sedentary life.

Smoking a pipe that glowed red, he had crossed his legs to be more comfortable while reading to an imaginary audience from his raised book. He looked jovial and obviously happy with his latest rendition.

I stood and stared for some time, but, as I walked on, I began to hear a soundtrack in my head. Matron was showing a family around the nursing home. They were looking for a suitable place to park their aged parent. She was saying:

'Last of all, we come to the sitting room. Roger usually takes up residence here in the mornings. You will see he is holding a book. He thinks he wrote that book. Apparently, it is about a walk he claims to have undertaken from England to Italy, but no one believes him. Just look at him – do you think he could have done such a thing? Don't worry, he is utterly harmless. We just let him do his reading every day. Anyway none of the residents come to listen any more, they have generally heard enough after their first few days in The Rhineland Care Home. Now let's move on to my office to discuss fees, shall we?'

As the morning progressed, the noise on my side of the river became almost unbearable, but luckily it drowned out Matron and her derisive banter. I was trying to keep to narrow roads but, between the busy river that was crowded with barges and me, there was a main road jammed full of heavy lorries. There was also a railway line along which long snaking freight carriages clattered their way to the industrial towns higher up the Rhine.

I took a short break in the Weingut Scheidgen, which sold glasses (with green stems) of their estate wine accompanied by a plate of nibbles, but generally it was an ear-splitting slog to reach the crossing point that would take me over to Koblenz.

On a factory estate near Neuwied, I stopped at a café to ask them to fill up my water bottles. Because I sensed some non-verbal hesitation on the part of the people behind the counter, I quickly followed the request up with some details about why I was walking and the charities that I was supporting.

I was met with the same kind of sarcastic comments so recently displayed by the Matron in my head. I was told in full-flowing German something along these lines:

'See that – there is a refrigerated cabinet, with bottles of water that you have to pay for. So there is no way that we are going to fill your bottles with our precious tap water for free. If that is not good enough, the door is over there.'

I had not been spoken to so harshly since the police in Holland insisted that I got in their car, NOW! I escaped quickly from that café feeling for the entire world like an unwanted immigrant.

Turning the next corner, and just as I was imagining telling the woman behind the counter where she could put her bottles of water, I saw the most unusual advertising poster that I had ever seen, and strangely on a similar theme.

A shapely, virtually naked, young woman (except for a slender G-string) with her back to the camera had a mobile phone stuck firmly up her backside. I was not in the least bit shocked but reflected that this sort of graphic would never be allowed in the UK. A quick WhatsApp to a family member in the UK, who translates for a living, coupled with my own use of Google Translate led me to understand the legend written above and below the young woman, which read: 'Is your mobile phone a pain in the arse? Then don't worry, we can mend it for you.'

Not a Rhineland chocolate box in sight.

9: A Pilgrim in Koblenz

I crossed the Rhine on a footpath beside the railway line and felt an enormous gust of wind hit me when a train went careering past trying to get to Koblenz before I did. The extremely prolific graffiti all over the struts and stanchions of this metal cuboid of a bridge made me ache with a sense of foreboding about what was to come. Who were these people who had time and the inclination to crawl all over this bridge, making these obscene marks, risking their lives every time a train went by?

The walk from this bridge into the heart of Koblenz proved again that every so-called beautiful city has a back door entrance, which appears in no guidebook. A kind of Dante's Inferno way in, which is reserved only for the hardy or the foolhardy.

At one stage, I passed a railway siding that was used for storing old trains and carriages, which were decidedly past the end of their working lives. They were rusty, falling apart and faintly flecked with paint signifying their former glory. Right at the end of this siding was a slaughterhouse of sorts, in which these metal beasts were killed off for good. Their death rattle could be heard from the road. It was sickening. As was the lingering odour of greasy food being served in countless fast-food outlets on the road ahead of me.

Where was Walt Disney version of the Middle Rhine when you needed it?

Having walked through the 'valley of the shadow of death,' certainly for the unwanted railway rolling stock, I came, in the end, to the place where two of the greatest European rivers met in union: the Mosel (Moselle in French) and the Rhine. By then it was nearly 5pm and I had been walking since about 7am. My brain had turned to jelly in the last five miles, but it was re-energised when I crossed the bridge over the Mosel towards Koblenz's Altstadt.

A blanket of grey cloud covered the entire sky above the city. The surface of the river was like corrugated sheet metal only interrupted by the thin islands running down the length of the Mosel's final approach to the Rhine, and the long, white river cruisers moored up near the Altstadt. These floating hotels had just disgorged their passengers to wander round the fairytale streets before dinner.

Standing in the centre of the bridge, I was imagining the choices that had been made, over the course of 3000 years, by the Celts, Romans and Prussians, for example, who had come this way. Whether to march straight on down the Rhine or veer left up the Mosel and head towards what is now France. Either way the possibilities for trade, exploration and wine growing were enormous.

In front of me was German Corner. An island, once owned by Teutonic Knights, on which now stands a statue of a mounted Kaiser Wilhelm I to celebrate his work towards the unification of Germany. Just beside it were three slabs taken from the Berlin Wall when it was dismantled, to commemorate an even grander unification.

While deep in thought about this inspiring area, I tried to imagine the point on the riverbank where PLF jumped ashore from his cement barge. At the same moment, I received a call from Adrian, my Airbnb host for the night. Where was I? What time would I be arriving? Where shall we meet? I was dangerously near the end of my 10-minute period for a break. I had discovered, over the last three weeks, that a stop of more than 10 minutes led to a stiffening of the legs and a loss of motivation. After those two brutes took hold, it was desperately hard to get going again. So now I had to push on before my day ended there and then.

Adrian was a student living in a skyscraper of student flats. He was wonderfully polite and helpful. He was Polish and had made a great effort to come and study in Germany. I liked him as soon as we met in the street near his place. I guessed that these meetings are common in the Airbnb world. They gave the host a chance to call it off, if you did not look like a suitable guest, because at that stage you still had no knowledge of where they lived. Anyway, I must have passed the test, because very soon I was soaking my aching legs in a hot bath. A better end to the day, I could not have imagined. I felt that Matron had stopped watching over me and that the morbid feelings inspired by the city's backdoor entrance had been washed away completely.

In the early morning of the next day, I walked through the grander part of Koblenz, which was bathed in bright sunlight – I saw how the other half lived. Yesterday's inferno had become today's paradise. Well-stocked shops full of beautifully designed goods sat underneath four or five floors of neat-looking apartments. The top floor often had dormer-type windows stitched into grey slate roofs. Yellow, orange and pale green facades topped off in a smart grey hue: the buildings looked both regal and comfortable. There was a spring in my step brought on by the bath, Adrian's good hosting, the smart side of Koblenz and the fact that today's journey to Boppard was only 13 miles.

I had decided not to try and find PLF's route because the account in his book was very vague about the exact path he had taken. With a few miles to cover, I took a forest trail that, with any luck, would lead me directly to Boppard. My plan was to miss out what I later found out was the largest bend in the Rhine by going straight through the forest. However, as Robbie Burns said: 'The best laid schemes o' mice an' men…'

After the city, it was a welcome relief to step inside the forest. I was alone, totally. Unlike the stiff ranks of conifers which I passed through near Goch on my first day in Germany, here many varieties of deciduous trees surrounded me. Oaks and linden were prolific. Countless shades of green revealed themselves as the wind shook the trees. To begin with I walked on tarmac but, after that ran out, I spent the rest of the day on tracks or paths clogged by dead leaves.

At mid-morning, I found a functional but comfortable hut in which to take a break. As there was no hurry, I had time to sit and wonder. I was perched in what looked like a glorified bus shelter, with bench seating on the inner three sides. It was fully open at the front. A sloping roof prevented the weary getting wet. I saw some signs and stickers, attached to the woodwork.

There was a prominent sign in large letters, which informed me that the hut was called a Merkurtempel-Hutte. That meant nothing to me. But, while having my drink and snack, I looked it up. I discovered that the name of the hut was related to a story told by the Roman poet Ovid. In his work called Metamorphoses, we learn about Jupiter and Mercury and their visit, in human form, to Phrygia (a region of Turkey many miles south of Byzantium). They were looking for a place to stay the night but were turned away by the unfriendly people who lived there. All except an old couple called Baucis and Philemon. They welcomed the travellers, offering them food, drink and a bed for the night.

When the old couple realised that these two men were Gods, not just ordinary travellers, Philemon wanted to kill their goose to make a special meal. Jupiter refused the dinner, saying that they all had to leave immediately and go to the top of a nearby mountain. When they got to the top, without looking back as they climbed, the old couple were staggered to see a flood had destroyed the entire land which they had called home. Everybody in the entire region had been drowned and their houses destroyed because the Gods were angry at the inhospitality they had encountered. The only place left standing was the old couple's hut, which had been transformed into a temple.

Baucis and Philemon were granted wishes, as a way of rewarding them for their kindness, but all they wanted was to live a simple life as guardians of the temple, and when one of them died, so should the other. They lived happily serving others in their temple and in time, their last wish was granted too. Upon their death, they were turned into two trees that grew intertwined as one: an oak and a linden. In death they stood together, in the grounds near the temple. In the years to come a forest would have grown around them, just like the one in which I sat.

What an incredible story, I thought, and how moving to find the hut named in honour of Baucis and Philemon, and their temple, in such of an out-of-way place.

On the top crossbeam of the hut, just next to the words Merkurtempel-Hutte, there was a sticker, with a blue background. Emblazoned on this was a bright yellow scallop shell. I knew this to be an indication that I was actually on the St. Jacob's Way. This was one of many paths, in this part of Germany, which led to Trier. This ancient city was a kind of focal point where paths from all over the north of Europe converged. Pilgrims on their way to Santiago de Compostela in northern Spain, to worship at the shrine of St. James (or Jacob as he was known hereabouts) would gather at Trier before walking south and over the Pyrenees. The sea creature from which this sign derives lives in a home of two, hinged scallop shells: one signifying the spiritual side of life and the other, the material. Pilgrims who follow the way of the spiritual shell hope to find the strength to live a peaceful and caring life, such as that discovered by St. James on his way to Spain after Jesus' death.

Lastly, there was another sticker between the temple and the scallop shell. It, and its message, was the most difficult for me to fathom. At first, I thought it was an ultra-rightwing sticker because it consisted of a woman with a full burka standing next to a man in traditional dress but holding a machine gun. The typed words beside the pictures were in German and I struggled to translate them on my phone. The nearest I got was: 'We Must Stay Outside.' On further investigation, I found that these words are used in the title of a recently published book by Kathrin Hartmann, which is called 'We must stay outside – the new poverty in the consumer society.' The blurb told me that: 'More and more citizens in Germany are excluded from the economic wealth of the country. Not only the unemployed or pensioners, but also many people, who are in an endless spiral of cheap jobs and temporary work.'

Whether that particular sticker held a message that was in support of disenfranchised Muslims or advocating keeping them 'outside' – I could not be sure.

Nevertheless, here I was, sitting in a temple dedicated to a couple whose welcome and generosity were amply rewarded; on the St. Jacob's Way that led pilgrims to a life of peace and care for others; and signposts to a book that warns of the social and economic problems of leaving some sections of the community on the 'outside.'

The day before, two cyclists had hurtled past me quite near the awful café, where the owners had refused to give me water. The lead cyclist slowed and called out to me, in an encouraging way, 'Are you walking to Compostela?' I now knew why he was asking. 'I am a pilgrim,' I wished I could have shouted back to him, 'just not going to that destination.'

10: Deep in The Forest

I decided it was time to move on, but not before taking a final look around for an entwined oak and linden. I wished that Baucis and Philemon might be there, just beyond the clearing. But even without seeing them, I knew that this place was a waypoint on my pilgrimage that would fuel my thinking for a long time to come. At the end of the afternoon, I looked back on that moment of solitary elation, and realised that it was a brief moment of happiness before the misery began.

My downfall started when I thought it would be a good idea to take a shortcut. So instead of walking the ridge ahead of me all the way down to Boppard, I wanted to veer left and follow, what looked like a dry riverbed down to the main road. I guessed that the road walk at the end of this route would get me to my bed for the night quicker than sticking to a track all the way.

It was all right to begin with, but I was soon out of my depth: literally, in very deep gullies filled with ages-old leaves in which I sank above my knees. I started to panic. I had come too far to turn back. The steep slopes behind me, some of which I had slid down, looked treacherous to climb back up again for someone with a heavy weight on their back. I did try it just to make sure, but I started to topple backwards, as soon as I began.

Then it became impossible to move. The deep leaves were acting like quicksand. I was spending too much valuable energy by lifting my legs above the surface level, just to take a step forward. I undid my rucksack and rolled to the edge of the gully. Up to my left, I saw that the ground hardened and, although there was no actual path, a route, the shape of knuckles on a close fist, looked possible.

I kept telling myself that I could not get lost. As long as I was going downhill I should come to the road in the end. Dragging my rucksack, I crawled in all fours to the edge of the gully and clambered up on to the craggy slope in front of me. Turning to face downhill I set off, only to be stopped in my tracks by fallen trees. The forest must have suffered a fairly recent disaster, because in front of me, at regular intervals, tree trunks (some huge ones) had fallen over the knuckles of bruised earth.

Owing to the height of their clod-dripping roots, the trunks were levelled somewhere between my knees and my hips. I clambered over them, but that was very time consuming because I often needed to snap off small vertical branches, which threatened to puncture my trousers and my skin. After about half-an-hour of these gnarled hurdles, they thinned out and in front of me was only thick, seemingly impenetrable forest. In the far distance, I could hear the sound of an occasional car on the road below. This was cause for a break.

Having fallen, rolled, crawled, slid and clambered through this unforgiving forest for about two hours, I stopped to compose myself. Nagging questions would not go away. Was it wise to try a shortcut with no proper map? Should I not have turned back after the first steep slope instead of ploughing on? Would the emergency services, which I could have called out using my SPOT device, thank me for having taken such a risk?

'Now tell me Herr Gill: how old are you? So, you thought, at your age, it would be a good idea to leave the proper path and slide down this gully for several kilometres?'

I could hear the ambulance driver saying that I was a fool and I knew it. I was a long way from the gently winding St. Jacob's way. My pilgrimage had gone pear-shaped.

My understory was told.

Luckily, my bruises, scratches and cuts were only minor ones. So, after a break, I straightened out one of my collapsible walking poles and began hacking through the thickets between the road and me. After a steep drop at the edge of the forest, I skidded down to the road and began walking towards Boppard as if nothing out of the ordinary had happened. I felt like Charlie Chaplin waddling, whistling and twirling his cane after narrowly escaping a ton of bricks hurtling towards his head.

Pasted prominently on the first lamppost that I passed was a sign that read: Gengen Nazis, which translated as – Against Nazis. Thank goodness I was back in civilisation: a place where people rage against the slumbering dog of fascism. I was not alone any more: no longer surrounded by thick knots of trees, which lacked the grace and goodwill of the entwined Baucis and Philemon.

Later, I looked up the word deciduous. It comes from the Latin dēciduus, which translates, in one sense, as 'tending to fall.' That was certainly true of me in the forest between Koblenz and Boppard. At many times, along the way, my progress through the forest was decidedly deciduous.

11: Lorelei, Cuckoo Clocks and Hildegard van Bingen

Boppard was another stylish resort along the banks of the Rhine. Grand buildings sporting grey spires, of different shapes and sizes that attempted to puncture a sympathetic grey sky. My evening was spent drinking a celebratory glass of Riesling out of a large cupped glass with a tapering, thick-ribbed green stem, and then a meal of beef soup with marrowfat dumplings followed by the obligatory bratwurst and chips. I asked for a Mosel wine, since I had just come from the confluence of the two great rivers, but was told that the soil and angle of the sun in Boppard were not suitable for that grape, so the local choice was Riesling or Riesling. I chose Riesling. I was celebrating, not just because I had survived a disastrous afternoon in the forest, but more importantly I had been walking for three weeks and had covered 376 miles so far.

I was hoping for fine weather the next day because I had planned to make my first camp, beside the river at a site in Oberwesel, on the west bank of the Rhine: the Roman side. The campsite was only a short distance from the famous Lorelei Rock. However, when I set out in the morning, the wind was strong and it looked like rain: not ideal camping weather. If yesterday had been a solitary interlude, today looked as if I would be sharing my experiences with many another, as I had hit a tourist hotspot. Even as I left Boppard, the coach parties were gathering and I could hear the tour guides on the pleasure barges warming up over their microphones.

Because I had missed the spot where Siegfried killed the dragon, I was determined to see the Lorelei Rock. I guessed that it would be lunchtime when I arrived in Sankt Goar, which is the town that dedicates itself to keeping this harrowing tale alive. As I walked along the riverside, the rain became even heavier and the wind scuffed the water violently.

My jacket was buttoned up like it had been when the hailstones in Holland attacked me. It all seemed quite fitting because I was approaching the most dangerous section of the River Rhine. Just past Sankt Goar the width of the river is reduced considerably and the undercurrents become severe. This is where boatmen have always had to take special care. The last major disaster happened in 2011 when a barge carrying 2,400 tons of sulphuric acid capsized near the famous rock.

The rain had eased by the time I reached the town. Before I looked for somewhere to buy food, I gazed intently out over the river, following the progress of a heavily laden coal barge going upstream. It was being navigated with caution, sticking well inside the white buoys and avoiding the red ones, which floated above the dangerous currents. I was gripped, but the bored-looking teenagers just descending from a coach only gave the river a cursory glance. They looked stubbornly disinterested. Their teachers herded them towards a nearby cuckoo clock museum and factory.

I learned from reading a postcard outside a gift shop that in 1824, Heinrich Heine, one of Germany's favourite poets, revived a story about a love-thwarted blond-haired girl from a poem written 20 years earlier. This maiden sang songs from a high rock luring sailors to their death in the turbulent Rhine. His poem became a huge success. It spawned other versions of the tale and a clutch of musical tributes. I read it while standing among other tourists who were also scanning the postcards. I thought the poem absolute dross, totally uninspiring and wondered if it accounted for the teenagers' apathy today. Perhaps they had been required to read it for homework in preparation for their day out.

As I sat perched on a concrete slab near the public toilets eating my sandwich, I saw the school party emerging from the museum. As is often the case with pupils on day-trips, stolid boredom often turns into giggles and poking by lunchtime. True to form, several members of the group sat themselves on blocks near me and frolicked beyond the gaze of their teachers. It was clear – they had been left cold by the cuckoo clocks.

As a child, this type of clock had saddened me, immensely. My mother and I once went to a house owned by someone who possessed a German mechanical clock. It struck the hour by sending out a woman from one door and later a man from another. They were never out together. Each one looked sad and lonely, never realising that, had they waited, they might have had a moment of warm human contact. Of course, I never verbalised it like this at the age of eight or nine, but the dull ache, inspired by this hourly-mechanised scene, remained with me for a long time. Maybe I felt sorry for my widowed mother seeing her as the lonely wooden figure? Caught in that moment of re-alisation, I was nudged back into reality by the young people beside me asking what I was doing and where I was going. When I told them, they seemed impressed, at least more so than by the clocks, though this was not much of an accolade.

I almost missed the actual rock on which the statute of Lorelei stood. Of course, it was on the far side of the river, but even so she was tucked out of sight near a telecommunication mast, which could be seen. I stood beside two young women who, like me, were poised to take a photograph. It was pointless. So we shrugged our shoulders in unison, concluding, I guess, that the blond temptress was either purposely evasive, had jumped, or was just fed up with the attention.

I supposed that a good view could be had from the hotel, tourist centre or hostel, all of which were conveniently situated near to the statue. 'This is not the real Germany,' the words of the bar room-know-it-all sprang to mind again.

I arrived at the campsite at Oberwesel in time to book in, find a spot and pitch my tent – all before the mobile restaurant opened for evening meals. My tent was next door to an English couple who were biking back home after cycling around the world for 19 months. An incredible adventure.

This campsite (on the Roman side of the river) was on exactly the same line as the Roman Limes. In fact, I saw that there was a cycle route with the same name running just outside the gate of the campsite. From the word 'Lime' we get the word 'limit' because this was the limit of the Roman Empire. Lying in my tent, recovering from the day, with the River Rhine flowing only a few paces from my door, I felt really at ease with the world. Peace reigned and I drifted off to sleep.

All was well, until a freight train went by on the other side. The racket was deafening. It echoed round the hills of this cavernous valley. I realised then that, despite being two days away, I had simply walked further up the same valley, which had been so noisy on my way into Koblenz. I was even more anxious when a voice from the next-door tent, said: 'We were here yesterday and the trains over there kept us awake most of the night.'

It seemed that raucous trains on the eastern side had supplanted the uncivilised tribes that held sway on the eastern bank in Roman times. Despite my having indulged in enough beer to act, as I had hoped, as a sleeping draught, the trains made such a racket that I did not sleep for more that 20 minutes at a time through the entire night. That is, until the light came up and, for some reason, the trains took a rest until breakfast time.

So far in my journey, I had never suffered from a hangover or awakened lacking the will to set off again. The morning, after my night's camping at Oberwesel, was a first in all respects. The effect of being woken up every 20 minutes; being disturbed by the heavy rain in the night and being depressed by having to break camp in drizzle, dampened my enthusiasm for walking anywhere.

A breakfast of two brioches, eaten as I walked out of the campsite, was the only yeast in the loaf that morning. Although the next large town along the Rhine was that of Bingen, it was not my destination that day. I was actually heading for Rüdesheim, owing to a cheap deal in a hotel there. It was only a short ferry ride away from Bingen across the Rhine. Both Rüdesheim and Bingen are noted places on PLF's route. One Christmas Eve in 1933, he stayed at a guesthouse in Bingen, but I was saving that town for my free time, the following day. Apart from it being the place that PLF awoke on Christmas Day in 1933, Bingen was reputed to be a spiritual focal point where mysterious things had happened.

At the age of eight, the famous 11th-century Christian mystic called Hildegard von Bingen was placed in a convent. She was already hearing voices and seeing vision at that young age. In Bingen she grew to become a brilliant scholar, naturalist, musician and artist. She was centuries ahead of her time for her understanding of the natural world, health and spiritual matters. Only one of four women who have ever been designated as a Doctor of The Church for her contribution to Christian Theology, she stands head and shoulders above most religious thinkers. These are the reasons why so many people are drawn to this famous town on the Rhine.

Her status as a mystic even placed Hildegard on the Share International Foundation list of potential Spiritual Masters. Most people would be absolutely unfamiliar with the theories behind Spiritual Masterhood and the works in general of Benjamin Creme and Alice Bailey. I find them fascinating, although they are somewhat obscure. I think talking about these ideas would place me in the same league as individuals who walk along chatting in a childishly squeaky voice about life in a medieval German castle; the sort of bespectacled geek to be avoided at parties.

According to the central ideas expounded by Share International, individuals who are capable of attaining the highest spiritual levels do so by being incarnated many times, typically five, before they can be designated as a Spiritual Master. Apparently, Hildegard von Bingen is at level 3.5 and is now living, somewhere in the world, as a man who works helping others as a social worker. Has anyone seen him, I wonder?

Irrespective of Hildegard's sometime position at the esoteric far-end of the spiritual spectrum, she is absolutely mainstream among the majority of people interested in the development of religious and environmental ideas.

As the day went on, rain sleeted down on me relentlessly. I spent most of the day getting wet while walking beside the B9. This is a very long German main road that is busy, noisy and best avoided. I had to take this route for the sake of directness, not out of choice. By the time I got near to the ferry landing in Bingen it was late afternoon and I had eaten no lunch. So, wet to the skin with water running off me in small rivulets, and sodden socks, I found a place to eat even though lunches had finished hours ago. The only person being waited on, I stripped off the top layer of wet clothes and sat in miserable glory eating a hot Thai coconut curry with saffron coloured rice. The food stopped me shivering, but as soon as I donned my wet clothes to leave, I started to shake again.

12: Christmas Day 1933

The ferry across to Rüdesheim ran diagonally across the Rhine, taking about 10 minutes. At the landing point, on the far side, I looked for evidence of a vineyard, because it was here that PLF drank a glass of hock on Christmas morning before walking along the east bank to find an inn serving Christmas dinner. There was a sizeable vineyard directly opposite the place where we disgorged from the ferry, but unfortunately no longer any sign of a tasting booth. I was interested to find out that the word Hock, often used as a generic term for German white wines, was made popular because Queen Victoria loved it. She and Prince Albert had their favourite German wine from Hochheim am Main shipped home to England. So, people wanted to buy what they called, Hock to emulate the royal family.

Not long after, my bedroom at the Rüdesheim Hof looked like a campsite drying- room. My tent and sleeping bag were hung between the wardrobe and toilet door. Dirty clothes had been washed in the shower while I was wearing them, and hung over chairs and the shower cabinet to dry. I set my alarm for seven and slept until it was time for my evening meal. It had been a long day.

I grew to like the evenings before a free day because I could go to bed a bit later. In the old centre of Rüdesheim I visited a themed restaurant run by a brewery. The theme had something to do with a romantic era in Germany when waitresses wore pink checked dresses and platted their blond hair in pigtails. In this one, The Breuer-Rüdesheim Schloss, there was also a dance floor and band area. The restaurant tables spilled over into a courtyard festooned with vines and exotic plants.

I ate roast guinea fowl and drank several glasses of the local Hock, just to be like PLF. Soon after I began eating, the band sprang into action, which forced me to take a bet with myself. I thought it would not be 15 minutes before they played 'Val-de Re, Val-de Ra,' Or as it was formally called, when it was a hit in 1954: The Happy Wanderer (Val-De Ri, Val-De Ra) by Henri Rene's Musette and Chorus. I used to adore this song when I was seven and just recently sang it at the top of my voice when 'wandering' through the forest after Koblenz. That was before things took a turn for the worse. Now, it seemed the perfect song to play in this palace devoted to nostalgia. I won my bet, because in 10 minutes the first notes wafted across the restaurant and several couples left their food and rushed towards the dance floor.

After my meal, I took a beer and sat at the edge of the dance floor watching couples gyrate to Elvis Presley songs like, 'Always on my mind' and 'Wooden Heart.' Even with my limited German, I joined in, always one syllable behind though, with a hearty rendition that echoed round the room: 'Muss i denn, muss i denn, Zum stadtele hinaus, Stadtele hinaus, Und du, mein schatz, bleibst hier?'

Some of it had stuck in my mind from Two-Way Family Favourites on the BBC Light Programme on a Sunday lunchtime, in which records were played for loved ones back home, and, in return, for those on West German bases in exotic-sounding places like Osnabrück and Wuppertal.

I slid down in my seat when the entertainment organiser began looking for volunteers to play the cowbells. Finally, without my assistance, a line of willing tourists produced a spirited version of Edelweiss to great applause and hoots of appreciation from their friends who, like me, had also sunk below the sight lines of the master of ceremonies.

At the end of the evening, nostalgia triumphed over me and, without a cliché in sight, my eyes bubbled with tears when a middle-aged couple beside me danced the last waltz to: 'Can't help falling in love with you.' He was dressed rather like Al Murray's Pub Landlord in a smart, dark red blazer and she in a black leather mini-skirt, a white frilly blouse and shiny black high heels. I was sure that he had Brylcreemed hair and her bouffant must have been held stiff by the spray from half a tin of hair lacquer. They looked marvellously in love. In that moment, they represented all that I missed.

I left before Elvis finished, walking straight back to my damp drying room of a bedroom at the Rüdesheim Hof.

Thankfully, my free day to be spent exploring Bingen began in sunshine. Crossing the Rhine on the ferry reminded me how busy the river was. To get to Bingen, just after breakfast, we had to dodge the early morning barges heading in both directions. This traffic was just a fraction of the 50,000 barges that navigate up and down the Rhine between Basel and Rotterdam every year.

The museum showing the life of Hildegard had a subtle but shocking effect on me. It built up over the two hours that I took to wander around the exhibits. I forgot all about the fantastical theories propounded by Share International. Rather, I became overpowered by a story of a medieval woman who conquered, in middle age, the awful legacy of what we would now call an abusive childhood that festered darkly for much of her adult life. I realised that her life contained a very modern message for us all because everyone is faced with the problem of coming to terms with the karma of their past.

As a child she had visions and heard voices. Her parents concluded that these unwelcome skills would prevent her being eligible for marriage. So, she was offered to the Church, at the age of eight, as an oblate – a kind of spiritual apprentice. A gifted child who saw things that others didn't had to be locked away for her own good. She stayed heavily cloistered for decades; forced into a life of self-denial, religious strictures and pious punishments. Her tutor and spiritual guide, Jutta von Sponheim, was an anchoress in a monastery who lived in a small cell receiving food through a tiny porthole in a prison-like door. She was so devotional that, underneath her habit, she wore a chain with sharp prongs attached to inflict righteous pain at any time of the day or night. Hildegard, at the age of eight, was imprisoned in a world of self-flagellation and spiritual penance.

During her very long confinement, Hildegard learned to read, write and play the psaltery – a medieval stringed instrument: skills that would serve her well when in later life she broke free from her shackles. Jutta died, probably of self-neglect, when Hildegard was 42 years of age. At that point, instead of being crippled by circumstance, she found the strength to make her own life blossom.

Hildegard basked in the sunlight of her freedom, discovering that her visions had not been buried too deep. These visions provided the spur and substance of her profound interest and creativity in music, painting, cosmology, botany (especially the medical qualities of herbs), human sexuality and gender equality. She wrote very influential books, painted beautiful pictures, composed hauntingly mesmeric music, founded two monasteries and gave lectures that even castigated male clerics for their narrow-minded views and religious bigotry.

I left the museum with a strong sense of elation. I had been in the presence of someone who had led a victorious charge against a hobbled childhood: an adult who flowered against all odds. Her music, which played in the decompression zone of the gift shop, resonated round my brain as I reeled into the narrow streets of Bingen looking for some strong coffee.

It was not even lunchtime but I had a powerful urge to cross back over to my hotel, pack my rucksack and be on my way. Inspired by a woman who died 837 years ago, I felt the need to keep moving, striving, experiencing; but then I remembered my soggy trousers hanging over the bathroom door and walking socks on the radiator, and felt resigned to spend the afternoon on this side of the Rhine.

A little later, as I hovered round the town's centre, I came across a small crowd of purple-capped men standing in the street chatting outside a bar called the Binger Bleistift or Bingen Pencil. More men in similar apparel were crammed inside the bar as I tried to worm my way through to see what food was being served. I was told politely that the bar was closed today for a private function and that I would have to go elsewhere for lunch. On asking what event was being held, I learned that I had stumbled across men of all ages, attending the annual meeting of an ancient student society.

I began to chat to the talkative society members who were heading outside for some fresh air after the formal business had finished. Apparently, this was the kind of society that used to practise duelling with fencing swords – a tradition that dated back to at least the early 19th-century. I found out that the whole idea was to inflict a scar to the face of your opponent called a Mensur or bragging scar. Custom had it that the real victor was the man who showed enough courage to stand and take the blow. The proud recipient went back home with a cut across his cheek. In reality, there were two winners: one who showed enough skill to inflict the wound and the other brave enough to withstand the blow.

One of the men on the pavement told me that there was a secretive aspect to this kind of student society in that, until quite recently, men attending interviews for important jobs often scored a crucial advantage if they were sporting a Mensur type scar on their cheek – even easier than a secret handshake, I volunteered.

Men in purple caps, resembling the type that Billy Bunter and his chums wore at Greyfriars School, surrounded me. I couldn't resist feeling a little uncomfortable in their company.

They were deadly earnest about their traditions, beliefs and antics but I could not resist seeing them as comic book characters who lampooned themselves with every new story: Billy Bunter and the Bullingdon Club boys all wrapped into one. I had gravitated from a victorious, saintly woman to a bunch of overgrown schoolboys in the space of a few hours. This left me vaguely depressed.

All I wanted to do was to be on the road to Mainz. It had been quite a day of flesh wounds and mortification and I felt exhausted. So, I made a polite exit and headed for the ferry.

When I got back to the Rüdesheim Hof, I got my belongings neatly packed up, went downstairs for dinner and turned in for an early night. My head was fractured with thoughts of Hildegard, incarcerated until the age of 42, and men willingly offering to have their cheeks

sliced open to gain a badge of honour. Needless to say it was an uneasy night's sleep. I tossed and turned marvelling at a woman's fortitude in the face of suppression and despairing of man's intrinsic
vanity.

13: A Cage of Rats

I awoke to Day 25 of my travels feeling ready for the road despite the
dampening effects of a restless night. The sky was thinly coated with
straggly clouds and the air was decidedly cold. I had a couple of
hours' walk on the eastern side of the Rhine prior to crossing on the
Oestrich-Winkel ferry. Before that, the owner of the hotel wanted me
to pose for photographs outside so that they could advertise my walk
in relation to PLF's visit to the town in 1933. He also gave me a small
pocket-sized book of inspirational quotes to help me on my way.

I realised, once again, that the people I met used my experiences
to summon up all that they aspired to do in life, when the time was
right. As I waved goodbye to my hosts, I could feel their love and support, fuelled by their growing understanding about what they wanted
to achieve for themselves in the future.

By mid-morning I had seen fields full of shut-up caravans, ready
in a few weeks to be opened up for a new holiday season beside the
Rhine. One of the most famous wine growing districts in Europe was
a draw to millions, but today – in the cold air of a mid-May Sunday –
I was left virtually alone to watch my breath vaporise in front of my
face and contemplate what lay ahead.

I had read about Mainz and looked forward to finding out more
about Johannes Gutenberg who, in around 1440, invented his world-
changing printing press in this famous city. Also in a notable act of
reconciliation, the famous Russian, Jewish artist Marc Chagall was
asked to create a stained glass window in St Stephans' Church after
its post-World War Two reconstruction. He was 97 years old when the
last window was fitted in 1978. Ever since then the entire creation has
shed a mystical blue light over the interior of the church, allowing an
onlooker to be bathed in the blue-glow of fabulously illustrated biblical stories and a host of watchful, benign angels.

The Jewish connection with the area became more apparent after

I crossed the river and walked across the headland. I was effectively crossing a large bump of land, which was fringed by the river as it skirted round its ankles. After buying a much-needed lunch at a café next to a Lidl in Ingelheim, I came across a statue of one of that town's most famous sons: Sebastian Münster. He was a 16th-century polymath who produced, among other works, the first German Hebrew Bible and his Cosmographia of 1544 (a description of the world) which was so successful that in the next 100 years it exceeded 24 editions in many different languages – it was one of the century's bestsellers. This incidental bumping into famous people of the past kept me going for hours on end.

I was thinking about all the bestsellers in history that Johannes Gutenberg's work must have facilitated as I wandered through the fertile farmland that surrounded me on what was now a warm Sunday afternoon. The clipped lines of fruit trees, fields of strawberries and heaped-up rows of white asparagus proved what good growing soil this was. Sebastian Münster must have walked the same route to Mainz, looked at the same view of the Rhine and marvelled, as I did, at the beauty of his homeland.

I was heading for a house on the outskirts in which lived my next couchsurfing host, Kurt. He turned out to be a charming young man who lived with his family and a couple of rats. These rats were in a cage in his bedroom-cum-sitting room. I breathed a sigh of relief when I learned that when out of their cage they played only in his room while he was busy killing people, on one of his many video games.

Kurt was training to be a chef, a job he would be able to fall back on once his real passion of joining the German navy for a tour of duty had run its course. He delighted in telling me that he had just gained his entry qualifications for the navy and was off to join up any time soon. We chatted like this as he gave me a tour of the city. As we waited for the bus, he kept glancing sidewise at me because, as he said, he was struggling to believe that a man of my age could make such a journey. The bus dropped us near the centre from which we quickly found the Gutenberg Museum, which was closed.

With only one night in Mainz, I had no hope of seeing the first wooden bed of movable typeface, which after being composited with letters was laid under a massive screw-operated press to produce the page of a book. Rather like grapes being pressed for wine, words were squeezed onto paper to make readers dizzy with their power. Before Gutenberg, all books had to be written longhand and then copied longhand. In the 1440s Johannes showed that metal letters could be moved around in a shallow wooden tray that, after being pressed, produced pages. Sewed together, they made the world's first printed books. Simple. But staggeringly revolutionary.

Invoking the memory of my father, who was a compositor for the Glasgow Herald until 1950, I missed seeing the history of his trade by about an hour - 60 minutes adrift in 35 days of walking or 66 years of living since his death. I hoped he would have forgiven me for being late.

Neither did we get a chance to see St Stephan's Church and its famous stained-glass windows. But we did marvel at a staggeringly evocative memorial to the people who died in the mass bombing of Mainz in the final months of the war. Between September 1944 and March 1945, just before Hitler was finally defeated, British and American bombers unleashed hundreds of tons of explosives: enough to wipe out 80 percent of the buildings in Mainz along with hundreds of its residents.

St. Christoph's Church remained standing but only just. It survived as a shell of outer walls and empty windows. Having stood for about 650 years and been the local place of worship for Gutenberg himself, St. Christoph's skeleton of a building was preserved in exactly the same way as parts of Coventry Cathedral in England. It was a reminder of the bombing and a place of meditation for those that remained: the living who had rebuilt the city or who came to remember. Sitting on the benches in contemplation, Kurt and I stayed a few moments in silence before strolling down to the Rhine to look out across the water and remember the ghosts of the Germanic tribes who used to gaze in awe, frustration and anger at the Roman legions. Fearful of the Romans' killing ways, but determined to be their match.

We looked for somewhere to eat while quietly considering the seemingly pointless slaughter of the ordinary people of Mainz, going about their daily lives regardless of when it happened: Roman or modern times. It was during anxious, vulnerable moments like this that I became worried about my own human frailty: my aching limbs, my still-ticking – but precarious – heart and my severely battered shoulders that yearned to be free from the painful yoking caused by my rucksack. So, it was a relief when Kurt suggested we caught the bus back to his house for a good night's rest.

While we waited for the bus, I asked him what people in Mainz thought of the proposed EU referendum in the UK. There was a silence before he answered. He eventually told me that no-one had spoken about it. It was not on the news and it was likely, he thought, that no-one cared. What a salutary reply for me to hear... Many of the people I had met along the way had a view one way or the other, but here was a blank cloud of indifference. Quickly, I felt anger on behalf of a self-important UK but I managed to quell it with the realisation that, ultimately, we had no right to expect people in the Middle Rhine to care that much about us. Especially, since we had destroyed nearly the whole of their city only 71 years ago.

He wanted to show me his video games. Looking round his room again, while he booted up the computer, I saw a single bed, a sofa, and the table on which stood the rats. I guessed that after he had showed me how to kill several dozen enemy soldiers, he would take me through to my room. Instead he told me, over his shoulder, that I could take the cushions off the sofa and place them on the floor to get more space on which to sleep. 'Where will you be?' I asked, thinking that being alone with the rats was my fate for the night.

'I will be in the bed,' he replied matter-of-factly, as if there ever had been any doubt. 'Don't worry about the rats,' he said calmly, 'they might wake up and play in their cage, but I won't let them roam around the room tonight.'

So there I was, watching how to survive in an alien landscape by shooting everything is sight, while longing for the kind of deep sleep that would help me forget about the rats.

Convinced that I had learned enough about gaming that I could buy my own setup when I got home, I slid into my sleeping bag while Kurt carried on to the bitter end. I woke up several times to find him still playing but then, much later, it was just the rats running around their wheel who kept me company, when the early morning light told me I had survived unscathed.

Kurt slept off his late night of intergalactic slaughter while I tiptoed around the house. His brother saw that I was fed while he got ready to do his holiday job of selling asparagus and strawberries beside a main road outside the city. I waved goodbye to a slumbering Kurt and wished him good luck in the navy, but I whether it registered I'll never know.

Negotiating the suburban streets that skirted Mainz, the indifferent sky was a deathly grey. An eerie quietness hovered over the land as if I was traversing the landscape in one of Kurt's video games. This was the moment when the aliens were regrouping before their final attack. Then I saw a bakery open and sidled in for a second breakfast of brioche. It was there that I found out that no-one was around because it was Pentecost Monday, what in the UK we call Whit Monday. It was a public holiday and people, I was told by the baker, traditionally did nothing in the morning.

They might have been staying indoors on his dull morning, but I had 16 miles to walk to Nierstein, a small town further up the Rhine. I intended to do everything I could to keep away from the heavy freight and fast cars on the Bundestrasse 9 (B9). So I hiked through a terrain of arable fields interspersed with the odd flinty slope of upland. I had plenty of time to think deeply about where I was and where I was going. Way across to the east, in the furthest distance, I could see the skyscrapers of Frankfurt. Then to its south began a range of wooded hills that stretched like the rim of a teatray on the horizon, marking out the entire sightline to my left. I knew that I had to get to that rim in three days' time. There lay Heidelberg to the south, on the River Neckar, where I was going to meet Alice and Max for a day's rest and recuperation. I felt very at home in the landscape. It was a tremendous feeling to see a range of hills in the distance and know that my journey lay that way. I could not see a single tree on that hillside but the dull green shading told me that the slopes were not bare. I promised myself I would cheer the moment that the individual trees became identifiable, but that was three days' hence – I guessed.

This sense of being at one with my surroundings and seeing myself as a figure in the landscape was, I thought, a turning point in my journey. I was beginning to process the extent of this feeling when hunger overcame me. I realised that some toast and a brioche were not enough to sustain me, so I looked around for a place to eat even though I feared that most places would be closed. Near Bodenheim, a small town on the route, tucked in beside a roundabout, I came across a small restaurant, called Gaststätte Zur Hasenklause, serving food. I almost wept I was so wobbly with fatigue.

What I ate was immaterial; it was somehow the quantity that mattered on that cold, inhospitably Pentecost Monday. The hosts welcomed me in to the fug of a jovial, holiday lunchtime with several large families being fed. There was an eat-all-you-can buffet for starters followed by piled plates of meat, potatoes and greens. What more in life could you want? The entire company of eaters made me feel at home, asking me about my walk and making all the expected noises of disbelief and encouragement. I even risked a beer, which I had discovered was my fifth big mistake if taken at lunchtime, making the snowball even larger, because then depression inevitably grabbed hold of me while walking in the afternoon. But I threw caution to the wind and after that I asked for a steamed pudding to finish it all off nicely.

I was wobbly going into lunch and possessed by a different kind of wobbly feeling coming out, probably due to the unnecessary steamed pudding. The fabulously friendly owners wished me good luck especially since the only direct way now to Nierstein was on the dreaded B9. If I was lucky, they said, I might find the cycle track but it was hard to spot and anyway it went way up through the fields on the hillside a long way from the river. Did I really want the extra distance after such a Friar Tuck style lunch? Not really, I replied to my own question.

14: Another Police Car

The B9 lived up to its reputation. There was a narrow cycle strip within a painted white line, wide enough for a thin walker. But after that lunch I am not sure if I qualified. I strode courageously south against the hoots and honks of massive lorries and a legion of mostly

grey cars that typified the spirit of the afternoon: tarmac, fine rain
falling from grey clouds and a chill headwind.

Then, as soon I could see a church spire in Nierstein beckoning me
towards it, I saw a blue light up ahead flashing in a lay-by, on my side
of the road. I knew what to expect after my encounter with the police
in Holland. These two young and very efficient German police officers
wanted to see my passport and to know what I was doing on this busy
road. I was given a polite lecture on the foolhardiness of walking beside a busy road such as this and told to get in the car because they
were obliged to get me to safety as soon as possible.

'Where are you going?' The officer in charge asked.

'Well, you see that church a couple of hundred metres away?' I
replied, thinking they might let me out again realising it was so close.

'We'll drop you there then,' he said while negotiating a hasty U
turn and putting his foot down so as to keep up with the busy traffic.
I was probably in the police car for no more than three quarters of a
minute before they set me down to find my riverside guesthouse
called Klabautermann. This was only my second time ever in a police
car; I promised myself not to make a habit of it.

I had read about Nierstein when I booked the accommodation, and
had formed a totally different impression about it compared to the
drowsy, rain soaked, shuttered-up town that I saw in front of me at
half past five on a bleak afternoon in May. Was this depressed outlook
on my part brought on by the beer at lunchtime or the aftermath of
my second police interrogation? Whatever it was, it was made doubly
worse by the welcome I received at the Klabautermann. I was shown
to my room by a Lurch lookalike from the Addams Family. In hesitant
monotones, he told me that I was the only guest tonight and that I
would be the only one in the dining room tonight if I wanted food.
Service finished at 9pm. I said I did and, as soon as he had departed,
I fell into bed for a sleep of avoidance and disappointment. It definitely
was the beer.

I woke up with a jolt, still fully clothed in my walking gear, at
about 8:30pm It took me 10 minutes to get changed and down to the
dining room only to be told that since I had not arrived the chef was
closing up. After much pleading, he agreed to cook me soup, steak

and potatoes. Since that appeared to be the only thing on the menu, I agreed hastily.

On any other day, Nierstein is a fascinating place. It is the home to the oldest vineyard in Germany, boasts some animal footprints in Permian rock that date back 290 million years, holds a festival of Maypole Dancing that welcomes in the growing season and of course it was a Roman Township because of its position beside the Rhine. Now the town is famous for Wingertsknorze (rye rolls with caraway), Fleischworscht (meat sausage), Worschtsupp (sausage soup) and several kinds of unique local cheeses – none of which I was offered that night.

Before the Romans, the Celts had discovered a sacred spring, which they dedicated to their goddess of healing, Sirona. She walked around with a snake over one arm and in the other she clasped a basket of eggs. The Romans, when they arrived, called her Hygeia from which we get the word: hygiene. They also believed that the snake is symbolic of medicine and healing.

As I ate my reluctantly prepared meal, I read about the name of the place I was staying at. A Klabautermann is a child-sized sprite or Kobald, similar to Dobby, the house elf, in the Harry Potter series of books. A bit like the elves in Cologne, but the sprite in my accommodation had a nautical bent. It was a boatman's helper, dressed like a pirate and smoking a pipe. He kept an eye on the sailors and saved them if they fell overboard. With all this wonderful history and cultural associations, how could it all be so dull on my visit? I was still trying to fathom the answer when Lurch told me that the restaurant was closing and what time did I want breakfast? To avoid the rush (sic) I said 7:30am and hurried off to my room to FaceTime home for some much needed cheering up.

15: Walking with Martin Luther

When I woke up on Tuesday 17 May, life was back to normal. I could hear trains, road sweeping wagons, hearty voices of people on the pavements going to work, and the family downstairs in the kitchen getting ready for a more energetic day.

As I walked away from Nierstein towards Worms (pronounced Vermz for the squeamish) I was determined to find some smaller roads and tracks to prevent me having to take to the B9 again even though it looked like the cycle track, to the south, was now double the width.

Walking first thing in the morning was always a trial. I had to get my body back in the swing of things. It was hard. Not just after a day's rest, but every day. I got into the habit, like this morning, of stepping gingerly to begin with to make sure that no sudden movements pulled or tweaked any muscles. Gradually, in this fashion, I worked up to a steady pace, so that I felt relaxed again in my own stride.

At Oppenheim, I decided to take the wine-village route, keeping well away from the main road. Immediately, I felt better. I was moving smoothly and listening to blackbirds singing lustily: marking out their territories, calling to their mates, and heralding spring. I saw ancient farm buildings latticed with wooden beams. They had courtyards for the vineyard equipment, which included thin tractors specially de-signed to go up and down the gangways between the vines. Every now and then, between the farm buildings, I breathed in the musty scent of nettles or cut grass.

While plodding along, I resurrected my recent thoughts about being a figure in the landscape. I was even more convinced now that I was in the middle phase of my walk. The first phase was all about leaving home, looking back, concentrating on how far I had come and feeling overpowered by the distance still to travel. But now, I was fast becoming at ease with where I was. The halfway point of my endeav-our was only about a week away, so I would soon be looking forward more than looking back. My life had become a daily round of living at street level. It was just like being a child again. I actually had time to breathe in deeply when standing next to a nettle bed. The warm, tarragon-tinged fragrance made me light-headed. In that stretch of countryside, before Worms, I had the same compelling experience in front of wild roses, honeysuckle, lilac, wisteria and grass. I was re-minded of Dylan Thomas' poem: The Force That through the Green Fuse Drives the Flower. It was as if I was imbibing that green fuse: I had the time; there were no interruptions. I was free to experience my surroundings. Twenty miles a day was a reality to which I had become accustomed. My mind was opened enough to embrace it. This was definitely the second phase.

In advance of walking into Worms, I had been reading a lot about Martin Luther. He was an astoundingly brave monk and theologian who stood up boldly for what he believed in and by doing so gave birth to Protestantism. The currency of his thinking has lost its value in modern times but in the early 1500s he was a lion roaring against the corruption of the Catholic priests. He pinned a paper containing a list of 95 statements onto the door of All Saint's, the church of Wittenberg Castle, saying why he was at odds with the then current practices in the Catholic Church. It was nothing more than an agenda containing thoughts that would be discussed at a meeting to be held at his church. Those not able to attend were asked to write a letter containing their ideas on the matter. In those times, Catholic priests were going around selling indulgences (spiritual notes of forgiveness) that absolved people of their sins – wiping the slate clean by greasing the palms of greedy priests. Martin challenged the sale of indulgences, but more importantly the whole position of the Pope and his clerics as intermediaries between an individual and their God.

At once, Luther became for some a hero and for others, including the Pope and the Holy Roman Emperor, a dead man walking. In January 1521, he was excommunicated and later summoned to Worms for an imperial council meeting, known as The Diet of Worms, led by Charles V – Holy Roman Emperor. All Luther had to do was retract his list of grievances and Pope Leo X would welcome him back into the fold. He stuck by his beliefs, would not withdraw his 95 Theses and by 26 May 1521, was declared an outlaw and heretic.

As an outlaw, he could have been killed by anyone on his way home, without the threat of punishment. However, instead of crushing his cause, the European Reformation was given life and its growth was accelerated. On his way home, Luther was spirited away by his supporters to a castle in Wartburg to lie low while his ideas flourished. The fledgling printing press helped his ideas circulate right across Europe. Eventually, no longer an outlaw, he died in 1546 of natural causes, the father of a new church and six children!

I revelled in this story not only for the courage shown by Martin Luther but also for his physical stamina. When walking to Worms from Wittenberg, at the age of 38, he covered about 280 miles in 14 days – an average of 20 miles a day. There I was on the same approach road to Worms, much older than him and 495 years later, keeping up the same pace. There were major differences though. He was applauded in every village on the way by people who supported his stance against the religious culture of the time. By contrast, I was a solitary figure stopping occasionally to sniff beds of nettles, drooling over the roadside strawberry stalls and gazing ahead at the skyscrapers of Worms, protruding sharply on the horizon, in the late afternoon of my Day 27.

I stayed that night in a hotel so cheap that it bordered on being a hostel. Everywhere, the walls seemed to be lined with a dark brown wood that was echoed in the plywood doors of the wardrobes and the fronts of drawers. It was a depressing visual experience: a symphony of brown. I hesitated to open the drawers because they looked the kind that would stick or come apart in your hand. The shower dribbled and the basin was slow to empty. I felt in need of a bath. Lucky then that, as a diversion, I spent the time during which I usually had a nap before dinner exploring the town for statues of Luther and other Diet of Worms related places of interest.

I was thinking how many days it was since I had soaked in a bath. Too many – came the answer from the Greek chorus in my head. I needed some cosseting. So by bedtime I had booked ahead a discounted hotel room, in Mannheim, which had a bath. All I had to do was get there. It meant leaving the Rhine. This was a major shift in focus for me.

16: Leaving the Rhine behind

The next day, crossing the Rhine on the Nibelungen Bridge, going out of Worms, was like leaving a friend at the station after a holiday in each other's company. The excitement of our experiences, the gossip, the gazing into the future and the pondering on times past were all on the verge of disappearing into the abyss. Enjoyment in places beyond the river was almost unthinkable. I was walking over the water into which Hagen had thrown the Nibelung treasure in the famous German epic poem called 'The Song of The Nibelungs.' Siegfried, he of the dragon's blood, whom I had marvelled at further downstream, had been murdered, and Kriemhild, his widow, gathered together all of his treasure for safekeeping. The story tells how the hoard of gemstones and gold was so large that it took dozens of carts to bring it to Worms over a period of four days and nights. Hagen, the killer of Siegfried, decided to steal the treasure, sink it in the river and come back for it later. Apparently, he never came back or, if he did, the treasure could not be found. Surely, even the dimmest of murderous criminals could have foreseen that?

It was a warm, sunny day. The kind that dries out the damp that stays lurking in the seams of one's clothing, days after being drenched. The heat penetrated to my skin making the rhythmical movement of walking a luxurious experience to be savoured. The fields seemed to be lower down than the river so the clanking noises made by the barges drifted over towards me at head height. The only people I met were cyclists going the other way to Worms. Occasionally, I passed dense woodland and heard the bark and scream of agitated animals. A cloud of terror enveloped me. There were wolves among the trees, I was sure of it.

I realised that this was the first day out of 28 in which I had not had a painkiller to take away the throb of blisters, shin splints or any other kind of muscle pain. Despite this being a kind of turning point in physical endurance, it had been an enormous psychological challenge to even get out of the chair after breakfast this morning. Stuffed with cheese, hard-boiled egg, ham and salami as usual, I had sank into the chair in my bedroom and searched for the mental strength to get started. The middle of the walk, I reflected, might be laced with moments of being present in the experience of it all but it was also a time when weak resolve crept up unexpectedly. The purpose of the walk and the strength of mind needed to carry on day by day had to be summoned up every morning – otherwise I might just stop altogether.

I was on the lookout for signs of another river to make friends with: the Neckar, which flows into the Rhine at Mannheim, was the ideal choice. Following its course would lead me to Heidelberg after which I would head for Pforzheim, which sits on the northern edge of the Black Forest. Being an industrial centre, Mannheim had suffered badly in World War Two, which is why so much of it is new. Industry bloomed in the 1960s and 70s once the city had got back on its feet after the bombing. Among other industries with heavy plant, it is the home of Daimler, which builds Mercedes Benz cars.

As I approached the outskirts of the city, heading for the Radisson Hotel on the far side with its cheap last minute deal (with a bath), I felt overwhelmed by my own ignorance. I realised that I knew too little about heavy industry, the development of the automobile, the Black Forest, and rivers beyond the Rhine. I was like a walking dust jacket from which the pages containing all of the facts had blown away in the wind. It all happened so quickly that I have no memory of what the pages said. However, I reminded myself that was precisely the point – to walk in order to open my mind and learn. Slightly placated, I entered the hotel's reception.

More snow rolled onto my sixth mistake because as soon as I walked towards the desk they spotted my rucksack. This was the kind of hotel that I used during my working life. I saw men parading in their slightly loosened work clothes, heading to the bar for a pre-dinner drink, and I felt intimidated straight away. A silent pep talk to myself reminded me that it was the bath that I had come for; the rest was mere wallpaper. After soaking for a long time, I joined the businessmen grazing on their up-market burgers and thick-cut chips while watching Liverpool play football on a huge TV screen.

Lying in bed that night I went back over my afternoon encounter with a couple of charming Turkish girls wearing the hijab. At about afternoon tea time, I was walking through what must have been a Turkish quarter of the city. All I recalled was a maze of old factory buildings, small corner shops selling everything on earth, and a smattering of cafes and restaurants that offered me the tempting prospect of a second lunch. Second breakfasts and second lunches had become a necessity to stave off the hunger, which cropped up at very regular intervals. I read that I must be burning about 3000 calories a day. Sometimes if felt like many more.

One of the girls I encountered was running a bakery-cum-café and the other was her friend but also a customer sitting at my table. I was filling up on a slice of pizza and a fizzy drink, while the girls chatted away in Turkish. After a few minutes they asked me what I was doing and in turn I asked them about themselves. They were the children of immigrants from Turkey who had come at the invitation of the German government in the 1960s. They were born in Mannheim and loved the life they led. As far as they were concerned, the city lived up to its 30-year-old reputation as a Welcome City. Mannheim had, they smiled broadly, been very welcoming to their parents and others from Greece, Italy and Yugoslavia when they came in as guest workers, and now the Syrian refugees who had arrived recently for humanitarian reasons.

The positive outlook of these two young women had made me buoyant and optimistic. All along my way, I had seen evidence, through stickers on lampposts and graffiti in places like underpasses, of Nazi-style racism against immigrants, but these young women seemed too gentle and positive to even mention this. I asked out of interest: 'where are these Syrians?' I had read about them and seen them on the TV news, but not come across them in my walk apart from in a tiny village just on the German side of the Dutch border. They told me that, since I was walking to Heidelberg tomorrow, I would see them housed in US Army bases (the biggest was The Benjamin Franklin Village) on the way out of Mannheim.

Apparently, more than 80,000 refugees had arrived in Germany in September 2015 of which 12,000 had been given shelter in this city. In fact, I learned later that the city's commissioner for integration and migration, Claus Preissler, has done a fantastic job in a situation where 44% of the local population has a migrant background. Everyone in the city realises that the recent influx represents the biggest challenge ever faced by the council but Claus is determined that 'we as a city can shape the coexistence of different cultures we have here now.'

As I settled down for sleep that night, I was thinking about how positive the young women in the café had been and how I was enormously inspired by the work of Claus Preissler. All of which helped me overcome the feelings of loneliness that beset me occasionally. Sometimes I felt that my treasures, like those of Siegfried's killer Hagen, had sunk to the bottom of the river, but now I was ready to scoop up some more along the way. I remembered that reinforcements were close at hand. Alice and Max were getting ready to drive to the Hull ferry port tomorrow. The day after, they would be arriving in Heidelberg for a jaunt. For me it was a day off from walking, but for them it was a motorway drive, from the Europoort near Rotterdam, following the direction of my walk. The day after that, I planned to walk with Alice for a morning towards Pforzheim, while Max cycled in the area. In the afternoon, as part of this whirlwind tour, they were to head back to the ferry via Belgium where they planned to visit Max's aunt, Madeleine, in Brussels.

17: Refugees Welcome

It rained hard in the night. Setting off on my 12-mile walk to Heidelberg, it was dry but the air was still dank with the smell of wet bushes. I had become accustomed to having my lungs filled with the scents of my surroundings: nettles, hay, wet cut grass, meadows, thick woodland…and now rain-soaked bushes – they all had an intoxicating effect on me. Something that a life spent mainly in buildings never allowed. It was a short walk that day, so there was plenty of time to get involved in what was going on around me. Having weaned myself off any medication for the constant pain in my legs and feet, today I had taken some paracetamol just to nip in the bud some shin twinges. The hills I had seen in the far distance a few days ago now loomed large. The trees were almost visible, though not individually, so I could not yet give a triumphant shout. I was on the verge of getting close to the chain of hills which seemed to run south into the Black Forest.

With the lingering scent of the bushes still in my nostrils, I bumped into a woman who was curious enough to ask me about my journey. In turn, I asked her about the whereabouts of the Syrian refugees and she pointed ahead, round the next bend. I might have known I was getting close because there in the long grass, beside the track, was some entertaining graffiti on two hydrants a few metres apart, which read: Refugees Welcome! Smoke Weed; and Refugees Welcome! Fuck Racism. Clearly by the same author; one who had the ability to sum up popular opinion quite succintly.

Then I saw the entrance to The Benjamin Franklin Village. There were official-looking gates, a sentry box and a red and white striped barrier, but no actual Syrians to be seen. It all looked well-kept and organised. My anticipated moment of chatting to Syrians to find out how well they were settling in after escaping the bombing at home never materialised, neither did the refugees themselves. I walked on. Disappointed, but glad for them that in this vast complex of yellow painted barracks they could find some rest, peace and security. The problem for them was where did they go after life in the barracks? Would there be enough room for them elsewhere? Could Claus win the day?

The land around me was flat and fertile. I was heading for the River Neckar, to follow it into Heidelberg, but running across my path were busy motorways fringed by small towns. Alongside these trappings of civilisation, the cold, blue sky was peppered with birdlife. White storks circled the fields sizing up the waterways for food. They were arriving from Africa having over-wintered there, maybe as far down the east coast as South Africa. I loved the idea that I was seeing them swoop around in fields near me just after their monumental flight from Africa over Egypt, Israel, Palestine, Syria, Turkey, the Balkans, and now Western Europe. It looked to me as if they were in a royal procession along a curving flight path, circumventing a gang of proletarian blue tits and chaffinches that gossiped in the trees, beside the road along which I trudged.

Still caught up in the amazement over the migratory route of storks, I arrived at an underpass with the motorway booming above me. I stood transfixed at what I saw sprayed on the walls. The paintings spanned the width of the entire underpass; four wide panels forming an intricately sprayed montage of political angst.

German street artists, I was discovering, are knowledgeable and eloquent about their political stances. I felt stunned by my ignorance of the particular subject matter in front of me on this underpass. Elsewhere on my journey, I had been engrossed by ideas on anarchy, but here was a statement the kind of which I had not seen before. It was an elaborate howl about the 1915 genocide of Greeks, Armenians and Assyrians in what is now Turkey during the First World War. The painting told me that nearly three million Christians were slaughtered.

I had previously thought that The Ottoman Empire was famed for its tolerance of different religions within its boundaries, but according to these artists the embryonic state of Turkey committed nothing but the genocide of Anatolian Christians.

Subsequent governments there have refused to accept that these atrocities happened at all. The Turkish state has always been in denial and the descendants of these brutally murdered people are still fighting to get recognition of the crimes and to recover some of their homeland. The struggle goes on, led primarily by a group called The Restore Nineveh Now Foundation, which was the signatory of this powerful history lesson.

I entered the underpass thinking of graceful birds that wintered abroad and left it feeling crushed by a genocide of which I knew nothing. Once again, I was confronted by my own limitations and forced to question my narrow perspective on life. I prayed with crossed fingers to keep an open mind in my old age.

I used my phone to read about the Armenian atrocities and felt sick at what I discovered. The brutality meted out seemed just as bad as that used by ISIS or the Myanmar Army in persecuting the Rohingya. Apparently, Hitler even tried to justify his own exterminations by saying, as if parading a convenient truth, that no one remembers the Armenian Genocide. As I started walking again in my much-rehearsed slow gait, which let my legs find their own rhythm, I reflected that we don't change much: like the storks do every year, we once made our own way out of Africa, but all too often our behaviour lacks their grace.

Soon, I found the River Neckar and saw that it was narrower than the Rhine, but still deep enough to allow quite sizeable barges to make their way past Heidelberg. Its banks were covered in thick grass and thickets until the city's tentacles started to appear. A hydroelectric dam appeared on my left, which held the river back towards the city. This increased the width of the water to about 200 metres. Then there were footpaths, cycle tracks and sweeping bends of painted fences, all leading to what I discovered was the jewel of Baden-Württemberg. With a university founded in 1368, no wonder Heidelberg has appealed to young people over the years. Currently, almost a quarter of its population is made up of students. In the 1930s many of them were members of fencing clubs that practised Mensur, before Hitler stopped them in favour of his brown-shirted youth movement. I had read that some of the bars which were the haunts of these students still existed, so I looked forward to drinking in them.

At mid-afternoon, on a day that had threatened rain continually, but was now deciding to shed sunlight on the old city, I rounded a bend and saw the warm-coloured stone of the magnificent arched bridge, which spanned the river. A leaflet picked up along the way informed me that this 250-year-old structure is the ninth bridge over the Neckar. The Romans erected the first. Many of the subsequent bridges were destroyed by ice flows, including the sixth, which interestingly was designed by the cartographer named Münster – I discovered his statue on my approach to Mainz. The fact that ice flows were once, but no longer, large and strong enough to demolish bridges as huge as these proves that global warming has been on the march for centuries.

I remembered seeing a film set in Heidelberg called 'The Student Prince' (1954) on our nine-inch Pye TV when I was fairly young. Its theme song, 'The Drinking Song', sung by Mario Lanza, sprang to mind. In the film, the scenery of timbered houses looked flimsy and wobbled like hastily erected cardboard would do, but what I witnessed in front of me was beautiful, solid buildings, square and enticing, with honey-coloured tiled roofs that sloped steeply down to the eyebrows of their dormer windows. Seen from a distance, I was looking at wealth, comfort and stability. There was not a hint of the concrete wastelands, factories and breakers' yards with which I was familiar at the back-door entrance to other German towns. I couldn't wait to shed my rucksack and start exploring the narrow streets of the old town.

I was particularly looking forward to eating at a restaurant that I had booked in advance, as a special treat. It was called The Gasthaus Zum Roten Ochsen (The Red Ox). I had wanted to take Alice and Max there but it was closed for a function the following evening. Luckily, I could get a table on the day I arrived. Quickly, I unpacked my rucksack in the Hotel Schönberger-Hof (a stone's throw from the river), paid them the princely sum of 5 Euros to get my washing done, in a proper washing machine – the first time since leaving England – and set off to savour my surroundings before finding The Red Ox.

18: At Patrick's Table

Dressed as always after a day's walk in my turquoise all-purpose sweater, easy-wash mufti trousers and lightweight rubber slip-ons, I entered Vetter's Alt-Heidelberger Brauhaus and felt a wave of contentment flow over me.

Luckily, my footwear was no longer torturous, so wandering around the old town was bearable. I sat with a taster tray of beer gazing at the menu to compare it later with the fare provided by The Red Ox. It consisted of the most tempting comfort food imaginable: potatoes and pork in many guises. By now, I was very fond of these brewery restaurants, but this one was particularly special owing to the huge copper vats that sat on the bar, obviously containing the beer in the process of being made. The taster tray comprised several school milk bottle-sized glasses containing the main variety of beers on offer. You could have a blond or dark tray of beers. That was another thing I had grown to appreciate – the limited choice of high quality beers. If I not had booked a table elsewhere, I think I might have settled down for a plate of Palatine stuffed pig's stomach from the region, liver dumplings and grilled sausage on a bed of sauerkraut with bread.

Later, standing outside the Gasthaus, I tried to transport myself back to 31 December 1933 when Patrick Leigh Fermor had arrived here looking for somewhere to stay. Fortunately, my efforts were helped by the fact that the place had hardly changed and it was still owned by the same family who, 83 years before, had welcomed PLF. Of course, I realised, it was not unusual for a fan of PLF to turn up wanting to imbibe the atmosphere of this historic gem, but – as is probably always the case – I acted as though it was. Philipp Spengel and his 10-year old daughter welcomed me in. Philipp introduced her as the next generation of ownership. I had told him over the telephone about my walk and got the impression that most other aficionados came by car. At least I could claim the added distinction of having followed in PFL's footsteps thus far.

The dining room's dark oak panelling was festooned with pictures of the family dating back well into the 19th-century. Artistic cameos of some young gentlemen engaged in sword fighting showed evidence of the fixed-stance fencing that I had discovered in Bingen. Ornate pottery beer tankards were scattered about the room on high up shelves, which gave the dining room a Student Prince vibe. As I sat at my table, I learned that the proper name for a scar to the face or head was Schmiss and that Couleur was the coloured uniform, sash, ribbon and cap. Single diners, like me, were placed on a long table together.

On that evening I was on my own rather like PFL who 'longed… every day…to settle at a heavy inn-table, thawing and tingling, with wine, bread, and cheese handy and my papers, books and diary all laid out; writing up my day's doings…' My table was carved with a thousand pieces of graffiti as if the duelling students had just gouged it and left. I jotted ideas in my notebook while waiting for my food, and in a few moments I was served with potato soup, sausages and lentils (laced with pasta strips), a dessert of Black Forest ice cream, with dark jam mixed in, all rinsed down with local red wine (my first red in Germany) – I was in ecstasy. As I left, Philipp gave me a shot glass with the red ox's head on it as a memento: something to treasure as a sign of having sought out such an historic restaurant. After that, I was so tired that I went straight back to my room and slept the contented, blissful sleep of a long distance walker who knows that tomorrow is a day off.

So far, I had walked eight miles short of 500 miles, which meant that on the way to Bruchsal the day after tomorrow, I would pass that significant milestone. Actually, the stopover in Heidelberg represented several milestones, not just the number of miles walked even though that was the furthest I had even covered in one journey. I realised that this city was the last of its kind for some time. Before me lay the Black Forest, Lake Constance, the Austrian Alps and the Italian border at Lake Resia. This was 19 May and I did not expect to be crossing the border until 10 June, which was just over three weeks away. In that stretch of my 1200-mile hike, there would only be Bregenz, on the shores of Lake Constance, as a town of any size. When I dug deeper into my 'several milestones' quandary, it wasn't the lack of city life that was the problem but the fact that the Alps might be an even bigger challenge than walking over 500 miles to reach them. I could not imagine what it would be like to cross this mountain range. They might defeat me. I might fall and end the prospect of reaching my destination. I might not just be up to it. It was a dread that never went away and I was walking towards it. Lucky then, that I would have Alice and Max to help me brace myself for this seemingly impossible feat of endurance.

They arrived after lunch. I had spent a leisurely morning folding my washing, visiting The Church of the Holy Spirit, which used to have one of Europe's most envied libraries until, after The Thirty Years War (1616-1648), nearly the entire collection of books and manuscripts was taken by Maximillian I and presented to the Pope to keep at the Vatican. This probably angered not just the students at what was already by then a 300-year-old university. I found out that in the early 1970s, hippies adopted the church steps for their gatherings and just before that in 1968 the student riots, which began in Paris, reached Heidelberg and its market area. Beyond that, I just idled my time away in cafes mulling over the challenge of the Alps and getting depressed at the thought.

As predicted, my visitors boosted my morale greatly. I introduced them to the delights of the Alt-Heidelberger Brauhaus. We tried the blond and the dark selection, before taking the funicular railway to see the castle. In the evening we ate so much local pork, after a huge bowl of potato soup, followed by apple strudel, that not one of us could lick their platter clean. I staggered back to my room while Alice and Max sought out an Irish bar for a nightcap. I had to keep up my routine of early nights especially since I had a 23-mile walk the next day.

I was sure that anyone could do what I was doing as long as they were prepared to stay focused and disciplined for the entire journey. That was the trick: the hardest part. There was a danger that these cities – along, or near, the Rhine – were so interesting that they could take my mind off the main task, especially when one's brain was addled by a combination of good quality beer and potato soup.

The plan, for the next morning after I left early, was that Max would drive his car to my 15-mile mark and drop Alice who would walk with me until about 1pm. He would cycle back to the car, collect Alice and take them both off to Belgium. Alice felt confident to walk a minimum of five miles. That was her objective and we would both be proud if she could achieve that.

19: A Newfangled Bicycle

I set off just as the bakery vans were delivering the breakfast bread to the shops and cafes across Heidelberg. Much later, at a quarter to nine, I read a sign that told me I was on The Bertha Benz Memorial Route. I learned that this was the way that Karl Benz's wife took when, in 1888, she drove the first ever long-distance journey in a motorised vehicle (about 120 miles). Later that day, after Alice had left, I came across a chemist shop on the spot where Bertha had stopped for a bottle of 'ligroin' – a type of petroleum spirit. The history of this world-famous journey, accompanied by drawings of the automobile, was writ large on a billboard by the road. The Benz Motorwagen mark 3 was actually a three-wheeler with bicycle-style wheels, solid rubber tyres, wooden block brakes and a small cylinder engine behind the carriage seat, high up above the two back wheels. The whole contraption was steered by a two-handed joystick that worked the smaller front wheel. When going up hills, Bertha's two teenage sons had to push her. The route was from Mannheim to Pforzheim via Heidelberg, which was exactly what I was doing because Pforzheim is a gateway to the Black Forest.

Mrs Benz was quite a wealthy person and had invested in this – her husband's sideline project. He had invented this small cylinder engine a couple of years before but had not done much to develop it as a commercial enterprise. Karl was loath to let it take over from his main occupation of making heavy machinery for factories. Bertha was passionate to see the Motorwagen succeed, which is why she was taking it to Pforzheim to see her mother. Her two boys had to walk alongside, as there was too little room for them on the driver's platform.

Being very resourceful, Bertha used her hatpin to clean out the carburettor and unwittingly invented brake linings when she stopped at a shoemaker's to have leather pads nailed onto the wooden brakes, so as to give them more resistance when going downhill. After three days with her mother she drove home again to strongly persuade Karl to go into production – thereby starting the whirlwind of technological development in which we are caught up today. What is more, Bertha told her husband he needed to introduce another gear to make going up and down hills easier. Ironic then that, at the moment I discovered this woman who changed the face of motorised transport, Alice and I were simply walking along this most famous driving route in history.

The day became quite hot and we had to ration our drinking water. When I started out in April, every morning I would fill my camel pack with up to four litres of water. It soon became very tiresome to carry this extra load in addition to the 18kg in my rucksack. So, I began to fill two one-litre collapsible bottles and carry them in my trouser pockets – the ones that ran down the outside of my legs. This worked well, but in the heat I was forced to buy extra bottles of water along the way, except when there were kindly householders in their gardens who could be persuaded to fill my bottles for me. Today, we had used up our supplies quite early and came across no shops or convenient houses at which we could fill up.

The road was long, straight and busy. Bertha's route was being used by hundreds of cars that day. Many of them would cover the distance to Pforzheim, which she took all day to accomplish, in about an hour. Apart from the volume of traffic on the B3, the whole aspect of the route had a different feel to it compared to most of my journeys along the banks of the Rhine and Neckar. Gone were the sloping hills covered in vineyards stretching down to the water's edge. The boatyards and ferry landings had given way to petrol stations and flat fields on either side of the road.

The route ahead was forever undulating giving an intimation of the hills, uplands and steeper inclines to come. To the west, in the semi-distance was a medley of thick woodland. I began to long to be in a forest again. Apart from wading thigh-deep through pits of leaves and risking serious injury in the forest outside Koblenz, my days among trees – in Holland and Germany – had always been magical: a time of contemplation. Trees somehow made one feel more connected to life. Now the fingers of the thickets beside me were always pointing south towards the Schartzwald (I was getting used to the German word for the Black Forest).

Whenever this place had popped up in conversation at home in England, the famous gateaux had been uppermost in people's minds. I was reserving judgement. I could not decide which would be more fascinating: woodland elves, unicorns, gingerbread houses or the forest gateaux. I vacillated continually between unicorns and gateaux – only time would tell which would triumph.

Throughout the rest of the morning, Max criss-crossed our path on his mountain bike, while Alice became increasingly confident in her stride having walked much further than her anticipated five miles. She was very supportive particularly since it dawned on her that what she was undertaking for a few hours, I had been engaged in for exactly four weeks. Drawing close to the small town of Wiesloch, we searched for Max and his van. Finally, desperate for some water, we knocked at a partly open front door and asked a kindly but confused woman for a drink. As was becoming typical in these parts, she came back with a cold 1.5 litre bottle of mineral water from her kitchen, which she gave us with a huge smile. Looking bemused at the 'walking to Italy' stabs at German conversation, she waved us goodbye as she retreated back inside looking worried that something strange was being lost in translation.

Just after 1pm when my two companions had set off for Belgium, I turned to head south again knowing that I had another five or six hours to walk. PLF had stayed in the Schloss-Bruchsal at Bruchsal, which was, in those days, a massive palace owned originally by a Prince-Bishop (a relatively unusual combination of a Prince who was also a Bishop): the only one of its kind this side of the Rhine. On the other hand, I did not have those kinds of aristocratic connections and chose to stay at a very cheap hotel in the more rural village of Kraichtal. Bruchsal would be the only place so far in which I had not stayed where Patrick had laid his head, but I was coming to the end of my connection with his walk and felt the need to begin a process of decompression. Coupled with the fact that the Kraichtaler Hof would put my budget back on track after a few days of comparative luxury, with treats like a bath and getting my washing done in Heidelberg.

By about 6:30pm, having walked for 11 hours, I was about to enter the village of Kraichtal. The evening was becoming cool quickly because the clear blue sky persisted. Blackbirds seemed to monopolise the trees giving an English country garden feel to my approach to the hotel. I looked to my right, over a hedge on this country lane, and saw a long row of portable cabins being used to house refugees. Several families were sitting outside. Some were smoking, listening to iPods, playing, chatting…it all seemed very civilised and peaceful. I had no idea how integrated they were in the community or what plans had been made for them in the future but, at a glance, they seemed content with their lot. I waved and got several waves back.

My hotel, which offered the cheapest deal in the whole area, was empty except for me. I was given the key to my room and told that breakfast was at 7am in the morning – and that was that. My bedroom was another symphony in plywood. I guessed that I was so used to melamine in England that bare plywood could jar the senses. As the evening chill grew even deeper, I hurried to find something to eat. The only place open in this seemingly empty village was a Turkish Doner, Kebap and Pizza shop. It was perfect for my needs. Here I was in a village deep in the heart of rural Germany, on the fringes of the Black Forest, being served by Turkish guest workers with only Syrian refugees to be seen in the surroundings. I was happy because they were all happy to be in Germany. We were all a long way from strife or discord. In my case, hardly featuring on the scale of international strife, the preparations for the EU referendum were hotting up. Boris' Red Bus had begun its tours on 12 May, so by now it was a well-established item in the news, which I read about on my phone every day. I was amused to learn that, ironically, the bus was made in Germany and Poland. To make up for that, I guessed, he was pictured on its maiden run to Truro getting off it waving a Cornish pasty.

I was on the brink of a big change of direction. Tomorrow, I would reach the end of PLF's walk – as far as I was going on it. I would assume the role of the itinerant chimney sweep, except that he was 18 years old and dressed in a black cord jacket, a scarlet waistcoat with brass buttons and a top hat. This was the typical garb of a chimney sweep's apprentice from Hamburg in 1934. Like him I would strike south for Italy. I was nervous, not just because of the Alps but also because from now on the route was my own. Despite this, I was determined to turn these nerves into strong sinews, making my own path – cutting a unique swathe through Austria and Italy.

Outside the Kebap shop, the evening had become too cold to be strolling around getting even more hyperbolic about paths, routes and self-determination, so I decided to go to bed early and prepare mentally for tomorrow's turning point. It was lucky that I did because I could never have guessed how depressed I was going to feel at the end of Sunday on Day 32.

As I drifted off to sleep, Boris Johnson came back to haunt me. Such strange confidence, I thought, for a man who had so recently been strongly in favour of remaining in the EU. Almost as if he had changed sides as a favour for an old school chum. 'No, that couldn't be true – could it?' I said to myself in my cold, plywood bedroom. I was asleep before I could even attempt to answer my own question.

20: Goodbye Patrick

After breakfast, I walked out of Kraichtal with the sun already shining strongly; there were no clouds in the sky, only jet trails from the planes taking off from Mannheim. There were more people around today than yesterday evening, mostly old ladies with dogs and cyclists in full regalia. I always like to get off early to cover the first 11 miles before lunch, so that the afternoon seemed easier. At least that was the plan.

Beside me on both sides, the woodland seemed full of cuckoos. They were making a great deal of noise as if at a convention. I wondered why? Of course this was the land of the cuckoo clocks: they were invented in the Black Forest. My previous musings on the loneliness of the man and the woman on the clock came back into my mind. Now I began to formulate another idea. Remembering that cuckoos have given us the name 'cuckold', I wondered whether the clock was just a huge sexual joke. Perhaps the man and the woman were not lonely at all but when one was out the other entertained a lover indoors? Either way, the continual calling of the birds around me became slightly annoying. It was at the zenith of their irritancy that church bells booming over the fields told me it was Sunday. Lately, I never knew what day it was until reminded by an event of some kind. So now the inescapable image of sexual infidelity while the partner was at church kept me fascinated until I reached the brow of the very steep hill in front of me.

From the top I could see a high range, to my right, accompanying the equally high hills of yesterday, to my left. They seemed to be shepherding me south in a pincer movement. I guessed it was mainly due to the reappearance of the Rhine valley that snaked off to my right, towards Basel in Switzerland. The excitement I felt was not about the place names but about being part of the geography, part of the scenery. It was not just the big features that thrilled; it was also the small and insignificant.

Yesterday, on the track, there was a host of beached giant beetles in various stages of decay. It was as if they had just fallen out of the sky; some were crawling with flies already. Their dark golden wings were shimmering gloriously in the afternoon sun. Just as I had been before in the first couple of weeks, I was drawn to what I called my 'pavement friends.' How could these highly unusual sights not fascinate? Similarly, the man-made towers built in fields for the storks from Africa to use for nesting. They resulted in acres of land to explode suddenly with white wings churning in the sky – moments of inescapable splendour: insignificant, temporary but hauntingly beautiful.

With 11 miles still to go, I stopped for Sunday lunch at an Italian restaurant in a small town called Bretten. The owner and his girlfriend were incredibly kind. They fed me very well and let me charge my phone and backup charger. The owner/chef cooked while his girlfriend chatted to me about my walk. It turned out that during the week she worked away at Düsseldorf Airport and that to get there she took three hours on the motorway (thanks to my friend Bertha). We laughed when I looked back at my diary and saw that I was in Düsseldorf two weeks and three days before.

Upon leaving the Italian restaurant, the weather turned very cold and showery. The main road beside which I walked, albeit on a cycle track, was extraordinarily busy with Sunday traffic. So I decided to find a woodland path running parallel: quieter and with a better view.

I found woodland that was interspersed by open fields.

I was just emerging from a copse when I glanced to my left and saw a couple in the long grass without any clothes on. There I was, Forrest Gumping along with my walking pole in full swing trying to make light of the whole affair. Without thinking, I shouted out in a friendly and supportive fashion: 'Just carry on, and don't mind me,' before I struck out down the side of the field towards a clump of trees in the valley.

Glancing back at regular intervals, I saw them frantically dressing in the way that suggests that arms and head cannot find the correct hole in which to slide as quickly as the brain wants them to. They were also laughing uncontrollably. I could hear them on the wind and see them shaking as if being struck by lightning. Of course there might have been an innocent explanation: they could have been practising an ancient German tradition of naked wrestling in order to summon up good weather for the crops, but I found it hard to sustain this theory when I saw them covered in such embarrassment. At least, I thought afterwards, passion in Pforzheim has an intrepid face: there must be something in the backbone of the city that inculcates such a brave spirit in its lovers.

Soon the outskirts of Pforzheim demonstrated my back-door theory very well indeed. The utilitarian design of seemingly endless rows of cramped houses, the unimaginatively designed factories and littered patches of wasteland all conspired to depress the spirits of a traveller who had only recently seen darkling golden beetles and the angelic white wings of storks.

Look on any travel site and you will see the glories of taking a break in Pforzheim. So, I must have caught it on a bad day. The weather was closing in and the streets mirrored the grey skies: dreary with their cheap postwar facades. I had booked an apartment so that I might cook my own meal for a change but, on a Sunday, it seemed I was too late to buy any decent provisions for dinner. The supermarkets were shut and the corner shops did not rise above the level of pot noodles.

From the outside, my apartment looked like a tenement in Stalinist Russia. The idea was to use a code of entry gained from telephoning a guy who sounded as if he was on the other side of the world. When entry was achieved, I found the room cold, dull and musty. I could not get the heating to work; the TV handset was one of those long thin ones with a trillion buttons. It defeated me! There was no hot water to be drawn from any tap. I rang the owner who said that everything had been checked and that if he came over it might take a couple of hours to get there. I told him not to bother. Anyone who could check this and pass it as serviceable was not someone I wanted to meet in person.

I went out to search for some food. First in a bar that only sold bottled beer and crisps and that had a shelf of what looked like stuffed rats above the counter. It was an establishment that still allowed smoking inside, so I came out reeking of smoke. Did we really suffer that for decades in England?

I soon found what appeared to be the only restaurant open, which was Italian again, only to be told that service stopped in 10 minutes at 9pm. I gobbled down a plate of spaghetti and regretted it immediately. Within 15 minutes I was in bed, shivering terribly and telling myself that the forest tomorrow would heal any of the hurt caused by this hellish apartment.

I had telephoned home for commiseration while slurping my meal, so the lack of any Wi-Fi or phone signal in the room only prevented me from reading Twitter or Facebook. For one night I was Brexit-lite, which was probably the only blessing to be had.

21: The Black Forest

The next morning, I took extra time in applying my foot cream, plasters, toe guards, and liniment. I lingered because I was sad to be saying goodbye to PLF and Nick Hunt. Our world together was ending – as T.S. Elliot put it in The Hollow Men: '…not with a bang, but a whimper.' There was certainly no crescendo in the way PFL failed to remember the city: 'Of the town of Pforzheim, where I spent the next night, I remember nothing.' Nick Hunt remembered it all too vividly and declared: 'Pforzheim was a dismal hole.' How could I summon up a positive slant on a city from which I was also glad to be walking away? I vowed that one day I would come back and seek out the best of its charms. If only in memory of the naked couple that I had came across the day before, who seemed to be a month or two early for their own comfort.

Mulling over the disappointment of Pforzheim, I wolfed down two apricot pastry slices for breakfast while sitting at a bar stool in a café on the way out of town. Through the window, I could see the rain pouring persistently as I sipped my cappuccino. The cheerful, stout woman behind the counter said: 'Walking to Italy? How I would love to come with you.'

'Why not?' I said. 'All you need to do is grab a bag and you could join me on the road.' I joked, guessing that some people would do anything to get out of Pforzheim.

There was a fleeting, almost imperceptible, moment when she looked as if she was going to leave the café and set off to Italy with me, but then reality kicked in and she said: 'I would love to but there's my husband and children...' It showed one thing though, which cropped up many times during my three months on the road – people saw my journey as a way to reflect on their dreams and ambitions to the extent that sometimes they almost put their boots on. At times like this, I felt like a Pied Piper for adults.

Not long after that, I came to a sign, which told me I was entering Naturpark Schwarzwald. The sights around me could not be more different from the grey dreariness of the city centre. Here were green copses, elegant houses and well-groomed gardens. It was still dull with rain but I became happier with each step that I took. What followed in the next few hours showed me that the healing process was beginning: the forest had a will, which was exerting itself in my favour.

I walked for more than an hour along a forest track, beside a river. The trees were flushed with vivid lime green leaves but even more spectacular was the moss on the tree trunks, which was thick, ragged and matted. In places it looked like the strands of a dyed sheep's fleece. To some extent the trees shielded me from the incessant rain, but I was well and truly soaked by 11am. It was then that the benign forest helped me out. A voice in my head blurted out: 'I would just love a coffee,' without the rational side of my brain thinking I had no chance of that in a forest like this. But round the next bend, I came across the most fabulous conference centre and hotel complex that I could ever have wished for. It was called Hohenwart Forum. At the desk, I asked if I could dry off and have a coffee. I was welcomed heartily and told to help myself to coffee and sit in the dry for as long as I liked. All it needed was gingerbread tiles on the walls and I could have believed in magic. Instead, the walls were full of posters about yoga, meditation, poetry and the visual arts. Magic of a different kind.

After about an hour of sitting in the warm, and still damp but not dripping, I started to walk again. I really needed to find a cashpoint if I was to buy lunch later on. Miraculously, in no time at all, one appeared in a small village that I came to. Then, to cap it all, my third wish for sausage and chips – my default lunch in German cafes – was granted at about 1:30pm when I stumbled out of the forest, down a steep incline, on to a busy road and found a log-cabin style restaurant, which was still serving food. My three wishes had been granted and there beside me, at the same table, was a friendly looking man dressed in a lumberjack shirt, tweed jacket and forester's hat, to whom I could regale my story of the morning's enchantment.

He was also very keen to hear about all my other adventures, but like so many other times when people said that, what they really meant is that they would like to tell me about theirs. I had come to understand this and forgave immediately; anyway his story was genuinely fascinating.

A few years before, he and his friend decided to explore Namibia in South West Africa, which until the 1919 Treaty of Versailles, was a German colony. They hired a Land Rover and motored across the Kalahari Desert, presumably to end in Windhoek, the capital. It all sounded an awe-inspiring expedition. I was captivated by his tale of two friends in a jeep skirting over orangey-red sand dunes surrounded by patches of parched grass, dotted with stunted trees. His eyes stared longingly into the distance when recalling the game animals they saw enroute, and the orange sheen across the landscape as the sun was setting. It was only then that I found out that he had dropped off the same friend for his cancer treatment that very day and was idling away the time talking to me while his friend was being treated. Another case of people in Germany driving miles to take friends or family to the right hospital for some high quality treatment – it was all so well organised, giving people a strong confidence in the country's commitment to their welfare, in a hospital of their choosing.

When I started walking again, I carried with me a picture of two mates having the adventure of their lives; cementing a friendship that made sure that they would stick together, even when cancer struck. It gave me a sense of elation but, at the same time, I had to fend off a momentary feeling of emptiness, tinged with jealousy. This was the downside of walking solo: when loneliness struck, it packed a hefty punch.

I also carried with me his reflection on our forthcoming EU Referendum, which was salutary to say the least. I asked him what he thought of the impending referendum and he replied by telling me how the EU was a brilliant idea because it brought together countries which has spent centuries fighting each other, such as Germany and France. He believed in a community of different countries in Europe coming together for peace.

'But what about us, in the UK?' I asked. He was silent for a moment while, I guessed, trying to find a way to be polite about it.

'Well, you have always been a bit hesitant about making a full commitment to the EU. There are many things that you disagree about. You have always been looking for opt-out clauses. Perhaps it might be best if you went your own way,' he suggested. Nothing like the cold truth on a damp day, coupled depressingly with my anxieties about the downside of walking alone. I thanked him for his honest reply, and drained the last of my beer. I struggled to put on my rucksack, which seemed to get heavier as the days progressed.

22: Hermann Hesse

It was while I was walking through a rain-soaked village marvelling at how different from the grey barracks of Pforzheim the houses were here, with their exposed patterned beams that I made a decision about where I was going to stay that night. In England, before I left, I had booked a campsite about 5 miles south east of Calw.

Being soaked already I could not imagine spending the night

under canvas even though I did have a groundsheet! So I booked a cheap hotel room online and made for the centre of Calw instead, which was only a few miles further down the road. Little did I realise that Calw was the birthplace of Hermann Hesse, one of the most famous novelists of his generation. I remembered that he was extremely in vogue when I was a student in the 1960s. Students raved about his novels such as Steppenwolf and Siddhartha.

Later during my delicious evening meal of rump steak and noodles lying in a puddle of Baden-Württemberg-style onion gravy, I read about Namibia and the way native peoples belonging to the Herero, Nama and San tribes had been subject to ethnic cleansing by the Germans in the early 1900s. It was the first genocide of the 20th- century: more than 60,000 people were killed brutally. I wondered how many more genocides I would find out about, along my route, which would prove my ignorance of world affairs.

My route through the Black Forest was to lead me in a diagonal direction to the eastern end of Lake Constance, or Bodensee as the Germans called it. The border between Germany and Austria lies at that end, but before reaching that I planned a day off in Friedrichshafen, the city by the lake in which the Zeppelins had been designed, test-launched and manufactured. Apparently, there was an interesting museum there. I was going to take minor roads, footpaths, cycle tracks and forest trails – of which there were many. All I longed for was some good weather. So far this must have been one of the wettest springs in continental Europe. I had the chaffing marks on my legs to prove it. A weather forecast, on AccuWeather in February 2016 seemed to be coming true: 'These persistent storms will elevate the threat of flooding across southern Germany where the ground is already saturated following a wet winter. The greatest threat of flooding will be in Baden Württemberg and Bavaria where frequent rain and early spring mountain snowmelt will combine to produce high river levels and flooding.' Here I was on 24 May, walking 18 miles that day in clothing that was still damp after a night in my cold room in Calw.

My sun hat, which I purchased on the Internet just before I left, was made from the tarpaulin coverings of lorries that once trundled along the dusty roads of Brazil. I clearly remembered needing it to keep the sun off me on the approach to Düsseldorf, but apart from that it had often been perched on my head because its wide brim kept the rain from my eyes. I also liked it because the catcalls of 'Forrest Gump', which I received from youths in passing cars, could be alternated with 'Indiana Jones' when wearing this Tarp hat.

People asked me whether I spent my time listening to recordings on my phone while walking, to stave off the boredom. I never wanted to do that because there was always too much to see or think about. That morning, while walking along some very quiet, but wet lanes bordered on one side by slender trees and on the other by yellow fields of rape, I was trying to answer my own question about Black Forest gateaux or unicorns?

The least likely to be seen might appear obvious, but I was beginning to think that both might be a rarity. Every time I asked if there was a BFG (my shorthand for this mythical cake-like beast) for dessert I received a laugh in reply. Most recently, it happened the previous evening when, after my rump steak, I casually inquired about a slice of BFG and was given apple strudel with only a knowing grin to explain the denial of my request. This morning, in the spirit of scientific research, I popped into three cake shops in the villages through which I passed. Each time, I was told that they had no BFG. Reasons such as 'the last slice had just been sold,' or 'we were not delivered any yesterday' were trotted out in an unconvincing way. What were they trying to hide? I wondered. At one shop, I counted eight oozingly tempting cakes on display but no BFG. At last, I concluded that if I had a slightly better chance of spotting a unicorn, I had better stay more alert on the forest paths.

I also wondered 'where are all the pigs?' I had been passing through Germany for a few weeks and consumed my own weight in pork products but never seen a pig in the flesh, as it were. Today, by contrast, when I was not staring at bedraggled wheat or rape, all I saw was a flock of dirty, brown sheep.

By lunchtime, I was passing through the town of Herrenberg, with its church topped off by an enormous grey, slate onion-shaped dome. This imposing building was embedded in a background of only slightly lighter grey cloud. I felt that I was in a completely different country to the one in which I had seen the twin spiked church steeples at Cologne. Seemingly here they had swapped their steeple for an onion about 200 years ago. Why? It was a mystery to me. Was there a Russian Orthodox influence here in Baden-Württemberg, I wondered? Perhaps it was something to do with the eastern reaches of the Holy Roman Empire? Or being so close to the Danube, the people hereabouts had ventured down the river into the Ottoman Empire?

I found a welcoming bakery shop where an amiable assistant made me a plate of two hot meat rolls (the delicious meat loaf was a kind of warm, spicy, moist spam) and a non-BFG cake, all of which I ate in seconds while sitting and checking on the Internet why one of the roads, which I had just passed by, was called Johannes Kepler Strasse.

It is little wonder that I end up talking to myself in the kitchen at parties, when I seem to be the only one interested in the development of the thinking about our solar system and the cosmos in general. I get so carried away that I sometimes bore myself to sleep. But here I was, passing a street named after a real hero of scientific thought and space in particular and I could have missed it.

Kepler was born in Weil der Stadt, which I found out was only a few miles away from my hotel last night. It was all very well to learn from the young student who served me breakfast that Hermann Hesse, the darling of students in 1960s San Francisco, was a local but she had failed to tell me that the great Johannes Kepler was born in the neighbourhood as well.

At a very young age he studied at Tübingen University (a day's walk from where he was born) and later taught there after spending many years in Prague while escaping persecution during the Thirty Years War. Among other wonderful scientific insights, he postulated the elliptical movement of planets in their orbit round the sun. The supposed circular orbits, which had been held as a belief since Greek times, did not correspond with observations now being made. Like Galileo – his more famous contemporary – his work also flew in the face of the truth propagated by the Church. His problems were further exacerbated by the fact that his mother was tried for being a witch. His was a fabulously interesting life story that began and ended about 300 years before, in the landscape through which I was walking. The same landscape that saw battles and skirmishes during the Thirty Years War fought between Catholics and Protestants, and the crash landings of several prototype Zeppelins, designed by Count von Zeppelin, much nearer to the present day.

How would I have time to listen to anything through my headphones?

After Herrenberg I came upon vast stretches of meadowland with long grasses packed with flowers including yellow daisies and delicate lilac-coloured field scabious. I was in what looked like a giant saucer of land with Herrenberg on its northern rim. I calculated that I had to walk across the bottom of the saucer to reach the small village called Oberndorf where I had booked a bed at the Gasthof Rössle. This guesthouse lay in a deserted stretch of farmland running alongside the north-facing side of heavily wooded hillside, which I could see from miles away. It was not warm enough for people to have yet dispensed with their wood burners so all afternoon I could see thin curls of smoke rising, like grey hairs lying on a tweed coat, over the trees behind the village.

I reached the Gasthof only to find that no one answered the door. I thought I might have to pitch my tent on the nearest piece of grass but eventually I managed to stir the owners. My room was ready for me but they did not serve meals on a Tuesday. I should have checked – it was my fault but that did not stop me feeling somewhat distraught. I needed calories!

The owner told me that there was a restaurant a few miles away but the idea of walking even a few paces was totally out of the question. Kindly, I was offered bread, cheese and sliced meat in my room. I begged for a beer as well. In less than an hour, I had washed, changed, eaten my frugal meal, drunk my beer and settled down for the night... I could not ring home because there was no phone signal in the village. I was in bed at half past eight.

Fortunately, I made up for lost calories at breakfast time and was most thankful to the owner to find that there was no charge for my meal the night before even though it had been my fault. Kindness surely followed me in random ways.

23: Fronleichnam

Trying to get going on the road after breakfast was almost impossible. I had a stabbing pain in my right hip. I had noticed it slightly the day before but put it down to tiredness. Now after a long sleep, I began to think it was more serious. Sitting by the roadside after only a few hundred yards, I readjusted the straps on my rucksack. I imagined that the weight might have been misaligned yesterday and caused the pains on my right side. It could also have been due to my worn boots, which were beginning to lose the black layer on their heels.

I thought it might be wise to change my route and revise my mileage for the day. When pain struck I had learned to shorten the focus of my ambitions. I also had something to look forward to. Kate and her sister, Anna, who lives in France near Belfort, were planning to meet me in three days' time. They would join me for a day's walking to a town called Sigmaringen.

Luckily, outside the village I was able to pick up a signal, so I made a plan to walk 13 miles to Mössingen, stay the night and then 15 miles the next day to a place called Gammertingen where I would meet Kate and Anna on 28 June, after I had rested for a day.

It was not raining for a change. I was on a cycle track going south in a land of utter peace. On either side of me were vast meadows full of wild flowers; meadows that were dotted with bulbous fruit trees, clumps of bull rushes, and small copses. At the edges, on the rim of my vision, were the occasional spires of squat churches. Dotted in between were fields of wheat, which had also been sown with peas; they grew entwined, grain and legume clinging together among the wild flowers. I guessed that organic farmers planted peas to give the soil a boost of much needed nitrogen, which was then snapped up by the wheat.

Whole banks of wild lilac ran down the side of some meadows. These were often overshadowed by hawthorn trees heavy with may blossom. Wild strawberries poked up along the banks beside the path, and huge snails slurped their way across in front of me looking like I felt and, for their size, travelling at about the same speed.

When walking became a painful chore, I had developed a habit of zoning in on my immediate surroundings. Sometimes even saying to myself, 'try and make it to that tree up ahead, then take a break and then try moving on to the next tree…' In this way I reached the town of Rottenburg by coffee time.

The pain in my hip had subsided, but I knew to treat its presence seriously. So I enjoyed a longer coffee break than usual, which caused the owner of the café to come and quiz me about my journey, particularly, I guessed, since it was hard to keep my rucksack out of the way of other customers, their pushchairs and doddery feet. Unfortunately, my German did not extend beyond simple well-rehearsed sentences and his English was about the same, so try as I might, I could not convince him that I was not walking to Rome. I had read a poster about Saint Martin's Way, which ran through Rottenburg, just before entering the café – so I guessed that he was suggesting that I was on that route, but I gave up trying to correct him, and in the end I just smiled sweetly. He wanted a selfie with me so that he could put it up on the café's notice board along with his collection of Manchester United memorabilia. With much posing and backslapping I managed to extricate myself without repeating my real destination and telling him about my dislike of all things football.

Looking for a bakery to buy my rolls for lunch, I came across a street where shop fronts were being adorned with birch tree saplings. It looked as if Great Birnam Wood was on the march up Dunsinane Hill again. About 2.5 metres tall, they were in leaf and had elegant trunks the size of a well-turned ankle. I asked a man what was going on and he dived into the shop to get someone who could explain it all to me.

He rushed off leaving me to hold the tree trunk, which he was erecting. I did not grasp it quickly enough, because I was fiddling with my phone to take a photograph, and, like a row of dominoes, the trees along the front of his shop were felled in quick succession. I stood transfixed, flummoxed. Seconds later he came out with a women who could speak English and we all helped to pick up the trees. As we were working, she told me that it was a tradition to put these trees up when celebrating Corpus Christi (Fronleichnam – 60 days after Easter Sunday), which was the next day. I sensed a pagan-cum-Christian link that connected the new growth of the trees in spring to the Last Supper and the resurrection, but the language skills between us were too weak to launch into this.

'If there are no more disasters,' she said, smiling politely at me while looking at where, on my watch, the trees had fallen, 'we should be ready for the parade along here tomorrow. It is a public holiday, so we will be very busy.' I wondered how many public holidays they have in Germany. They seem to create a healthy economy in the time between celebrating every twist and turn in the Bible. Maybe, I asked myself, we should take more days off in the UK? That is where we must be going wrong.

It was not long before I found the River Neckar. I stood on the bridge and watched the slow waters creep along towards Heidelberg, Mannheim, and the Rhine – then onto the Europort from whence I had come, four weeks before. I began to get worried that too much backward glancing might hinder me from moving forward, so I made my farewells and turned to face south again.

Miraculously, the clouds cleared and the sun came out. The canopy of blue sky almost hurt my eyes. I felt a quick injection of energy and optimism, now I was looking forward to arriving in Mössingen, more so because I had booked a room in the B&B section of a traditional brewery. I considered enquiring whether, in this particular case, the real meaning of B&B was bed and beer, but quickly dismissed the idea. My hip had stopped complaining. It was enjoying the leisurely stroll today. It was the first time for two weeks that I felt it necessary to smear sun cream over me, which must herald a turn in the weather, I hoped.

I chose a forest path to get to Mössingen, even though above me the frequent and noisy aircraft interrupted any sense of real solitude. Despite that, it wasn't long before I did feel quite cut off and ready to enjoy life around me. I came across a semi-squashed fire salamander on the track in front of me. Its black leathery skin still retained a supple appearance and the egg yolk-coloured spots and longer daubs of creamy yellow that ran along its length remained bright even in the slanting sunlight that forced its way through the beech leaves above. I was buzzed by hornets with short red wings flying around like tiny helicopters and, after all the rain in the past few days, I had to step over bright orange slugs that littered the path like dropped shoelaces.

A notice told me that I should watch out for deer and wild boar. I just hoped that the boar were free of young ones at the moment because of the threat a Forrest Gump like me posed and the anger that they could show if I came upon them unexpectedly.

Almost at the dead centre of the forest, along a track – but sounding like a road – called Rottenburg Strasse, I became woozy with the scent of wild mint. There were clumps of it along the verges of the path, but almost hidden in the rampant brambles. Oak, beech and fir trees surrounded me. This was not a managed forest with phalanxes of fir trees. Rather it had a homely, Midsummer Night's Dream feel to it: a magical place in which to lose oneself entirely. If unicorns existed, they were in this forest. Being alone and susceptible to fancy, I imagined that I saw all kinds of creatures, even unicorns, slipping behind trees as soon as I looked in their direction. I felt quite at home in the disorientation of this place. Orchids in the grassy patches and garlands of mildly scented wild honeysuckle hung on low branches, completing the enchantment of it all.

In absolute contrast, and sometime later after I had emerged from the forest and meandered down a winding road to the outskirts of Mössingen, I could not resist – on a whim – the more mundane charms of a MacDonald's. The advertising at the time was 'Big is Back' and I wanted to see if that was really true. To give praise where it is due, the company had done a marvellous job of the lay-out by creating tastefully decorated areas like an ice-cream parlour and a quality play area for children. One still had to queue but after being given a ticket for collection, a screen told you when to retrieve your food. Rather like an Argos Store in the UK or as the builder beside me said: 'It's just like my works' canteen.'

The food, however, never ceases to amaze me. The burger bun still had a wet slippery feel about it. I was worried that the meat might shoot out of my hand on to the floor. These second lunches gave me much-needed calories but I wanted to leave as soon as I had proved that even if 'Big was Back', size certainly wasn't everything.

On my way out, I got a massive surprise. There in the chilled cabinet was my first sighting of a Swartzwälder Kirschtorte, the much sought after BFG. How amazing, I thought, that in the forest I could have so easily seen a unicorn lingering long enough to beckon me further in, and here in MacDonald's was my mythical cake on display. Two rarities in one day: I must, I vowed, slow down with a hurt hip more often. Actually, on hindsight, I might have known there were rare treasures to be found in MacDonald's owing to the trail of litter leading people to it. It was like Princess Ariadne's thread trail that Theseus used in the Labyrinth; only this time cake was the prize, not the Minotaur.

On the far side of town lay the Fisher's Brauhaus, my B&B, which lived up to all the hype. Guests were given a half-litre of beer to take to their room. The staff were pleasant in an off-the-scale way. Photographs on the wall of long beer wagons pulled by a team of dray horses gave the atmosphere a sense of history and family continuity. I took to the place straight away, but looking at the massive hills behind the brewery, which lay in my direction for the next day, I realised that too much of the local brew would ruin my chances of a successful walk to Gammertingen tomorrow. It was a distance of 19.5 miles with steep climbs thrown in.

Over breakfast I said goodbye to Heather and Dave, a most friendly couple from Fife who were engaged on a family research project. They treated me to my restaurant meal the evening before, because they were so keen to hear about my journey and my charities. Chance encounters like this were the lifeblood of my expedition. There was an unspoken freedom on both sides, which allowed a different kind of conversation to the ones that occur in so-called 'normal' life: conversations that set the blood coursing and remind us of our common humanity.

24: Last Days in Germany

Walking away from my bedtime brewery, I was so close to the countryside that I was quickly deep among some wild-flower meadows and brightly painted beehives dotted around in clumps, under the trees. The strong sun made me reach for the sun cream and, while I stood to apply it, I also plastered over some nagging blisters on my heels, and put a stretchy bandage sock on to strengthen my right Achilles tendon. Each day, these minor ministrations helped to stave off a major incident. I could not avoid listening to my body because its messages to my brain sounded loud and clear.

Looking up at the hills ahead, and knowing the route I was following to Gammertingen, I had a feeling that this was going to be a warm, comforting but blissfully uneventful day. I had an apple and a banana for lunch, left over from breakfast, in case I did not come across shops or any restaurants open. It was, of course, Corpus Christi, so there was no guarantee that I would even see anyone, let alone find any shops open. My plan was to take the day in manageable sections, so my first job was to climb a long, steep hill into some fairly thick woodland.

After two and a half hours, I had a panoramic, sweeping view from the top. Quiet villages on the plain below suggested that coffee was out of the question. In one direction there was a sharp, pointed church steeple and in the other a bulging onion spire. It set me thinking that there was once a time when most people believed that their prayers were projected and guided up to heaven, by these pointing fingers of church architecture. They were the conduits through which the material connected with the ethereal. I guess most people would now have a different view based on a lack of belief in the invisible. Ironically, the same people, I reflected, have no difficulty in believing that a telecommunication tower, like the one I could see on the horizon, would transmit their speech directly into a handheld device to a recipient on the other side of the world. I was still deep in thought about what physical forms it takes for people to believe in the unseen (quite apt for Corpus Christi when the bread and wine shared during Christ's last supper became symbolic of things that would soon become invisible for the disciples) when I came to the village of Melchingen. Nothing stirred and coffee was certainly not going to be served.

The villages might have been empty, but the narrow country road I was following was busy with holiday traffic. To my right, I saw the bobbing helmets of cyclists, so I wove my way among fields to join them. We were all heading towards Gammertingen, but at a comfortable distance from the throng.

I chatted to any cyclist who was taking a break and was told that there might be one restaurant open at a village called Stetten unter Holstein. So I headed in that direction, past organic, fallow fields slumbering under their heavy coats of clover. Sure enough on a sundrenched bend in the road was a most welcoming restaurant serving huge bowls of pasta and cool glasses of beer. I sat, drinking and eating, talking to a young couple who were cycling around this part of the forest in training for a trip to Florence in the summer. I became envious of the ease in which people in southern Germany could just take off on cycling holidays. Everything was in their favour: cycle tracks, cheap places to stop for the night, cafes and restaurants – all geared up for this pastime. Even the buses had bike racks on the back so that people could get back home quickly from their destinations. They had no excuse for not enjoying their countryside and getting fit in the process.

I was already getting pangs of regret about leaving Germany. I had been here for over four weeks so far, and had loved every moment except for the 'pain in the arse' episode. So I became a bit morose during the afternoon, but beyond my regrets about leaving, my downbeat feelings could also have been the result of drinking a second beer at lunchtime. I had broken my own rule again and was paying the price.

I was kept amused by the tourist wagons drawn by teams of well-groomed horses, which passed me on the cycle track. These were the type of carriage that had a long table down the centre of the sitting section piled high with food, wine and beer. The customers ate, drank and enjoyed the taped traditional German music while the horses trotted along under a canopy of shadowy trees in this tranquil, late spring afternoon.

I also became fascinated with a large flock of sheep that were grazing beside the track, watched over by a raincoat-clad shepherd and his two brown Alsatian sheepdogs. It took me a moment to remember that Alsatians could also be working sheepdogs, as my only real dealings with them at home were when out jogging. I had vivid memories of them tugging on their leads, trying to get at me, while I was giving them a wide birth. Here, though, they were lying down, unleashed, in the cool, long grass with fixed eyes on the sheep. They took no notice of me, which was a relief. However, as I entered my second forest of the day, I still skirted round them, just to be on the safe side.

It was about 4pm when I entered the forest with only about three miles to go to Gammertingen. An hour and a half later, I was totally lost. Desperate for food and drink, I was ready to sit down and weep with exhaustion. 'What happened?' I shouted out loud. Invariably, in the last five miles something would happen to slow me down, and make me thoroughly depressed. I developed a theory that forest paths are altered owing to the arboreal programme of felling which changes the lie of the land. Vehicles, large and small, make their own tracks, which in the end can be mistaken for the proper path. Whatever the cause, I had no clue where I was. It was only when I emerged, eventually, from the woods and saw a road in the distance that my spirits lifted. As I made for the road, I looked back at the fir trees on the edge of the forest. The new green shoots on the tips of the branches were like fingers reaching out to grapple with something in the grassy verges. They seemed to want to keep me in their grasp. Uncharacteristically, I trotted the last few yards to the road. Frightened by the trees or craving food: I refused to make a choice.

I worked out from the setting sun which way to turn and, thankfully, in about half an hour I was on the outskirts of Gammertingen walking past a Celtic Tree Horoscope, which was displayed on a huge board beside the roadside. I only stopped for a few moments to glance at the board. It seemed an interesting project but I was too tired to take it all in – except to read that I was born under the influence of the Rowan Tree, which sounded a pleasant proposition. Especially when I read later that Rowan people 'are likely to be a keen-minded visionary, with high ideals. Your thoughts are original and creative, so much so, that others often misunderstand where you are coming from. This sometimes makes you aloof when interacting with others as you feel they wouldn't understand where you are coming from anyway. Nevertheless, although you may appear to have a cool exterior, you are burning with passionate ideals from within.'

With that said about you, how could anyone not admire the Celts for their perspicacity?

When I was settled into my room at the Hotel und Gastehaus Kreuz in Gammertingen, I worked out my mileage for the day and realised that when I stepped out in two days' time with Kate and Anna, I would be taking the first steps in the second half of my journey. I was at the 600-mile mark, nearly leaving Germany and looking forward to Austria: my fourth European country. I dressed up in my lightweight glad rags for a solo celebratory meal in the hotel's restaurant. As I had passed the dining room on my way upstairs, I had caught sight of the evening menu. I saw liver soup written at the top. Now I was keen to try this local delicacy as a prelude to an evening of gastronomic tasting. As was my Rowan nature, I was burning with passionate ideals, in this case, ideals about the quantity of food that I was just about to consume.

I was sitting in what I now knew was a typical, traditional German restaurant – a cavernous room with dark wood walls covered in sepia family photographs, and oozing conviviality. The atmosphere reverberated with the clinking echoes of waiters serving plates of comfort food. There were large heraldic shields, displaying the symbols of local families, surrounding a large crucifix supporting an intricate carving of Jesus. He presided over last suppers, every night of the week.

Fried eggs followed my delicious liver soup. They were slipped on top of hot roast pork, and served with a pile of sautéed potatoes. A just reward for a 20-mile stint, coping with getting lost in the forest and preventing the green tentacles of some burly fir trees from keeping me captive. Apple strudel was an almost obligatory pudding especially if one was on a massive calorie-replacement diet.

While finishing my beer, I gazed at a map of Germany and calculated that I had walked through three of its 16 regions: North Rhine-Westphalia, Rhineland-Palatinate and Baden-Württemberg. A success, even though there were 13 more regions to go. Remembering the ITV News at Ten graphic, I reconciled myself to the fact that it was still quite a large section of the TV screen.

When planning the walk, while sitting comfortably on my sofa at home in England, I thought that as I got nearer to the Alps I would need a couple more days off to do sightseeing and generally rest up before the onslaught ahead. In reality, I found myself in a lethargic state not due to the exhaustion (although I was running on empty quite a lot), but because I was losing the drive and passion needed to face up to the enormous task in front of me. I kept telling myself that to get to Lake Constance was good enough. I was too content with what I had done already, and I had given myself too many rest days, which allowed me more time to dwell on my achievements, so far.

I had a day's outing planned for the next day. Then two days walking, one of which would be with Kate and Anna followed by a day's rest at Friedrichshafen. After that, when I got to Bregenz in Austria, (still on the shores of Lake Constance) I had another free day in which to summon up the strength to tackle the mountains. It all seemed so sensible at home, but now I began to worry that I was building up trouble for myself.

How pathetic to be spooked by the mountains? By the time I started to climb up to my first booked campsite at Bezau it would be 3 June. Summer would be buzzing around me. The snow would have melted and the cows would be on the higher pastures. I kept seeing the opening credits of The Sound of Music streaming inside my head: Maria running across an alpine meadow. What was there to fret about?

Kate and Anna were sure to have some wise words about my dilemma. That was the beauty of family joining me for a couple of days. It helped to put things in perspective.

Meanwhile, on the following day I was going to catch the local train to Hechingen, because I wanted to visit Hohenzollern Castle. I was determined to see a fairytale castle before I left Germany and there it was, according to the leaflets at my guesthouse, perched on top of a mountain (about 2600 feet), standing magnificent in its Swabian, limestone landscape. With sturdy battlements, grey-slate conical roofs on towering turrets, and vast manorial halls full of medieval armour and storybook tapestry, it looked as if it would easily satisfy my craving for romanticism. It was going to be a cliché fest: a wonderful diversion from the main event. I was like a child at the seaside, hiding behind the sand castles instead of running into the sea and standing up to the waves.

In reality, the next day was everything I wanted it to be. I was swept along by the views, the grandiose interiors and the pomp of the owners' lineage. This was a castle that had been revamped twice since it was first built in the 11th-century. It seemed always to have been in the Hohenzollern family, along with Sigmaringen Castle, which I was yet to see. The current owner, Karl Friedrich, Prince of Hohenzollern became head of the House of Hohenzollern in September 2010. About five years younger than me, he is not a stuffy kind of prince – when not managing his estate he is the lead singer in a band called Charly and the Jivemates (with a healthy You Tube following). Not bad for the head of one of the oldest dynasties in Germany and a Knight of the Imperial and Royal Order of the Black Eagle. As if he did not have enough to do, he is also the heir to the now defunct throne of Romania; such is the interconnectedness of noble European families.

On the journey back to Gammertingen on the train, I thought of lineage and pomp. I remembered, a few years before, searching for the grave of my grandfather in East Finchley cemetery. I never knew him and my only token of remeberance was the funeral director's card that bore the number of his grave. When I could not find any kind of stone that showed the name of John Chadwick, let alone a grave number, the clerk on the desk at the cemetery offices was kind enough to point out that being a pauper he was buried in an unmarked grave with five other unknowns. They were all buried standing up to save room for the paying dead. I did not begrudge the Prince his velvet, garters, hunting lodge, racing cars, and forebears of royal decent, but I was always amused at my fascination for this kind of life when mine, and my family's, was so lowly and unremarkable.

25: A Family Reunion

Kate and Anna had stayed at Sigmaringen in the Gästehaus Pfefferle the night of my return from Hohenzollern, so that we could all walk back there the next day to spend the night and retrieve Anna's car. The next day, I was up early and ready on the doorstep of my guesthouse eager to meet them and take the first step that would break my 600-mile mark. They arrived in a taxi in good time, and luckily the sun was out and the forecast was fair for the day. Our fleeces were tied optimistically round our waists as we headed for the road out of Gammertingen, after, of course, the obligatory photo of me taking my monumental halfway step.

This memorable, but very quiet Saturday, passed in a cloud of family chat and my reminiscences of the walk so far. I never quite did justice to my stories because I found it hard not to give polished versions of a few choice events designed for public consumption. I did not delve too deeply into any of my despairing moments. This was to keep my spirits high rather than to protect my walk mates from the gory truth.

While the conversation rolled on, we passed some peaceful, verdant countryside with stalks of wheat up to one's waist compared to the hand-high shoots I had seen in Holland. At lunchtime we stopped in an otherwise empty café for three wooden boards plentifully covered with Flammkuchen, a kind of German pizza. Anna was particularly partial to this kind of delicacy because its cousin, Tarte Flambée, is so popular in France, but neither Kate nor I had tasted it before. In an instance, this rectangular, savoury feast topped with salty bacon, soft, rich onions, and creamy cheese had us captivated. To make the lunch even more precarious for people walking 20 miles, wonderfully refreshing beer was served twice in long, narrow fluted glasses. By the time we were finished, I was pleasantly woozy and wanted a sleep, rather than walk another 10 miles, but we braved the road again and struggled to Gammertingen for a pre-dinner lie down.

It was a day of extra special eating. That night we found a restaurant just outside Sigmaringen that served Galloway beef. Anna and Kate are proud of their Scottish lineage and Anna's daughter, Sara, is married to a Scottish farmer in southwest Scotland. So how could we miss eating steak from Galloway cattle? Apparently, at the Beim Rinderwirt, which first opened its doors in 1871, they have been rearing and cooking this type of high quality beef for about 10 years. The fields around the Rinderwirt are never short of water and so the grass is lush for most of the year. Galloway cattle are the only ones that can thrive in these wet conditions. In Scotland they are famous for their love of the damp. So there we were, eating Scottish meat in the heart of the Black Forest.

The next morning, having walked the 17 miles from Gammertingen, Anna's leg was too painful, to walk with us again. She planned to visit Sigmaringen castle instead, while Kate and I struck out on the road to Illmensee, a village beside a small lake that boasted a very scenic campsite with a commanding view down the whole length of the lake. From England, I had booked a place at this site with dreams of gazing through the tent door at an uninterrupted view of the setting sun on the lake.

As we walked through Sigmaringen, we crossed a bridge, underneath which ran the River Donau. I did a double take because although I had read about it I had somehow forgotten the significance of this name. Of course, here it was: the River Danube. It had started trickling way up to our right, but now it flowed strongly towards Ulm, at which point it became navigable. Ultimately, it ran out into the Black Sea.

Another river crossed. If I still had my I Spy books to hand it would have been ticked off with a large pencil.

At just before midday, the companionship that I had enjoyed so much came to an all too abrupt end. Anna collected Kate in the car from a lay-by on the busy road to Krauchenwies and with quick farewells I was alone and heading south. They were driving back to France. I would not see Kate again until I walked into Santa Vittoria on 10 July at 5pm. It began to rain.

26: On My Own Again

In need of a rest and to shake off the wet, I asked for coffee at an Italian restaurant that was not yet open as the waiters were setting up for Sunday lunches. I spoke in a mixture of Italian and German to tell them about my journey. They were impressed enough to waive the cost of my drink.

Not long after that I glanced down into the ditch beside the road and saw one of my 'pavement friends.' It was a buzzard that seemed to have just fallen from the sky. During my entire walk, I had seen thousands of these graceful hawks circling around in the sky. This one showed all the signs of having just died. The body was in perfect condition with only its eyes gone: eaten by insects. It had landed on its back, so I just stood and absorbed the beauty of it. Underneath its wings, there was a patch of white like a dipper's breast and the underneath of its tail had crosshatch markings of grey and white that seemed like Egyptian hieroglyphics scratched into clay. Its claws were clasped, not in attack but in reaction to the fall – gripping onto thin air as it plummeted to earth. I was beginning to feel that my 'pavement friends' were signs, or echoes in the environment that revealed my feelings at the time. There was something unspoken between us and this hawk was so newly dead that I am sure its spirit was close by and could detect my state of mind.

I ate my lunch on the move because the insistent rain made it unlikely that I would find a place to sit in comfort. Not even a bus shelter in sight. All the while, the weather darkened and thunder rolled around on the edges. After a while, I diverted onto shingle-covered cycle tracks and came upon the remote village of Judentenberg and, for a moment, the clouds lightened a little from the west.

Swathes of wet corn glistened and murmured in a breeze that agitated the three modern wind turbines that stood outside the village. As I got even nearer to them I could hear their groans and grumbles in rhythmic sequence. Nordex NX9028 was the turbine that demanded most attention as it was making the loudest noise. I was possessed by the idea that it was a beautiful, almost human, icon. Here it was grumbling and groaning while making power for the German National Grid. Countless households were boiling kettles because 9028 had conquered its anxieties about clanking away during this unpleasant afternoon.

Feeling inspired by 9028, and its grumpy but noble fortitude, I turned downhill and wove my way beside more wet fields into Illmensee. That Nordex wind turbine was so blokeish – doing the job well while moaning about having to do it: such a classic stance.

Thick fog surrounded me on my final approach. The campsite was unoccupied. The dream of falling asleep looking out at a shimmering lake faded quickly as I realised my chances of camping in this boggy field were about as likely as 9028 becoming ecstatically happy in its work. A passerby directed me to the only place of accommodation that was likely to have vacancies. Not only was it very cheap, but also the Gasthaus Seehof was one of the most homely places that I had come across. They found me a room, booked me a table for an evening meal and poured me a beer, all in seconds. After 19.70 miles in the road that day with the final two hours in thick fog, I was ready for a sleep before my meal.

My journey the next day to Friedrichshafen was downhill almost all the way. From the top of a sharp incline, at about 11am, I caught a glimpse of Lake Constance and the Swiss mountains behind it to the south and southeast. Austria, to the east, was shrouded in cloud. Having become a Thomas Hardy type character during my last days in the Black Forest, wandering through a Wessex-style landscape of seemingly endless paths carved through rolling grassland, I was now moving much faster down towards a huge expanse of water and mountain ranges that stretched across the entire horizon. I saw snow on the upper slopes of the Swiss ranges, but, as I told myself, they were very high and it would be unreasonable to think that, at the end of May, the snow would have disappeared from peaks at that altitude.

Strangely, I became very excited by the changing landscape. My sorrow about leaving the Black Forest was replaced unexpectedly, and very quickly, by an appreciation of the astounding Rhine glacial basin in which Lake Constance lay. At the end of the last ice age, the retreating glacier carved out the lake's bed in the shape of a tongue. The Rhine now enters the lake near Bregenz to my east and leaves it near Basel to the west. I thought that I had seen the last of this noble friend at Worms, but here was it was again in its infancy. The lake is 39 miles long, although with some massive black clouds occluding my view at the edges, I was only able to see a fraction of it.

Here also was the birthplace of Count von Zeppelin's air balloons. In the early days, they were sheltered in huge sheds floating on the lake. I was looking forward to visiting the Zeppelin museum the next day. First though, I had to get down to the water's edge and find an artist's cottage beside a small river that runs into the lake on the outskirts of Friedrichshafen. I had booked this through Airbnb. Sanne, the host (and artist), had written a charming email to say that she was looking forward to meeting me. She was fascinated, she told me later, that a man of my age could embark on such a journey and be raising money for charity. That is why she went out of her way to befriend me and treat me like a long lost relative and not a regular kind of

Airbnb guest. 'It is my contribution to your charities,' she told me over dinner.

So, with a renewed sense of optimism I had ascended from the ditch and taken flight again, circling on currents of warm air, rising. Something at the back of my mind even triggered the thought that 'the Alps might not be so daunting after all, now that I could see them.' I only hoped that this whim might not be a bit premature.

I might have guessed that Sanne would be a person of strong character, but the cotton sheet stretched over her front garden proved it, if there had been any doubt.

Sanne told me later that the runways at Friedrichshafen's airport had been extended to allow for more daily flights. Her cottage was now directly under a new flightpath and she had installed a sheet with 'Keep the noise down' (or words to that effect! In German, of course) writ large upon it. It was for the pilots to read as they roared over. She had also written letters to the airport's authority. She was a long-term resident of the city (in fact this was the cottage in which she was born), and an activist at heart.

She could not have done a better job of looking after me. She ran my bath and chose the right essential oils for tired limbs, she cooked marvellous food for us to enjoy together and presented a superb variety of delicious things for breakfast. Everything was vegetarian and organic. Her pet Jack Russell, called Alex, was an amenable dog. She had taught him to do tricks, which he was delighted to show me on my second night in her artist's studio, after a dinner of tapas and her own concoction of apple, ginger and mint tea.

27: Wopsie the Cat

The next day was one of my free (avoiding the Alps) days. Having driven me into the centre of town, Sanne left me to explore the museum. I spent two uninterrupted hours looking at everything on display. Just as I was amazed at the size of the huge gliders used in World War Two in Holland, now I was captivated by the size of these balloons, the metal structures inside them, the gondolas slung under them for passengers and crew, and the technology involved in ensuring that the gas bags were safe from explosions caused by static electricity. Since Scotland had been at the forefront of my mind for several days owing to Anna's visit and the Galloway steaks, the story of the first transatlantic crossing made by an airship stood out above all others.

Admittedly not a Zeppelin, but an airship made in Glasgow by Armstrong Whitworth – the R34, nicknamed Tiny – completed the crossing from East Fortune (near North Berwick, outside Edinburgh) to Mineola, New York in 108 hours and 12 minutes. This non-passenger flight took place in July 1919; just about 20 years after the first Zeppelins flew over Lake Constance.

R34 was the length of two football pitches and cost £350,000 to produce. In addition to the bags of hydrogen keeping it up in the air, its engines needed 6000 gallons of petrol to move it forward. This would have been fascinating enough, but then to learn about the two stowaways on the airship's maiden voyage was even better. It gave the story a real human dimension.

William Ballantyne was a 22-year-old from Newcastle. Previously a prizefighter, he enlisted in the Royal Naval Air Service (later called Royal Air Force from 1 April 1918) as an airship rigger. His job involved, among other things, looking after the gasbags and putting rubber patches on any leaks. He was originally on the crew list for the flight but was left out to make room for an American observer. The motivation for stowing away was understandable. He wedged himself between a metal upright and a gasbag, but he was discovered after 12 hours into the flight because some gas leaked and it made him so nauseous that he gave himself away by the heaving noises he made. After recovering in the airship's sickbay, he was allowed to help out in the kitchens. The second stowaway was a cat called Wopsie. William had tucked the cat, which was the ship's mascot anyway, under his arm when sneaking aboard. I assume that, to this day, Wopsie holds the record for being the first, and perhaps only, cat to fly across the Atlantic in an airship.

Having walked 657 miles since leaving home, I left the comfort of Sanne's cottage on Wednesday 1 June to walk into Austria. The first night was to be in Bregenz, which is situated at the eastern end of Lake Constance, 23 miles away. I would be keeping quite close to the water's edge, passing the small island on which the picture postcard town of Lindau was situated. Unusually, the sun had warmed the air quite early, the woodland paths were soggy rather than waterlogged and the absence of any grey or black clouds augured well. I was walking well that morning. The oils in my bathwater, the complete rest, and exquisite food had been of enormous benefit not only to my physical self but also to my sense of purpose. The route was completely flat but I could still see to my left the slopes that ran north to the Black Forest, covered in fruit of all kinds.

As I was passing an industrial estate at mid-morning, I saw coming towards me two people who seemed, at a distance, to be dressed as part of a pageant. As they came closer I could see it was a young man and a young woman. She had a black corduroy suit on, with large wooden buttons to do up the jacket. Underneath she wore a black waistcoat with two rows of small wooden buttons, and a white collarless shirt. His suit was similar to hers except it was made of thick linen and the jacket buttons were white. They both wore black felt hats and had pencils and rulers tucked into pockets that ran down the outside of their trouser legs, while the trousers were hoisted by wide elasticated braces. What was even more striking were the two walking sticks they were using. It was obvious that they were originally cut and shaped from an actual branch of a tree: ones that had become twisted somehow so as to resemble two sticks of barley sugar.

As soon as I enquired why they were dressed like this, I realised that I already knew the answer. 'Ah! Yes,' I blurted out, when the male walker started to tell me. Recalling PLF's adventures, I butted in with excitement, 'You are journeymen,' quickly altered to, 'a journey man and a journey women.' They relaxed and smiled when they knew that I understood what was happening. A rarity for a foreigner, they must have thought.

I considered this custom to have died out long ago, but here were two joiners spending a year walking round Germany getting work that would extend their credentials. Company owners were obliged to find suitable work for them, so that the trade could prosper. At the end of the year, they would produce a piece of work that represented their skills and were judged on it. If successful they were awarded a trade certificate and they could use that to practise anywhere in the country. It was prestigious and represented wonderfully how Germany still takes its crafts and trades seriously. I told these two all about PLF and his encounter with a German chimneysweep who was seeking work on the way down to Italy but I think it went over their heads. Something lost in translation, I feared. We parted in high spirits, but I got the feeling that it was a bit of an 'old school' encounter for them (with my references to 1934), which was strange because they were the ones who looked old school, or so I thought.

It was not long after that I reached the Austrian border and took a selfie beside the welcome board, which announced that I was entering the region of Vorarlberg.

Austria

1: The Alps

With my Tarp hat on, my uncut beard of nearly six weeks, and my severely weathered face, I looked like a backwoodsman who had just emerged from the forest after months of seclusion. Now, here I was entering the culturally rich, throngingly touristic town of Bregenz with smart looking people drinking Aperol Spritz in the cafes by the lakeside, with sadly no chance of blending in.

I forced myself to stop apologizing for taking a few days' rest so as to prepare for the mountains. 'Who would actually bother with what I did as long as I got to the end and walked all the way?' This was the gist of my internal debate. That evening after a quick meal at a nearby Chinese restaurant, I went to my room in the Gastehof Linde and was in bed as soon as possible.

I decided that I would mooch around town the next day just taking in the sights and exploring at random. I bought a visitors' ticket that gave me access to museums and art galleries and spent some time in them all. I enjoyed lunch in a vegan café, which reminded me dangerously of home in Hebden Bridge. This was a blessing and a mistake all in one go. The café produced in me a sudden pang of homesickness, which made the snowball even bigger as it grew with my seventh mistake. Luckily, the excellent quality of the food almost made up for the longing to be back at home.

Needing a seat for a longer rest, I entered a Turkish Barbers on a whim. I drank in the atmosphere of coffee, spray perfume and beard oil. This was a man's place and I needed and injection of that. There was fun to be had just hearing the chatter in German and Turkish, not knowing what was being said. The sound of it all made me want to slip down the queue and stay even longer. In the end, I asked for a Number 2 haircut because when the weather got hotter (hard to imagine at that stage) I would need as little as possible under my Tarp.

My barber asked me what I was doing and when I told him, he turned around and involved the whole shop in our conversation. There were three other barbers and assorted customers giving their 'Oohs' and 'Aahs' almost in unison. Then one of the throng said how it reminded him of all the people walking out of Syria and heading west. I shrank a little inside on hearing this; remembering the happy Syrian families that I met on the Dutch/German border about five weeks before. Mine was a luxurious indulgence compared to their plight. But I perked up again when they asked about my charities and the Turkish chorus gave its acceptance of my dedication to what they called 'humanitarian causes.'

I spent the rest of the day wandering on the lakeside among the chess players, street artists and workers erecting the scenery for an opera that was to take place in a few evenings' time. Interestingly, some of the set was positioned on stilts in the lake and so the water became part of the scenery. I wondered whether this was an ideal opportunity to be doing some busking, but I had not yet committed all of the lyrics to memory.

A keen reporter from The Yorkshire Post had written an article in April about my proposed walk with a bold headline that announced: 'Retired Headteacher to Busk His Way Through Europe.' I actually said, in my interview, that I wanted to busk when the weather allowed and, of course, when there were people around in the evening to make it worthwhile. Sadly, none of which had applied so far.

I had planned to practise my songbook in the remotest parts of the Alps where no one could hear my gaffs. Then when I was word-perfect, I would put my hat down on the pavement is some sun-drenched Italian town, just before the dusk gathered, with relaxed people settling into their first aperitivo.

As I turned round on the steps of my guesthouse to take in the evening's view before dinner, I got a glimpse of the mountain foothills where I would be walking in the morning. I hardly noticed my meal of beef, onions and rosti because I ate, distractedly, at a table near the window gazing at that same view. I was transfixed by the task ahead.

When preparing for the walk, I had browsed among my father's papers and found a copy of 'The Hiker & Camper' magazine for August 1933. I didn't have much that belonged to him but that was a remarkable coincidence. In the very year that PFL planned and started his walk, my father had bought this magazine for six old pennies: dreaming of adventure.

One of the leading articles was entitled: What Austria Offers the Hiker. After telling the reader that they can stay in a picturesque inn, in the Tyrol for 4 shillings a day, there was an inspiring invocation to the mountains: 'Up there is another world. The laggard and the stay-at-home never reach these havens. They are the meeting places of men and women of endurance, and there exists a calm understanding between them that dispenses with formality and claims comradeship. "Berg Heil," is the password; the ice axe, knapsack and rope are symbols that bind men together as allies in a perpetual battle with the elements.'

I had to admit to veering near to some laggardly behaviour when feeling worried about the Alps, but now I vowed never to be accused of that sin or of being a stay-at-home.

Day 44 started well. The weather was fine and the wind was light. The woman who ran my guesthouse recommended a different walking route. I had intended following the main road so as to cut down on the mileage but she was certain that the heavy traffic might upset me. There are few main routes through the Alps and those that exist tend to get very busy. The lorries, I was told, can be overpowering for a walker. So I chose a minor, more twisting route, but one which would get me up high without the stress of traffic.

Reaching the highest point on my route that day would be about the same as climbing Snowdon and a little less than getting to the top of Ben Nevis.

This staggered me because I had not thought of comparing my

walk to heights in the UK. Anyway, these individual climbs would not be done in isolation. They were part of a two-week stay in these mountains. I was entering a world that I would inhabit for quite a while. It was to be an adventure in a different land not a quick one-off blast up the side of a mountain to bag a Munro as it were. I was in this for the long haul.

To make the challenge even more demanding, I discovered that my boots had worn completely through at the edges of the heels. I thought that once I wore through the black rubber layer on the heel; there would be solid sub-layer underneath. I was wrong. When I peered at what was left, I was confronted by a flakey, honeycomb, green foam section underneath the black layer. It emitted some green powder every time it came into contact with the ground. I only noticed that after breakfast when getting ready for the day. I saw tiny green mounds of powder and immediately thought of termites.

My spirits sank. How could I prevent them getting worse? What would I do if the entire sole gave way while I was in the Alps? Should I have brought a spare pair with me? The only hope was to buy a pair of boots at a mountain equipment shop along the way: as long as I could find one open at this time of the season.

This panic about my boots kept my mind busy until coffee time when I stopped at a bakery. I ate a very rich, sticky, nut circle and drank a cappuccino.

The minor road, recommended to me, provided a couple of hours of blissful walking. I climbed round what seemed like endless, hairpin bends and through stretches of forest until finally I emerged and joined the main road, but of course much further up than originally planned. That was a real shock. The lorries were careering past me so close that they almost sucked me along in their slipstream. Instantly, I felt unsafe. I realised then that any thought of walking on major routes in Austria was out of the question. Anyway, I did not want to be picked up by the police for the third time.

So after a quick check on the map, I decided to cut across the mountain to my right. A route that would take me over the top and down to a place called Schwarzenberg, which was only about six or seven miles from Bezau, and my campsite for the night. Another booking made, with the best intentions, from my armchair in England.

About half a mile later, I turned right onto an unmade up road and from then on, for the next four hours I was encircled by fields, farms, woodland, grassy walkways between copses, and rough tracks. The views back towards Lake Constance were astounding. At one stage I got lost and asked in a farmyard where to go and some farmhands directed me onto a path they called the Lorena. It wove its way all the way down the valley side in long winding curves, past other farms and rough-timbered outbuildings. To get to the top, which was the start of the Lorena, I had climbed 34 floors – as informed by my Map My Hike App. Quite a shock to the system when in Holland it had regularly stated that no floors had been climbed.

The meadows were pricked with flowers. Several times I swore I heard the opening chords of The Sound of Music playing on the breeze. The sun was hot and my Tarp was being used for its rightful purpose for a change. Just to spike my pleasure, while I sat and ate my lunch, I watched several large storm clouds bulging up from the south. They multiplied quickly as if in a hurry to make me feel at home in normal surroundings.

Just before lunch I came across what looked like a milestone in the grass, beside the track, but instead, I read, it was a memorial stone to the Schwabenkinder. I searched for a reference to this while eating and realised that even though I felt joyful to be walking the Lorena path, others in the last few hundred years might have felt terror instead. Until about the time of World War Two, it was a tradition in springtime, for children from poor mountain families to be sent to children's markets in places like Friedrichshafen to be sold to farmers as cheap labour: basically, they were slaves because their parents were too poor to feed them. They were then sent home again at the end of the season. A local priest was often their only guide, substitute parent and housing officer who made sure they had access to a warm hayloft at night-time on their long trek over the mountains to Swabia. So much for listening out for the strains of Rodgers and Hammerstein, I was more likely to hear the ghostly whispers of frightened children swishing through the grassy meadows.

By the time I reached Schwarzenberg the rain was heavy, and I was so soaked that I stood under the roof of a petrol station to prevent the incessant pounding on my head and shoulders for a few minutes. The car owners had paid for their petrol, but all they could do was sit and watch, because their wipers could not clear the water quickly enough to drive away.

Eventually, we could all get going again. I found a cycle track beside the road and settled in for the six-mile walk to Besau. The busy main road beside me was none other than the one I encountered a few hours out of Bregenz where lorries tried to ensnare me into their slipstreams. Actually, it really was a main thoroughfare as it went all the way to Innsbruck.

Not surprisingly, the campsite was afloat. There were two campervans marooned on slightly higher ground but in essence here was another slap in the face for my camping ambitions. My only option was to walk another 1.5 miles to the village and see what I could find. The rain had changed from torrential to merely tipping it down. No one was around. I was clomping onward with squelching socks inside my boots towards an unbooked bed, not daring to think what might be the alternative if none was vacant. The Schwabenkinder might well have come back this way when returning from their summer's slavery on the farms in Swabia. They might even have lived nearby. That day I knew first-hand how brave, strong and resilient they must have been. I thought that I had had a challenging childhood, but now I knew different.

Walking into Bezau with my fingers firmly crossed, I vowed to try every Gasthof in turn until I found a warm room in which to curl up. It was 4pm and I had just completed 18.4 miles in sometimes sunny but latterly, atrocious conditions. I was so cold that my teeth actually chattered in my mouth.

At the centre of the village, I saw the Gasthof Hirschen. I did not even flinch at the three stars emblazoned on the wall beside the steps up to the front door. This wooden tiled, four-storey chalet with flower boxes on every window ledge was going to be my savour – I could feel its warmth through my drenched clothing. When soon I stood in a pool of water in the entrance hall, a very friendly receptionist rushed towards me waving a key. 'You are in Room 15,' she said, smiling.

'Come down when you are ready and we will find you a table for dinner.' I obeyed instantly without even asking how much the room cost.

I found Room 15, snuggled into the eaves of the chalet, and stood fully clothed in the shower for 10 minutes. When I felt warm again I collapsed on the bed until I could summon up the strength to hang up my jettisoned clothes to dry and then manoeuvre my sore legs down to dinner. Stepping into the restaurant, I calculated that after one mile tomorrow I would have walked 700 miles from home. This called for lots of liver soup, noodles, dumplings, roast turkey, vegetables and beer.

2: A Good Talking To

I found it extremely hard to get motivated for walking the next day. Not for the first time, I had to give myself a strict dressing down in the bedroom after breakfast. I was morbidly dispirited with being wet and cold most of the time and I was worried about my boots. So far I had not found a shop open that sold boots or walking gear of any kind.

Trying to suppress my desire to throw in the towel, I needed a diversion to relieve me of the anxieties, so I thought of Antony Gormley, one of the UK's revered sculptors. I recalled that he had been given an Austrian commission that was fulfilled in 2010. He was asked to create an installation called Horizon Field, which featured 100 life-sized cast iron statues of the human body (actually, they were all replicas of his own) left across the region of the Alps through which I was walking. In the end, the entire piece covered an area of 150 square kilometres. Naturally, I was fascinated to look for these statues. In England, I loved driving past The Angel of the North, near Newcastle, so it seemed natural to enjoy his work here if I could.

As I walked away from the Gasthof Hirschen in the morning, and before I reached the 700-mile mark, my phone was placed at the ready to photograph one of Antony's metal figures, if I happened to stumble across it. Unfortunately, as I was to discover later, it had been agreed that the installation should be taken down in 2012, so my search was in vain. However, in looking for these figures, my eyes scanned the countryside with a sharper focus than normal, which made my day visually enchanting, even when seen through the inevitable outbreaks of rain.

As was the case on each occasion when I had a meltdown after breakfast, I was buoyant again once I got into my stride. That day, I was heading for Schröcken for no particular reason other than it was about the right distance away from Bezau and because it was a ski resort in the winter season, there would be plenty of accommodation available now that it was June. Importantly, it was in a generally south-easterly direction: I was heading for Trento, so I needed to choose my valleys and mountain tops with care to maintain a reasonable distance each day so as to keep on track with my finishing date of 10 July.

I had nothing booked in Schröcken, but that was exciting, because being able to choose at the last minute added a pleasant edge of unpredictability to the day. I had dropped down into Bezau, which was about 650 metres above sea level (still over 2000 feet), but Schröcken would be double that, so I was expecting quite a climb at some stage: more likely in the second half of the day.

Within an hour of leaving Bezau, I found myself walking beside a very fast flowing river pumped full of snowmelt, called the Bregenzer Ache. This brawny river flowed with an arrogant pride in its strength. The noise it made told the surrounding mountains it was coming through. In places, even in this plateau of a farming valley, it had scored deep gouges out of the rock to secure its violent pathway. Beyond all that, its colours excited me. Below the pure white froth, which churned aggressively, was a pale green and turquoise body from which a cold influence emanated. Far away from the muddy brown and iron ore colour of the River Calder at home.

Since leaving home, rivers had become my friends, but here was an untouchable: a personality that bucked and pranced with a rage that eschewed any advances of friendship. The more I walked towards the source of its anger, a 2544-metre high mountain looming over Schröcken called Mohnenfluh, the noisier and more hostile it became.

When I arrived at a village called Mellau the weak sun was strong enough to finish drying my clothes, still faintly damp from yesterday, and it was time for a break. A mass of walkers, cyclists and countryside potterers had grabbed all of the outside tables at the Hotel Bären und Café Deli, so I went inside and settled down beside a radiator. Of course there were crowds outside. It was a Saturday and once again I hadn't noticed until I saw the front page of a newspaper lying on my table.

An impressive range of pastries was obviously the draw for the weekend crowds.

The very pleasant co-owner asked me what I was doing. When I told her, it acted as a trigger for her to tell me about her adventurous father who was always defying people's expectations of what he should be doing at his age. I listened intently to what she said; she had a warm spirit that was especially poignant since the callous river flowed so close to this oasis of a hotel.

With my coffee this charming young woman gave me a home-made biscuit packed with seeds and nuts, all stuck together with sweet, sticky syrup. It was divine. They had a long chalkboard on the stairs up to the toilet and she invited me to write about my walk among the other messages left in German, mostly. On leaving, she refused any payment for my cappuccino and biscuit, in an act of generosity which I had to be careful not to take for granted because it happened so often.

Occasionally, the cycle track I followed took me away from the river and into pastures choked with tall ox-eyed daisies, dandelions with silver heads ready to blow apart in all directions, and rag rugs of yellow rape. The clouds were gathering around the mountains and rolling down the slopes. It was going to rain again. Of that I was sure. And then it did.

It was about a 19-mile walk that day, and by the time I took a rather late lunch of ham rolls at a café in Schoppernau it was already nearly 4pm. I had at least another two hours of walking up some of the steepest slopes of the day.

Schoppernau, I learned, was the place from which much of the planning for Antony Gormley's art project was masterminded. Little wonder that I actually stood no chance of seeing any of his figures, apart from the fact that they had been taken down, because they were all placed at exactly 2039 metres above sea level. With the cloud level as it was today, a male figure at half that level might have been fully shrouded.

It dawned on me, after walking on for 20 minutes, that Schoppernau was the last relatively flat village in this valley. Now the angle of ascent was steep, the valley sides were oppressively close and the main road disappeared into several long tunnels, the like of which had not appeared before. When they were not tunnels they were overhung, concrete cloisters, over which shot torrents of runoff water down into the river below. I knew I had to cross the river to arrive at the village of Schröcken, but I had no idea how I was going to do that. My mind had stopped thinking clearly because the deafening noise of the Bregenzer Ache had numbed it into submission. Not only that but its spray, complemented very well by the continual rain, conspired to drench me to the same degree of waterloggedness as yesterday.

I tried yelling with the loudest shriek that I could muster, but it was as if I had a bag over my head. No sound that I emitted made an impression on the air around me. The only thing to do was give into it. This angry swollen personality absorbed my whole being and, having given myself up to it, I felt strangely at peace. If that was what people meant by being at one with nature – that was me, there in the 'here and now.'

For the last mile or two of my trek that day, every atom of my being was melded with the river and its roar. In this out-of-body trance-like state, I found a wooden bridge over the water that carried me towards the village. Looking up among the tallest branches of the trees around me, I saw the hoists and pulleys of the Abenteuerpark just down the hill from Schröcken. This adventure centre provides a combination of rock climbing and suspended rope walkways. Too tired to even contemplate a sneaky swing on a rope, I followed the steep path up to civilisation and came at last to a large sign that blessedly read Schröcken. I had made it. Now I could find a place to stay since I was back in my own body having wrestled myself free: I was born again from my recent oneness with the river below.

Ahead of me was what in England would have been called a village green. I could see a notice board. I guessed that I might find details of places to stay since this was a ski village and tourists would be a major source of income. The board was quite a sophisticated affair.

There was a 3D map on which accommodation spots were marked and accompanied by a short script advertising their wares. There seemed to be a coloured light system to show when places had vacancies: green for vacancies and red for full-up or closed. There must have been a fault in the wiring because all the lights were red. I banged the front of the display to shock the lights into action. 'Surely,' I pleaded out loud into the thin air, 'there must be some vacancies? There must be a fault with the green lights.'

I stood soaked, cold, weak and with the river still ringing in my ears; overcome with the slow realisation that the entire bank of red lights meant fully closed. There were no beds to be had because the village was shut up for business. 'This is June. It is the summer,' I whimpered, 'where are all the walkers? There were plenty of people around at the Hotel Bären.' I felt my eyes filling up with self-pity: the kind of pity that you only let loose when you are on your own. There was no one around to whom I could turn in my desperation. Camping was my only option, as I was unable to walk any more that day.

My efforts to ring home, just to hear a kind voice, were thwarted as there was no signal, but then I noticed a built-in, landline telephone on the notice board. I scanned the accommodation details and chose to ring Villa Natur in a forlorn hope, because it used key words like: natural, local, simple, farm, homemade... My plan was to beg for accommodation, without a semblance of dignity, always assuming that someone was in.

3: Guardian Angels

I almost choked when someone picked up the receiver at the other end. 'Hello, do you speak English? I am looking at the board in the village. I am desperate. I need somewhere to stay tonight. Please help me.' I am ashamed to even relive the pathetic way that this plea was delivered.

'Listen,' said the most calming voice imaginable, 'we are all closed in the village. It is not our summer season until the third week in June. But wait there – I will come and collect you in two minutes.' I realised then that, in all my preparations, I had not imagined that the first week in June would not be within the summer season. What a fool I was.

First the rubber nailed shoes and now this even bigger blunder. My snowball of mistakes kept growing with this my eighth mistake.

Angelika Jochum drove up in a big SUV, and within five minutes from picking up the telephone I was being ferried towards Unterboden, a small hamlet just outside Schröcken. How apt, I thought as I bundled my rucksack into the boot, that my saviour was named after an Angel. The very large wooden chalet-style house that we stopped outside looked a modern building constructed on traditional designs. It was surrounded by some much older houses, forming a clutch of wooden resilient, solid looking dwellings tucked into a basin of farmland, at an altitude of over 1200 metres, fringed by forests and tall peaks.

Because I was three weeks early, the bedrooms were not ready; Angelika, her husband Josef, and two daughters were relaxing after a busy winter season. Despite that, she made me feel like a long awaited guest. I was shown to a wonderful bedroom in which the natural pine finish, and little wooden ornaments, gave me an all-embracing feeling of connectedness to nature without it being achieved through the violence of the river, which was running only a few hundred metres away.

While I was eating my evening meal, cooked by Angelika, I was introduced to Josef who had just come in from his farm. His herd of cows was kept indoors near the house until it was time to take them to the higher pastures for the summer in a few weeks' time. The cheese that I ate, after my huge bowl of pasta, was made from the milk provided by this herd. Cheese from this area is of such high quality that, as Josef told me, 'it is sold all over the world – as a delicacy in Harrods, for example.'

While we were all chatting after dinner, and I was drinking my second bottle of local beer, Josef and Angelika asked me all about my walk and what I intended to do the next day. I told them that I wanted to walk over the mountains to Lech. The main road, I emphasised, would be far too dangerous and anyway it was a much longer route.

They both laughed and looked at me as if I had said that I wanted to put waxed wings on my arms and fly up to the sun. 'Do you know what you are?' said Josef when he had calmed down. 'You are a very crazy man.' Funnily enough, this was not the first time I had heard this since I left home. I conjured up a vision of the teenagers in Hull who backed away from me in case they caught some of my madness.

'You can't do that on your own. The paths are still covered by snow. You would just lose your way and never get there. It is too dangerous. In three weeks' time it would be fine, but now it is impossible,' Josef spoke in a warm, sincere way but he still managed to prick the balloon of my ambitions. I saw my plans come to an abrupt halt. If I went by road I could be knocked down by massive lorries, and if I went over the tops I could get lost in the snow. He carried on, 'It would be all right for me because I know every route even when it is covered in snow. I grew up here and rambled on those slopes as a boy.'

'Do you think you could draw me a map?' I said clutching at straws.

There was a long silence after which he replied, 'You are crazy, but would you like me to take the day off from farming tomorrow and lead you across the mountains to Lech?'

I did not kiss him but wanted to – my reply came out in a jumble but the essence was clear. I would be eternally grateful if he did that and how could I thank him enough? Although he was probably about 20 years younger than me, his whole manner was that of a supportive father: an outward reflection of the father who had been walking with me all along. I retired to bed wondering how a telephone call from a completely red-lit village notice board could have led me to such a house full of warmth and harmony.

Before I fell asleep, I looked up the Villa Natur website on my phone. The facts proved my feelings to be correct. Schaschl, a firm of architects that specialises in 'harmonious' projects, produced the designs for this house. The wood used is called 'moon' timber, harvested during the waning moon when the sap in the trees is at its lowest point. Then the wood is left to dry vertically, but upside down. A bit like a yoga headstand for wood. Gravity pulls the remaining sap into the branches, which are then cut off. This method produces wood that does not crack, split or warp. All this is achieved without toxins or the need of a drying kiln: an ancient process that leaves a minimal carbon footprint. A technique which has been used for thousands of years and provided, for example, wood for the temples in Japan.

That night, I drifted off to sleep so easily in my moon-timbered room. Excited to be walking the snow route soon with the best guide possible. I prayed for a dry day tomorrow and gave thanks for yet another pilgrim's waypoint.

4: Marmots, Museum and Mark

Josef Jochum had another surprise for me in the morning. 'I am going to carry your rucksack for you today,' he said, in a tone that brooked no objection. 'You can carry our lunch in this small rucksack of mine.'

I had a brief debate with myself as to whether this invalidated my sponsorship, but realised that people had given me money to do the walk not to lug 18kg of clothes and equipment for the whole journey.

'That would be wonderful,' I replied, already feeling my shoulders relaxing at the thought of it.

He was so fit and strong that when he hoisted my rucksack onto his shoulders it looked like a light, sandwich-filled day bag instead of the loathsome load that, by the mid-afternoon of every day, became my pilgrim's burden.

By the time Angelika dropped us at the starting point I was ready for anything but still full of trepidation about the snow and the altitude. This was what I had worried about in the latter part of Germany and that day had arrived. Nothing could stop me now. Without my rucksack, what could I possibly have to complain about? I turned from waving at Angelika's SUV and fell in line with Jochum as he strode off up a steep incline towards the snow line. My outer jacket was designed to keep me warm, and the wind out, but underneath it I had donned several other layers just in case of extreme cold.

Then it dawned on me that my guide had only a bright yellow, short-sleeved tee shirt on to protect him from the elements. I obviously felt a wimp but knowing that we would be walking to the height of over 7000 feet (2200 metres or more) was my excuse. At that altitude I might have been able to see a cast iron man, sunk below the snow – but I had no need of that because I had my own iron man walking up ahead of me.

Shortly, we came to a very old-looking building that had been converted, Josef told me, into a rural museum. It was then that I truly came to terms with how rooted the Jochum family was in these mountains and valleys. There on a large laminated poster attached to the outside of the museum was a history of Josef's family dating back to at least 1774, when J. Christian Florian Jochum was born in Schröcken. He later married Viktoria Bischof from Warth, which is only two villages along the very busy road to Innsbruck, but it would then have been a quiet morning's walk. Apparently, the museum was opened exactly 400 years after the first tree was felled to make the original farm building.

The Jochum family, having been in Schröcken for at least 242 years, put Antony Gormley's iron figures in to context, since they only stayed two years. According to Gormley his work asked the question 'Where does the human being fit in the scheme of things?' I was finding the answer.

As we walked higher, I found out more about this remarkable man. He farmed, that I knew, but he was also a very well qualified joiner. He made all of the furniture, fittings, and staircases in Villa Natur and had a strong hand in its construction. In a similar way to the journeyman joiners whom I met near Friedrichshafen, he travelled extensively (not in costume) as far as London, to learn his trade. He was always going to come back to Schröcken. It was then that my 'O' Level credentials felt that they had to flash across my mind: Woodwork – failed.

As we began a conversation about his farming, we came across our first snowfield. I extended my two walking poles and prepared for the traverse. The clouds closed in on the basin in which we found ourselves, with meadows and clumps of pine tree mere smudges through the thinnest sheets of cloud. At this height, the lying snow was intermittent.

Beyond the first expanse we came to an open stretch from which we could see Josef's two alpine lodges. This was where he brought his herd of cows to graze in summer. Between the huts, perched up on a slight hillock, the close-cropped grass was all that was left of last season's rich sward. This totally organic mixture of red clover, Italian ryegrass, annual ryegrass, hybrid ryegrass, meadow fescue, oat grass and timothy, is the staple diet of the herd and the reason why the cheese is so sought after. What is more, the cows are given the last cut of hay from these pastures to eat throughout the winter. They literally do live a life in clover.

After the alpine lodges, and the ski station close to it, we entered another snowfield, but not before Josef had picked two gentian violets for us to wear in the bands of our hats. This was an honorary alpine gesture. I felt a real Austrian mountain walker, particularly since we were standing at 300 metres above the height of Ben Nevis. It was only later that I found out that the roots of the gentian plant are used as an ingredient for Aperol, a drink that I was planning to overindulge in once I reached Italy and my destination.

We were just about to enter a high-sided valley with the intention of climbing up the very steep north-facing side, which was ankle-deep in snow, when we heard a series of high-pitched, whistling sounds. The cold air, low cloud and the untrodden snow cast an eerie presence in which it was disturbing to hear such unworldly noises.

Fortunately, Josef did not look confused at all. 'There is a family of marmots over there. Can you hear them whistling? They are breeding now, so there is plenty of activity.'

I had not heard of marmots before, but soon saw that they were about the size of a small dog, with the pointed face of a large squirrel. These fascinating mountain creatures, Josef told me, saw us as intruders on their domain. They lived in these Alps in burrows or under piles of fallen rocks, eating grass and other vegetation. Running from hillock to hillock, they sat on their haunches at each resting spot, sniffing the air and whistling at us.

In terms of distance, that day was probably going to be my shortest so far (8 miles), but for experiences, the distance travelled with Josef was immeasurable. Still listening to the marmots, we tramped our way up the valley side: my walking poles steadied me, as I high-stepped my way to the top. Once at the summit, we found the path for descent right beside another ski-station. This one sent its gondolas down to the Lech ski-schools. Looking back in the direction of Schröcken we saw Josef's friend's sheep grazing on a snow-free incline. Their neck bells rang every time they moved. We could just hear them across the valley. We were over five hours' walking away from his village but Josef could still pick out sheep belonging to a friend. I was elated to see this mountain landscape though his eyes. It was so cold up there, on the Sunday 5 June that even Josef put on his outer jacket. In keeping with his image though, he didn't zip it up.

We made our way down to Lech with talk about what the summers were like up at the lodges. Josef waxed eloquent about his Scottish Highland cattle and the cutting of the hay.

'You can come, if you like. We take our guests up there in the summer. There are beds. We stay over, work and just enjoy life up there.'

That became my ambition. To come back with Kate one day: if nothing else to smell the scent of the hay blended with alpine roses, arnica, gentian, thistle and berry bush overtones.

After the village of Oberlech, we reached the main road between Lech and Warth, where Viktoria was born. After I had heaped thanks on Josef, he hugged me goodbye and walked off intending to hitch back home. I waved until I saw him disappear into the scenery. Turning towards Lech, I felt numb.

My melancholy soon dissolved when my nephew Mark entered the restaurant where I was eating a large bowl of pasta. He had just finished his own mammoth walk from the Langen am Arlberg train station, which, in the first two hours, took him up a very steep scramble and over a col of at least 2000 metres. He had forded freezing streams and followed mountain tracks all the way into Lech. I had just said goodbye to one expert mountain guide and now Mark turned up with his own impressive outward bound CV, which included mountain biking with his father, in the Outer Hebrides and Iceland. He had with him some detailed maps of the area in which we would be walking tomorrow. Now I was the one rolling in clover.

I saw Mark in his first week of life and have remained in touch throughout his 40 years despite him living in France, Scotland and Switzerland, and flying across the world for his job. When he was a teenager we walked the Calderdale Way together, which was a memorable event not least for the time when, passing through an almost empty field, he said, 'What does it mean when there is only one sheep in a field?'

'Not quite sure, perhaps it is ill and needs to be on its own,' I replied nonchalantly. That was until the ram, as it turned out to be, was butting me in the back of my knees and Mark was sitting on a wall laughing uncontrollably at my folly.

Now, instead of the usual family gatherings, we had a chance to relive our mutual love of the outdoors. Mark has a passion for maps and finding the correct path. With a journey over the Galzig range of mountains in our sights for tomorrow, I was relieved to be in his company.

That night we discovered the delights of the only bar and restaurant open in the deserted centre of Lech and then busied ourselves getting ready for the next day, which was guaranteed to be a demanding one. Once again, there were no shops selling walking boots open. So I decided to use my fast eroding pair until the green skeleton was laid totally bare, then bind them up with duct tape. In that way, I hoped to limp to my Italian front door, kitted out with the same boots that I was wearing when I left Hebden Bridge.

Fortunately, in the morning we rose to brilliant sunshine. All my talk the previous evening of being soaked most of the time seemed a distant fiction as we donned shades and rubbed in sun block before we set off. Of course, we spoke in an intriguing jumble about all that had happened in our lives since we last met.

Then, eventually we came to the forthcoming UK referendum: the inevitable Brexit topic. I told Mark how everyone I had met so far had either been amazed that we had gone ahead with the idea of a ballot, or treated the issue as some sort of passing phase that would not come to anything. Most recently, Josef, from an Austrian perspective, had shown great admiration for the UK and its standing in the international community and could see no reason why the voters would put that high ranking position in jeopardy. Likewise, Mark who took an international financial perspective saw how foolish it would be for us to distance ourselves from such a powerful commercial unit as the EU. That also seemed to be the resounding question that all the Dutch and German people with whom I had spoken about the referendum, had left me with: why would anyone risk the uncertainty of leaving the

EU when we had advantageous opt out clause on our side anyway? According to the received wisdom held by many: we needed the EU as much as it needed us.

However we were both aware that on social media there was a significant amount of hatred toward asylum seekers and foreigners in general – it seemed to me like the frantic barking had really woken up the slumbering dogs of racism and xenophobia. I only hoped that those awakened dogs would not win the day. It was one thing to want to be in charge of our own laws and borders – to regain our sovereignty – but a system based on hatred was unthinkable. Unbeknown to us, even while we were walking, it looked like the big dogs were winning. That day in the UK, as I found out that night, a You Gov poll found 45% favoured the UK leaving the EU, with 41% wanting to stay. The small dogs on a Red Bus, and those leading UKIP, were doing their job. There were three weeks and three days to go before the referendum, and it was not looking good.

Having got that out of our system, we stood in awe of a commercial helicopter at a place called Zürs, which was taking huge containers of cement up to the top of a mountain where engineers were building a new ski station. Every few minutes the helicopter returned to have its hopper replenished with slop from the cement mixer; then flew off again, like a bird taking nesting materials up to its eyrie.

One sure indication that I was in the presence of hiking royalty was that, at about 11am, we were sitting beside a frozen lake, on the Flexenpass Weg, drinking coffee from a flask. Normally, I found a café (not possible today) or satisfied myself with water, but today was special.

In crossing a mountain ridge on the way to St. Christoph am Arlberg, we were forced to scramble across some snowfields. In one particular spot, there appeared to be a ledge of ice and snow, which formed a bridge across a very steep ravine that fell away to our right: a sharply sided gash in the limestone that disappeared into a boulder-strewn basin at the bottom, about 100 metres away. The track was probably somewhere underneath the thick snow, but there was no way of knowing, and we had come too far to think of turning back.

Mark led the way, treading as lightly as he could before jumping the last bit onto the solid ground beyond the ravine. I followed being very careful not to dislodge any more of the bridge, because when pieces broke away we watched them tumble for what seemed like minutes into the basin below. I thought I was doing quite well given that I was carrying a much heavier pack that could make me more prone to falling if it swung and off-balanced me. Why then, I wondered, was Mark laughing as I reached the middle of the ravine?

It was only then that I felt a nudge in the back of my knee. Thinking I was in the way of another walker who rudely wanted to pass at an impossible place to overtake, I swung round (probably a little too quickly for my own safety) and saw a crowd of inquisitive mountain goats. They seemed to be growing in courage and several of the leading group were now bending their heads in my direction ready for a group butt. With that I swung a walking pole in the air, shouting 'Go away and leave me alone,' in the same tone as I have found myself shouting at a dog, bully or assailant in a dream.

After jumping onto the rocky platform beside Mark, we collapsed and watched the panicked goats pushing each other back across the icy bridge. I wondered what the odds were on being knee-butted twice, on walking trips with the same person, 24 years apart?

After I had regained my composure, we headed down the winding descent to St. Christoph. On our way there we heard the distinct whistle of a family of marmots. I was able to display my deep knowledge of these creatures, while we both smiled at their antics. Shortly after, while walking through the otherwise silent village of St. Christoph we came across a coach outing of senior citizens: many looked no older than me. Once free of the coach, they made straight for the roadside gift shops and were cooing over the stuffed marmots on sale: little realising that only a short walk away, up the mountainside, they could see them for real. We ambled on, not wanting to point this out, in case it sounded churlish.

The climb over to St. Anton was joyous. The still hot afternoon sun magnified colours in the scenery so well that their vivid hues made me forget my aching limbs. On these south-facing slopes, the snows that still clung to the grass clawed their way uphill in a melting retreat. Creating run-off waters that would soon be roaring downstream to the North Sea, by way of the Rhine, or to the Black Sea carried by the Danube. The gentian violets like torches, forcing their way up through the bearded grass, shone with Demeter's gift of spring. The mountain-side was healing itself after the ravages of winter.

Once in St. Anton, we still had about 5 miles to walk to arrive at our campsite in Pettneu am Arlberg. Ironically, because we had climbed to more than 2300 metres (7546 feet) that day, this fairly flat section alongside a river was very arduous. We traipsed along hardly able to talk. While we pitched our tents at Arlberglife Camping, we were exhausted after our strenuous 22 miles, and in need of much food and beer. As a reward, we spent the evening in a comfortable, dark wood, wattle and daub inn at the centre of Pettneu. We chose local delicacies such as grey cheese soup and lamb sausages with mash: such tremendous comfort food.

A feeling of looking back while being on the verge something new overshadowed the next days with Mark. It all started halfway down the descent from the mountain goat incident. We passed through a wood on a path called the Senn's Wünder, Wanderweg, which was established by the enterprising Senn family to attract visitors to experience the delights of that part of Arlberg. In the middle of the wood was a natural pine door – just like any door in someone's house – but this one was fixed between two trees: an art installation. It would have been easy to go round it but it was so tempting to pass through. Perhaps Janus, the Roman god of doorways, who looked both ways, was drawing us in? It gave me a strong feeling of both remembrance and anticipation, as I clicked the door closed behind us. For me, it was the beginning of the end of Austria on the way to the Italian border. This is what I had come for, what I began 47 days before.

Mark and I spent our first Janus day, after the Wanderweg gateway experience, using our free bus pass, provided by the campsite, travelling to Landeck, my next destination, and St. Anton just to see whether the gondolas were running to the upper grassy slopes. We had a yen to see the valleys from the top once more, as a farewell gesture. Unfortunately the campsite at Landeck lacked the facilities of the excellent Arlberglife, and the ski lifts were about 10 days away from being ready for tourists. It all mattered little because the pleasure of touring the area by bus was just what we needed after our exertions of the previous two days.

While getting ready for our tents that evening I found myself wondering about the couples of my age that were lounging outside their campervans at dusk. Some seemed to have been there all day, reading newspapers and books, eating food and drinking wine. My life of foot plasters, shin splints and walker's rash seemed in such contrast: I wondered when I would want to succumb to the deckchair way of life. I was so locked into my regime at the moment that I could not countenance it, but there was a problem there for me to resolve.

That night was a prime example of why I had not camped very much along the way. The rain began as soon as we zipped up our doors and continued unabated until about 5.30am on Janus Day 2. By morning, because of the humidity in my tent, the outside was wet but so was the inside. What is more, everything around me in my one-man, green coffin-tent was damp. We both packed up that morning. Mark was catching the train back to Geneva and I was walking to Landeck to stay in an, as yet, unknown destination.

As I was eating my breakfast in the Arlberglife café, I had a good idea. Since it was inadvisable for me to pack up my wet tent and sleeping bag, why didn't I see if there was an apartment in the main building to rent for the night, hang up all of my wet belongings, walk to Landeck and come back here to sleep? I was overjoyed when the owner showed me up to an empty apartment. It included all the hanging space I needed as well as a luxurious infrared seating area (really for tired skiers) in which I could relieve my aching legs, when I came back later on.

Mark and I said a sad farewell. I really hoped that, in the future, we would have another walk of this kind together but perhaps without a goat knee-butting incident...

5: Next Stop – Italy

I followed a forest track, mainly downhill, that would take me to Landeck, little realising that it was yet another long distance path leading to Santiago de Compostela in Spain. This one was also called the Jacob's Way and it had the familiar scallop shell emblem. These tracks were, of course, all over Europe: they led the faithful pilgrims who were following the way of St. James. Mark's father, Maurice, had walked to Compostela from near Lyon in France split into three sections over three years. Mark had adventure in his veins.

This route seemed to run from Salzburg to Switzerland before heading south to Spain. I even met a retired couple from Hamburg who were taking two weeks to walk the route, stopping to look at the stations of the cross, intricately carved in local wood, which were dotted along the way. This meeting helped me resolve my deckchair conundrum. Shorter, one or two-week walks with Kate might be the answer in future.

Once in Landeck, I checked my route for tomorrow, bought bags of nuts and some dried fruit, and looked at all the places at which I might have stayed. I was glad with my choice, including the byproduct that this had become a no-rucksack day. I could not see the forest track from the bus on the ride back to Pettneu; it was as if St. Jacob's Way had been an illusion. Seen from the bus window, the evening sky was a mass of cauliflower-shaped grey clouds interspersed with black florets. There were patches of blue, which helped to lighten the scenery, but mostly the hills were a dull green, scattered with snow-bones. With Italy so close now, I was hoping for better weather soon.

Janus Day 3 started well with a second sitting in the infrared chair. The science was not firmly established in my mind, but the feelings of warmth and the beneficial easing of muscles were phenomenal. With my rucksack full of dry clothes and equipment, I caught the bus back to Landeck. My plan was to walk up bedside the River Inn to the small town of Pfunds. From there I could reach the Italian border the next day. The River Inn starts in Switzerland and, a long way after Innsbruck, becomes a main feeder of the Danube. I already knew, owing to my meanderings the day before, that the Inn was in full spate and therefore likely to be very noisy, but I found that the path quite often veered inland, into woodlands and meadows, and this helped my ears to stop ringing.

By 9am the rain was annoyingly persistent. While I was standing in a bus shelter avoiding the worst of it (for what other purpose were they designed?) a group of three dedicated German cyclists crowded in there with me. It was cosy. They changed some of their clothes to help them brave the weather on the way up to the border. As they put on their special pedal-gripping shoes again, I asked them where they were going.

'Lake Garda,' the leader replied, 'It will take us four days at this rate. The wind and rain is coming down the valley. We are catching it head on.'

Suddenly, my mood lifted. They had cycled this route before. 'All you need to do is just keep on up this hill for two days and after the Reschen Pass, into Italy, it will be steadily downhill until Trento (near Lake Garda).' I thanked them heartily, took their photograph for their Facebook pages, and left the bus shelter with them to face the elements again. Hope was on the horizon.

I carried on through the five small villages that lay before Pfunds. In doing so, I crossed the Inn several times using some beautifully crafted wooden bridges with tiled roofs that gave me an aesthetic boost as well as temporary respite from the rain.

At each village I rewarded myself with a handful of nuts and a sprinkle of dried fruit. While I stopped to wolf down my reward, I noticed that there were intricately carved crucifixes on the sides of barns in every village. There were also wreathes of dried flowers with mirrors and sometimes ornaments tied into them. The religious fervour of people throughout mainland Europe impressed me greatly. The act of walking became a pilgrimage, even if one wasn't going to Spain.

It was only as I was near to crossing the river for the last time that day to enter Pfunds that I saw a sign telling me that I was walking along the Roman road of Via Claudia Augusta. In 15 BC, the Romans turned an ancient footpath into a solid, raised road big enough to take carts and legions of soldiers. It took 60 years to build, but when opened it joined the Po valley regions with the River Danube and the Roman Limes. It felt right, having spent so much of my journey in the Roman Empire; that I would be staying on this route until at least Trento, if not even nearer to the Adriatic Sea.

From my bedroom window in Pfunds, I looked out over the town, which was shaped like a triangle, tucked into a valley between two mountains. At night, before I went to bed, I saw in between the mountains a layer of dark, oppressive clouds. They obscured the view down the valley. By contrast, in the morning, a vast transformation had taken place. Although the town was shrouded in a light mist, above it was a translucent blue sky. It was the kind of sky that promised a day of fair weather.

I stood and meditated for a while on the traffic down this valley in Roman times. The Alpine cheese traded for the Romans' oil from Spain, fresh oysters and spices from Asia. A world of possibilities had opened up for the people in this valley that would last, at least, until the Empire fell. This was a major trading route and a sky like the one I woke up to would have lifted their spirits too. They might have been going up and down the valley to trade, but I was going up it to discover what I thought was going to be my fifth European country.

My first destination on this breathtaking morning was the tourist information office in Pfunds. I wanted to make sure that I could take as many footpaths as possible up the valley because I had been told in my accommodation that the roads were busy and there was at least one long tunnel through which it would be extremely dangerous to walk. Equipped with a handful of maps and leaflets, I set out to find the path on the east side of the River Inn. Just to make sure, I checked my map while standing beside a large elderflower tree which was already covered with white umbrella flowers. Tucked in amongst some lower branches was another crucifix in a diamond-shaped box. Jesus was hanging on his cross among streamers of flowers, as if he was standing in an enchanted garden. The pure blue sky behind him was almost burning my eyes.

To my right was the wide expanse of the Inn. It was creamy grey and flowing frantically around some huge boulders that had the audacity to get in its way. On either side of the furious water, mountains rose to their full height without clouds to stunt them. This valley had seen some bloody conflicts between the Austrian freedom fighters and Napoleon's army in the early 1800s. I had read about Andreas Hofer, the leader of the Tyrolean freedom movement, and I felt his spirit leaping among the boulders on the mountainside.

What really struck me was his bravery in defeat. After many battles with the French forces, Andreas was captured in a mountain hut, having been betrayed by a neighbour for a bounty. He was taken to Bozen (now Bolzano in Italy; where I intended to be in less than a week) tried and stood before a firing squad. Refusing a blindfold, he paid the marksmen to shoot straight, remained standing so as to give them more to shoot at, and gave the command himself. What better way to inspire your followers and become a martyr? One man against the might of Napoleon: how could I not be impressed? An Austrian hero, even today, he is celebrated for his defence of the Tyrol. A contemporary artist painted his portrait posthumously and, seeing that online, I really took to his massive black beard and wide brimmed hat. He would have made the perfect hipster today. Even though my beard had remained uncut for seven weeks, it was still no match against his. He became my hero too.

It was just that kind of day. Optimism and freedom reigned in my mind. For once I was warm. I regularly rehearsed my sense of elation at the prospect of walking across the border with Italy, later that day.

I had to swap sides of the river several times if I was to keep away from the road. I found nowhere to buy a coffee, and without Mark I had to make do with water. With the heat that day, I calculated that I needed four litres to keep me hydrated. At 10.15am, I saw, across a field, an encampment of tepees looking like a gathering of Native Americans. It reminded me of the scenes from the Western films I adored as a boy. I thought I might stroll across and see if I could get a coffee by a camp fire, which was sending smoke signals curling into the trees on the other side of the river.

That was until I saw a sign telling me that this was an organization called Native-Spirit and please would visitors respect the privacy of course members and keep away. Apparently, they were being immersed in shamanistic lore and needed peace, and seclusion. Their website announced that 'we open the veils of consciousness, strengthen our intuition, heal at energy level, travel with our spirit body and much more.' Another anti-deckchair enterprise, I mused.

After the camp, the path wound its way through the skirts of a forest on the west side of the water. I found myself heading down the Finstermünz gorge. I always planned to walk through five countries and to avoid Switzerland owing to the high costs of living there. I was worried that a cup of coffee and a sandwich might hoover up most of my daily allowance. Now, it appeared that I might have to compromise my plans.

I saw a medieval covered wooden bridge ahead of me, built between two square towers with pyramidical roofs, I had a strong feeling that I was approaching an important place. I found out later that I had been walking towards the Finstermünz Fortress via a bridge that, from the 1300s, was the toll collection point between Austria and Switzerland. I was, at that moment, standing unwittingly in Switzerland. For hundreds of years all the traffic from Italy to Austria had to cross this bridge. Before 1300, the bridge had been Roman.

If one of my ambitions on this expedition was to walk past a castle steeped in romance, this was it. Except that it was more like a fortress. At this point in the gorge, the Inn cut the steep sides of the valley, vertically. Pressed into the rocks, the fortress rose steeply; clinging on stoically as the river cascaded by. The long sweep of the bridge and the riverside approach to the fortress led me from a brief stay in Switzerland back into Austria. I crossed without having to pay a toll because after the mid 19th-century goods could be moved along a road built some way above the river. This was the road that passed through Pfunds. It was only 10.30am and I had already been in Austria, Switzerland and back into Austria again.

After filling up my water bottles at the manned, but not yet open, fortress café, I climbed the very steep hairpin path to the main road at the top of the cliffs. Apparently, there were no other options but to get along the busy main road until the cycle track after Nauders, the last town in Austria, began.

On arriving at the roadside, I saw the tunnel immediately to my right. There was a sign beside it warning cyclists and walkers that they were likely to die if they attempted to go inside. No map or leaflet gave any indication of a path over the tunnel and my phone showed only a blurred image on Google Earth. As I stood there several cyclists blithely entered the tunnel, but I declined to follow.

I stood beside a bus stop hoping that one would come soon and drop me on the other side of the tunnel, but after 40 minutes I stuck out my thumb to hitchhike instead. A car stopped, the window slid down and I was quizzed by the suited driver about what I was doing and where I was going. There was logic to these questions because it turned out that he was a senior civil engineer who was going to the grand opening of a new section of the road just beyond the tunnel, so he had to stop there; he was going no further. He was just what I needed, but he was so cool and preoccupied I felt that he could have done without me. It turned out he was the guest of honour and that without him the new road would not have been ready to open today.

I could not have imagined the sight that appeared as we emerged from the darkness of the tunnel. Down a dip, beside our road, was a whole new section, much straighter and smoother than the existing route. On this virgin piece of tarmac were trestle tables loaded with a sumptuous buffet, tents with a bar and seats for the band. Instruments were being tuned up as we arrived. My chauffeur left me as soon as he had parked his car. I had to run the gauntlet between the tables trying not to look hungry and smiling at all the glamorous guests who were staring at me and wondering why the main man had brought along a ruffian with a rucksack; sporting an inferior Hofer-type beard.

As I levelled with the last trestle table, the band started up and everyone turned to watch my driver mount the rostrum. I kept walking and within seconds was out of sight – not that anyone was looking at me anymore. I had been a temporary and insignificant diversion from the buffet and speeches. My stomach rumbled as I veered off the road and crossed a field towards Nauders to find my own food.

I was really tempted to linger much longer over my lunchtime pizza than was entirely necessary. I was overcome by an unexpected glut of emotions, partly, I guess, inspired by the large beer consumed on a hot day while sitting outside on a terrace admiring the view. I wanted to get to Italy as soon as possible, but at the same time something was making me drag my heels. It was as if, somewhere inside, I was not ready to arrive in my sixth and last country: my destination. If it was difficult to motivate myself on a rainy morning somewhere on the Rhine, strangely it was doubly difficult on a dazzling afternoon in the Austrian Alps.

After giving myself a lecture about keeping to schedule, reaching the 800-mile mark by nightfall, having walked the equivalent of

Land's End to John O'Groats by coffee time tomorrow…I got myself moving again and set off for the border.

The only thing that worked in these situations was to focus on things close at hand and remember my male forebears who died far too early. They, I fancied, were watching my every move.

I quickly passed Naudersberg Castle, which had been standing there for more than 800 years. Andreas Hofer would have seen this stately home and courthouse on his way to being executed in Bozen. It had a courtroom, judges' chambers and a prison, so he might even have stayed there on the way.

I was away from the road on a cycle path among green pastures. This grassland was strewn with nothing but clover, dandelions and wooden huts. The horizon was fringed with mountains with some snow still in their top crevices and, lower down, blankets of pine forest that lay round their ankles. It took me about 90 minutes to reach the border, which consisted of an official building with an Italian flag, and a blue EU metal sign with gold stars that simply told me I was entering 'Italia.' These official interruptions in a continuous stretch of vividly green countryside were largely symbolic, but nothing could detract from my wobbly sense of relief. I had made it. I was so happy that I actually felt like busking a few songs, but once again I was on my own, except for the speeding cars and a few cyclists.

All I needed to do now was walk another 400 or so miles to get rid of my rucksack and put my feet up for a while.

Italy

1: Via Claudia Augusta – Again

I had to find a decent cup of coffee to celebrate being in Italy. I found it in the Gasthaus Irene, only a few metres along the road into Italy. Of course they spoke mainly German, but the coffee was, I thought, a bit better than the regular German push-button stuff, but I could have been wishing that to be true. The family that owned the Gasthaus was interested in my walk. The father had just returned from a nine-day cycle trip to Rome, so he had some idea of the rigours involved. They told me I had about a 30-minute walk to the lake and then about a further two hours to reach my hotel. Since it was 5.15pm already, I felt the need to get going, particularly since I had booked a room with a bath. A long celebratory soak was waiting.

I reached the lake and made instinctively for what looked like a tourist viewpoint. The blue waters of the lake virtually matched the clear sky. Just beside the edge of the water a group of students were posing for selfies galore. I asked if one of them could take a photo using my phone and this caused them all to gather round.

One confident member of the group spoke for them all: 'We're from an American university; we're here to study for six weeks at a sister university in Venice; we're tutored by our Professor Peter Brubaker; and have spent the day bicycling round the area. We are studying physiology for a year before majoring in some form of medicine.'

Phew, quite a whoosh of information for a solitary traveller to take in. I loved the way all of the snippets sounded like questions. I was also delighted at their friendliness and the interest that they took in my expedition.

Their professor, who was the epitome of politeness, said that: 'since his students were studying the body's capacity for fitness and endurance, they would be honoured if I would join them for dinner tonight, so that the students could quiz me further.'

We almost clapped at the coincidence that we were staying at the same hotel in San Valentino, which was at the far end of the lake. I arranged to meet them for dinner at 7.15pm, which gave me two hours to get there, 20 minutes to check in, half an hour to wash and get changed. Within minutes, I saw them cycling in a long line down the east side of the lake while I took off to the west on a slightly shorter route, which was actually the Via Claudia Augusta. In Nauders I was dragging my heels, but now I was walking at a speed faster than I had in the entire journey. I was keen because to speak with a group of young, lively, intelligent, students. What a pleasure...

For a moment, I forgot that my boots were worn down badly and that was likely to have a detrimental effect on my leg muscles or even my hips. What is more, I was in such a hurry that I did not really take in the full significance of the lake: that it was actually a man-made reservoir. In the process of being formed, it had swallowed up a couple of villages, 163 houses and a church. The church tower was still poking its head and shoulders above the water. It seemed an uncanny sight, but it provided me with yet another church spire analogy. This one, like so many others in Austria and now the Südtirol (Alto Adige in Italian), was as thin as a sharpened pencil that pointed up to heaven. Rose thorns, onions and sharp pencils: all symbols of a human aspiration to have our prayers heard, just different shaped funnels to get the message out there.

The conversation over dinner was fascinating; I learned so much by talking to these young Americans. They filled me with hope for the future of the US: their passion for change and optimism for their future role in health and medicine was inspiring. We did a deal over Trump: they would not ask me about Farage and I would steer clear of Trump.

It was agreed implicitly that to be defined by your worst nightmare (or local barking dog, in my jargon) was unfair. Professor Brubaker, who watched TV news daily, told me that there was a growing groundswell for Leave in the UK, which confirmed my suspicions. In the seven weeks since I left home, the messages from people I met on the way had gone from 'unbelievable' to 'believable' as far as the Red Bus was concerned.

They wanted to ask me about how I had trained for my walk and what shape I had been in along the way. I told them proudly that to get to dinner on time, I had walked at nearly double my normal speed, which I supposed was an indication of me getting much fitter as the journey progressed.

It felt strange to try and summarise my experiences for people whom I had only just met. I shared with them that I had learned quickly what was easily digestible and, by contrast, what was too detailed for regular conversation with strangers. Ultimately, I ended up telling a few well-rehearsed stories to give listeners a flavour of the adventure, which seemed to be acceptable. I also zoned in on particular body parts to suit my audience, because people wanted to know about my hips, feet, heart, shoulders or knees depending on their proclivities in those regions.

As guest of honour, Professor Brubaker announced that my meal was complimentary, which was a nice treat. He also invited me to deviate from my route and visit them in Venice, when I arrived at the Adriatic coast. It was a really tempting idea. I promised to think about it when, or if, I got that far.

On beginning my walk in the morning, the wonderful weather had disappeared and fine, misty rain cloaked the valley ahead of me. I was to walk its entire length. This was the valley of Venosta, or Val Venosta, which is the name on the small sticker to be found on many apples in some of our supermarkets in the UK. The valley was so wide that it could take hours to walk across it. The flat part was filled entirely with carefully manicured apple trees, which were planted in manageable-sized fields, set at an angle with each other, presumably, to make sure that the sun caressed as many apples as possible. Right ahead of me, in the furthest distance, was a snow-capped mountain called Ortler, which was nearly 4000 metres high. Initially, I was walking towards it, but I expected to walk around it, because I was following the River Adige toward Trento.

My night's stay was at a place called Schlanders or Silandro, if you speak Italian, which by cycle track was likely to be about 25 miles away. Any mileage over 20 in a day was to make up for the lower daily coverage over the Alps. After battling through low cloud and mist for the first two hours, I began to be passed by heavily breathing cyclists competing in a Bike Marathon that was to finish down the valley, in the one of the smallest cities in Europe, Glorenza, with a population about the same size as The Vatican City.

I stopped for a coffee in the cobbled streets of Mals. Everything was a little more Italian at every village. Here in this café the young Saturday morning crowd were drinking rounds of a cocktail called Hugo, which comprised a dash of elderflower syrup covered in prosecco, served with a tiny sprig of fresh mint. I would like to have joined them but I still remembered the depression that set in after that lunchtime beer at Nauders.

At Glorenza, meaning alder meadows, I was struck by the beauty of this miniature city surrounded by millions of apple trees, but had to be careful when staring up at the medieval timbered buildings as racing cyclists, heading for the finishing line, were rushing past my legs to the noisy cheers of friends and club members. Lunch was a board of mixed salami and cheese served with rustic bread, which gave an Italian edge to this city that had been Swiss and Austrian at various times in its 900-year history.

For the rest of the afternoon, I followed the River Adige downhill to Schlanders. Once I took the wrong turning at a fork in the cycle track. When I noticed my mistake, after about a mile, I tried to cut across the apple fields. That was my ninth big mistake. The network of ditches, draining channels and tiny canals - many edged with alders - was immense. I ended up sitting in a ditch full of water having thrown my rucksack across when I realised that I had to jump the gap to avoid retracing my steps. I should have remembered from childhood that walking any distance with a wet bottom is one of the most uncomfortable activities known to man. I also should have realised that if a medieval city is named Alder Meadows, one should expect alders and the water that goes with them!

2: A Hugo and The Queen of Fanes

Looking dirty, wet and bedraggled, I booked into a reasonably priced guesthouse called Pension Pernthaler in the aptly named Via Andreas Hofer – synonymous, in my opinion, with my rough, but astoundingly heroic appearance. Luckily, my obliging host was able to do all of my washing for me. Even better, I discovered that the forecast was fair for my rest day. I intended to just mooch about in cafes, make notes, stare at the mountains and drink Hugo cocktails. I made notes in several small jotters, but mainly recorded my thoughts and observations on my phone as I walked along. In that way, I had hundreds of, sometimes quite breathless, reminiscences to use in my writing.

I discovered that there was a French word that described me and exactly what I was about to do the next morning. Un flâneur is a person who, when walking about enjoying the place they are in, tends to stroll, lounge, saunter or loaf. Since I was going to do all four of these activities, I saw myself as an apprentice flâneur.

Breakfast was served on the terrace in a quiet garden dotted with fruit trees. Us guests were bathed in a warm gentle wind as we ate what I considered to be my best breakfast since taking to the road 52 days before. What is more, I was eating outside at a more civilized hour.

Although we were in Italy, the German influence was only declining slowly, just as the Italian influence advanced a little at a time. It was the human equivalent of plate tectonics. Most people know that in geology, continental plates move around on the soft, malleable rocks below them by as little as 2mm per year. Sometimes they collide and one slips under the other. It was like this here, and at every border I had travelled through. Travelling in a car, you might miss the subtleties, but on foot they were obvious. They were part of the sheer enjoyment of being alive in a crossover plate region.

The subtle collision of tectonic boundaries at this pension was represented by the black German bread that featured proudly on the breakfast table and the fact that it was moistened by an excellent cappuccino, of which any Italian barista would be proud. More than that, we were presented with seeds, nuts, cereal, fruit, dried fruit, eggs and homemade kiwi jam. I lingered over breakfast, long after other guests had gone, until the employee who washed the sheets came out to hang up not only the sheets, but my washing too. So as not to be flapped on by wet washing, I then left the table having already got a tick on my imaginary chart for high quality 'lounging' and spotting the touching of cultural plates.

Sauntering was next on the agenda. I wandered into town and sat for coffee in a bar that was joined like a Siamese twin to a post office. The bar itself was festooned like a Christmas tree with Lotto cards of all varieties. It was just the place to sit and people watch thanks to the busy and continual traffic to the bar and post office counter. I loafed for so long that before I knew it, an early lunch crept up to demand my attention. I chose the perfect meal to represent a tectonic meeting: a toasted cheese and speck Panini and a glass of very local, German-style, dry white wine.

Sometime later in the afternoon, when I woke up on my bed at the Pernthaler, I realised that I must have sauntered back and decided to give in to my overwhelming tiredness. I decided that for the rest of the day, I would try to understand why I had wanted to stop in this ordinary place with little on the surface to offer? After all, relaxing was a luxury that could only be infrequently indulged. I would dig below the surface, look for the extraordinary in the ordinary and enjoy relaxing without having to catch a train somewhere or visit a museum. This was going to be hard but having had a sleep, I was game to try and tick more off on my flâneur chart.

Before I went out into the late afternoon sun, I saw the owner of the Pension at the reception desk. I already knew that he spoke excellent English but then I overhead him talking in fluent German and Italian on the telephone. I found many people like him on my travels, so good at swapping easily between languages that it made me decidedly envious.

After I thanked him for my washing, he told me that children at school are taught these three languages as a priority. Apart from a commitment to the European vision of mutually beneficial coexistence, there was also the necessity of relating commercially with countries whose borders were so close. I could not forget the Dutchman on a bicycle who, in what seemed another lifetime, had gently berated me with his statement that 'there are no borders now; we are all European.' Borders or no borders, people felt it necessary to communicate with each other for peace and prosperity.

He also told me that children in Alto Adige (as well as Trentino – where I was heading next – and other parts of the Italian Dolomites) are taught the Ladin language in school, which was and is used by the original mountain dwellers in this region. Although only four per cent of people still had a history of speaking it fluently, it is now being preserved in various ways to revive its usage in everyday life.

By the time I had ambled to a bar with a fine view of the mountains and ordered two Hugo concoctions in fairly quick succession, the sun was losing its grip on the mountains. Sitting, sipping this delicate tasting cocktail; I meditated on the mountains that lay in the direction of my walk to Merano (Meran in German) in the morning. Beyond the belt of domesticity on the lower slopes, lay the shoulders, the ranges and the high peaks that shunned all efforts to control them. These parts touched me deeply. They were another country, a place where gods lived. They answered to no man, retained snow as they pleased, in bones stuck in clints and groins. And when the snow was full upon them, the mountains could treat those who deviated from the flattened piste with little mercy.

These mountains were not conquered with flags pierced into their summits: people walked in their private places hidden from the public gaze. It was there that secret alliances were made. When, in a dreamlike state, adventurers return from these high uplands, they often looked with glazed eyes into the distance with a longing full of melancholy; aching in regret for losing touch with the mountains' remotest places.

The Ladins have passed down an ancient folk tale called Reign of Fanes, which tells of the almost primeval relationship they had with the lands beyond the cultivated skirts around the mountains. At the heart of this story the lineage of the Queen of Fanes is intricately connected to the marmots that live in the mountains. Her husband, the

King, who came from another land, had ancestral connections with an eagle. In a very Tolkienesque fashion the tale twists and turns with the help of a wicked sorcerer, magic gems, infallible arrows, twin princesses – one of whom gets swapped for a little marmot, and a secret door under the lake behind which the defeated Fanes lie waiting for the correct time to return and reclaim their kingdom.

However fantastical the legend of the Fanes is, it seems to touch the nerve that connects us to our environment – even in the remotest of places. Chemically, we are all stardust; even the mountains vibrate with the same basic ingredients as us.

With a jolt, I realised that light had finally faded and it was time for dinner. The food at the Hotel Goldener Löwe was ideal: German-style meat with noodles and some fresh fruit. More than the food, though, I was interested in what was going on around me. A hen night was taking place in the bar, but unlike anonymous celebrations where passers-by have no knowledge of the hens, in this small mountain town the women in the conga line knew everyone they bumped into. This seemed to make the fun even more effervescent. There were table games, dancing in the street and raucous practical jokes. It was all a mix of Tudor revelry, holiday-camp style forfeits and modern drinking games. Just as I was about to leave for bed, someone shouted: 'Here come the stags!' and with that the hens gathered up their long, satin dresses, shrieked and hightailed it to another bar.

I walked back to my Pension down cobbled streets, yellowed by the streetlights, fanned by a breeze of warm air like the one that had wafted over us at breakfast. I longed to stay in this town for a week, at least, which was the biggest indication that it was time for me to get back on the road again. 'Never rest until your muscles stiffen and always leave before you want to stay' were my rules for long distance walking that I wrote with the sharp pen of experience.

3: Sissi in Merano

On the morning of Day 54, Monday June 13, I began a long walk down to Merano, which is the second largest town in the Alto Adige region after Bolzano. In the second half of the 19th-century, it became world famous as a spa resort. It quickly spreadto accommodate visitors from across Europe and the world. I was heading for an Airbnb studio near the centre of the town, but not looking forward to it because the second B seemed invariably to be missing. Why call it a place for bed and breakfast if you don't provide breakfast? Then you declare that fact in small print somewhere in the bowels of the 'app.' I was getting fed up of anticipating breakfast and then finding it not available, when my favourite Pension in Silandro offered a top quality breakfast and was still cheaper than some pretentious Airbnb places. I was not going to book them anymore. That was it.

With that rant over, I settled down to studying what was around me. I was walking steadily downhill in the centre of the Val Venosta valley on a cycle track. My leg was sore beneath my trousers because I had recently suffered an altercation with a hard-boiled egg. I had saved some food for my lunch from my breakfast plate: a brown roll and an egg, when halfway upstairs I felt a scalding pain in my leg. Rushing into my room to investigate I found that the egg, in my light-weight-netting pocket, must have just come out of the hot water and now my leg sported a bright red egg shaped mark. It didn't prevent me from walking, but I now knew what medieval branding felt like.

The route was really busy with bikes, as if it were a public holiday. Beside me, the River Adige, which began to slow now that we were getting further down its course, possessed a green, silvery sheen, which was echoed by the willows on its banks. Beside the trees were masses of wild roses, beech, elderflower, silver birch, wild cherry and lilacs. On a patch of earth, near the track, I smelled some wild rocket. I knew immediately what it was, but I had to taste it to make absolutely sure. It was delicious. I love rocket pesto. The thought of that gave me strength for at least another two miles.

That feeling you get when you walk into a bookshop and realise there is not enough time left in your life to read everything that you want to or learn all that you had planned to – I now transferred that idea to wild flowers. I wanted so badly to know everything about them, but felt that I had left it too late. I could spot trees and the more common flowers but the others I could never come to terms with – they were part of a faraway galaxy. Another project perhaps to keep me away from deckchairs?

The apples seemed to be bigger as the valley opened out and the river slowed down. It was a miracle of farming that there were so much fruit on each tree, albeit only the size of a small satsuma at this stage of the season. A few workers were deployed to inspect the leaves of apple trees with their fingers to make sure that any dead or blighted ones were taken off. I could see the whole cycle of the tree planting process at a glance. Saplings with caps of delicate blossom were in fields next to more mature apple bearers with fruit that would be picked this year. At the end of their life, trees were rooted up; the soil left fallow and the knotted bump at the base of the trunk was cut off and thrown on to a pile at the edge of the field. These discarded nuggets of apple wood looked ready for a kitchen stove. I would have given anything to breathe in the scent from it, as it burned with a heady perfume. Or watch the process of it being used to smoke some cheese.

There were only a few 'pavement friends' higher up the valley, but now that it was warmer creatures like ants were trailing across the paths, and lizards appeared and crouched waiting to pounce on these unsuspecting insects. Just after eating my cold egg roll for lunch, I saw dozens of lizards beside me on a pile of broken paving slabs. It seemed like a sign of summer. To wash down my lunch I drank a plastic beaker of fresh apple juice from a vat left for cyclists by the apple farmers. There, beside the vat, was a 'Trust The Cyclist' pot for half a Euro donations. I obliged gladly as it made a heavenly change from water. As I sat feeling the warmth of the sun on my face, I could see the serried ranks of vines ranging down the hillside and at the bottom two walnut trees heavy with their green, velvet-coated nuts.

From here, the steep path down to Merano was full of hairpins. The whole town was laid out before me. There was a car park at the top with a mobile shop. As I drew closer, I could see that it was a bar selling mostly prosecco and aperol spritz. I wondered how many car parks in the UK had bars.

Although I could see the town from on high, it still took another hour or so to walk down and find my studio. Luckily it was close to the River Passer, which runs through the centre of Merano to join the Adige near the motorway, at the edge of town. On checking into my studio, I looked at my mileage for the day and calculated that so far I had walked 21 that day, and 846.74 miles in all.

That night, I wanted to eat somewhere really lively. I wanted to revive the fun of 'people watching,' which I enjoyed so much at the hen night in Silandro, the night before. Walking was a lonely business and to feel part of a crowd in the evening was a welcome relief. The Forsterbrau restaurant fitted the bill perfectly. The male waiters were dressed in lederhosen and the women wore red gingham dresses with plaited hair either in pigtails or piled up in a bun on top of their heads, giving them an appearance of Heidi, a popular character from the stories by Johanna Spyri.

This venue was probably part of a chain: the welcome, service and menu were all part of a well-oiled business. Pork knuckle, with ginger bread sauce served on a cushion of sautéed potatoes and sauerkraut healed my tired limbs. Beer flowed continually, served in tankards or long, tall glasses with a foamy head, which added a comic touch to anyone like me, with a beard or moustache. Instead of a hen night, we watched the Euros on large-screened TVs: Italy beat Belgium 2:1, which pleased the diners greatly, so after that more beer flowed.

Merano became internationally famous as a health spa after Empress Elizabeth of Austria, known as Sissi, brought her two-year-old daughter Marie Valerie there in 1870 to recover from a lung illness. It was meant to be an incognito visit but that was hard to achieve with a retinue of 102 people. Turning up at the local railway station with that kind of entourage would have blown her cover straight away. She stayed at Trauttmansdorff Castle and when news got out about how the castle and the town had contributed to the recovery of the Empress's daughter, Merano became the place to stay for the aristocracy, and the rich in general.

Sissi's life was a prime example of a young woman who marries into a royal dynasty and from the start regrets the limitations imposed upon her. From then on she lived to travel, suffered from eating disorders, lacked confidence despite being incredible beautiful, all because she felt trapped in an unhappy marriage. She became obsessed with getting old and losing her beauty, which made her fanatical about health resorts and holistic treatments. The more I read about her, with only one eye on the football, the more I realised that each royal family, just like our own, must inevitably at some stage, produce their own Sissi as a result of the entrenched traditions, rules and customs that bind them together becoming too restrictive for the free spirited.

Walking back to my studio, I was able to balance the pork-knuckle experience with some more Italian touches: men in pink shorts, 'Ciao' used as a greeting in the street, men wearing scarves tied in a typically Italian way, and the fact that at pedestrian crossings people were now more nervous about walking on them or anywhere near them. In Italy a pedestrian crossing seems a target for a driver or a challenge for the pedestrian, rather than a sanctuary for people trying to cross the road.

Breakfast, which was NOT provided by my Airbnb, was taken at the wonderful Bar Bingo, down the road from my studio, in which I learned from the welcoming couple who ran it that more than 70% of people in Merano speak German (albeit with an Austrian accent) and only 24% speak Italian. Obviously, Italian is spoken more in the service industries. Today I was walking to Ponte d'Adige, which is on the bend of the river, next to the city of Bolzano. I was given directions for a shortcut to the cycle path; a very tasty couple of brioches filled with pistachio cream; a good cappuccino; and some interesting facts about the town. Perhaps I should have thanked Airbnb for not giving me breakfast?

The weather bode well; it could almost have been another sunny day in the making. The clouds were gripping onto the mountains, in early morning defiance. Over the valley ribbed clouds were laid out like a piece of corduroy with an undergarment of blue peeking through the threadbare, fustian grooves.

I walked through the back streets of Merano to begin with, past blocks of flats each with their own balcony. I counted as many Italian flags as German ones hanging from the balconies in support of the two teams in the Euro football tournament. I supposed it was a good indication of the way national allegiances went in this border region between Austria and Italy.

When I reached the cycle track I found myself wanting to speed-walk because everything else was rushing in my direction of travel.

There were early morning power-walkers and cyclists moving along my track; then there was the fast flowing Adige; which in turn was beside a railway line along which a sleek, smart local train was carrying commuters towards Bolzano. They were all running parallel with a motorway, which carried lorries and cars galore to anywhere on the east side of Italy or perhaps even Hungary or Croatia.

Actually, to begin with, I was carried along more quickly than I might otherwise have walked, but slowed down when I began to realise the significance of what was around me. After the sleek train emblazoned with Alto Adige on its side, I saw a shabby, ill-kempt train owned by the national operator Trenitalia going in the same direction. The difference in appearance of these two trains was enormous. In my mind, they represented a visual image of the up-market aspect of this Italian region, which is justly proud of its special, delegated status.

The whole area, through which I was walking, comprises two provinces: the Province of Trento (Trentino), and the Province of Bolzano (Südtirol). They make up one large autonomous region (Trentino-Alto Adige) and have had very many delegated powers given to them by the Italian government. For almost 1000 years this area was part of the Austrian Empire, which is why Andreas Hofer was taken to Bozen (Bolzano in Italian) to be tried and executed. However, in 1919, after the First World War, it was given to Italy in recognition for its part in joining the Allies in their fight against Germany. Today, the region has made the best of its natural resources, taken full advantage of its autonomous status and is, as result, incredibly wealthy: a great success story within the EU. So the sleek train I saw was not a surprise, but rather an emblem for the success of this region. Delegated powers given to a people who possess a strong identity and are willing to work hard for it, all within the context of a family of nations across Europe: sounds a good idea.

The overwhelming volume of this region's commercial success could also be measured by the mountainous stacks of crates destined to be full of apples by the end of the picking season. Some of the crates I passed were as tall as the factory they stood in front of. They were mostly dark green or blue in colour and were just waiting for their share of the harvest, which I read amounts to approximately 350,000 metric tonnes from the Val Venosta alone. One geeky thing I like to do is to practise mental arithmetic while walking. So for the next half-an-hour I tried to work out how many apples they were talking about and for how many people that number would help to keep the doctor away. There are 1000kg in each metric tonne, so that makes 350 million kilograms and obviously 350 billion grams. Assuming a typical apple weighs 125 grams then there would be something like 2.8 billion apples picked in a season from that particular valley. At a rough calculation that would be enough apples to keep a doctor away from the door of everyone in Santa Vittoria in Matenano (1500 residents at my destination) for 5000 years, allowing each person, or a descendant family member, an apple a day. Quite a healthy small town, but I would feel sorry for the decimated medical service. Of course, my calculations could have been faulty and the medical service would have been safe after all.

I needed a break after all that mind-stretching work, so I sat down on a bench beside a visitors' notice board. I was near the small towns of Terlano and Andriano. The tourist information was fascinating. My own home region of Yorkshire has a so-called rhubarb triangle, so I was delighted to learn that here in this valley there is an asparagus triangle. Most of my walk through Holland and Germany was dominated by the roadside stalls selling white asparagus and now I was close to the green variety grown on this sandy, silted soil beside the River Adige.

The Greeks first discovered asparagus' detoxifying attributes. Since Greek communities lived in Italy for centuries, including the one from which Archimedes hailed, it is no wonder that news of this medicinal vegetable travelled north to where there are such ideal conditions for growing it.

More staggering was the information that nearby was a stand of yew trees that also thrive in this soil and climate. Yew tree wood was used for thousands of years for making bows, such as the ones used in the Battle of Agincourt. Thousands of years before that, the Iceman of South Tyrol would have descended from the mountains to areas like this to cut his raw materials to make bows and arrows.

It was in September 1991 that a married couple from Germany was walking over the Ötztal mountains, which I could see on the Italian side at Nauders, just before reaching the Austrian border with Italy. They spotted a body buried in the ice of a glacier. They thought it must be a missing hiker, but after extensive scientific analysis it was found to be the preserved body of a man who lived nearly 3500 years BC. He was nicknamed Ötzi and turned out to be the oldest naturally pre-served European human mummy.

The study of his remains has given us a wonderful insight into his life and times. He may have been taken up to the top of the range to be buried but Ötzi lived at all altitudes. Among his belongings buried with him was a bow made of yew and arrows made from light, strong woods or bamboo. Just the kind of wood he might have collected from the area around where I was sitting. While humans and the water rushed by, low down here, I was in the midst of the Iceman's world. That was until he was buried up with the eagles and the marmots.

Not far from the cycle track, in a village bar, I ate a huge bowl of pasta and drank only water because I did not want to slip into drink-ing alcohol twice a day, every day. I ate automatically, because my mind was far way. If my limbs ached on a daily basis, my mind was glad of the gymnastics I forced it to practise. The Iceman and his life absorbed me. The image of him consuming his last meal, somewhere in this area about 5000 years ago. was powerful. The contents of his stomach were studied to reveal a last supper, taken only two hours before his death, of red deer, green-leafed vegetables, and some grain, probably in the form of bread. He and I walked the same mountains and valleys; we ate similar food, but I was sadly lacking the expert skills to make a bow and some arrows to kill my own dinner. How would I survive if society collapsed? Was I prepared? Hardly.

I needed to get a move on to reach Ponte d'Adige in time to find some accommodation. I had prevaricated when I was doing some ad-vance booking because there did not seem to be any cheap deals on offer. I needed to stay in that town since I estimated that walking an extra two or three miles into Bolzano would be too much. Conserving my energies after the Alps was vital, because there were more moun-tains to come between Rovereto and Vicenza, before I reached the Veneto. This is a huge area of flat land that sprawls right down to

Venice and along the Adriatic coast.

It rained heavily in the late afternoon, so when I reached the outskirts of my destination, I did what I always did: stand in a bus shelter until I had made my mind up what to do. Opposite was a hotel and, making a random choice, I walked quickly into the reception of the Premstaller Garden Hotel and asked if 'I they had any offers on?'

I said what I was doing and that it was 'too wet to camp, and that at my age I needed a comfortable room, I was wet through...' The receptionist took pity on me. I ended up with a spacious, comfortable room with breakfast and a three-course dinner for far less than the studio in Merano. It was a large hotel with only a few business people staying there who, I felt, saw me more like an Iceman in comparison to their modern civilised selves, but none of that mattered because I was in bed by 9pm and asleep by five past.

Over dinner, I allowed myself the privilege to be honest with myself. I realised that I was getting mentally drained by days of endless cycle paths. I had been on the same path since the hill outside Landeck, beside the River Inn, where I met the four cyclists in a bus shelter. They would have been to Lake Garda by now and be halfway back to Germany with their bikes on the back of a bus. I calculated that I had two more days of this cycle track before I reached Trento. I was going to have a couple of rest days there because, even in my armchair at home, I had anticipated physical and mental exhaustion at this stage. Besides if Trento was a place of rest for Roman Centurions, it was good enough for me.

4: On the Road to Trento

Trento was a Roman outpost town, so the soldiers would have found rest and recuperation there before they had to walk all the way I had just come, over the Reschia Pass to the River Danube. Or the same journey in reverse. I wondered whether they found it as draining as me. I was doing my best to find interesting things to engage my mind, but by now I was incredibly weary and badly in need of a change of landscape.

Little did I know how much of a change I would be getting in the Veneto, and what new torturous inflictions it would have on my body.

The next morning, as I passed Sigmundskron Castle, perched boldly on top of what looked like a lone mountain beside the river, on a sweeping bend outside Bolzano, I bumped into a man of about my age with whom I struck up a conversation of sorts.

We walked together for about a mile. He spoke no English, but had German, Italian and Ladino. I found out that he had had a heart attack and that the doctor advised him to walk briskly for an hour each day. I smiled when I realised I was doing a minimum of eight hours in a day. His walking made me think of the Zimmer frame brigade in Germany. Here you just had to walk under your own steam and that was that.

He had mapped out a loop, which took in the river and a view of this magnificent castle. We both stood in silent admiration of its wonderful battlements and then walked on as he told me about his life. He was born a Ladin, but I did not have the language to ask him about the folklore that was part of his culture. I desperately wanted to know more about the Reign of Fanes. However, thanks to my pidgin Italian and sparrow-like German I was able to have a sustained conversation, albeit in snatches.

What I appreciated from this random meeting was the resilience this man showed, his sheer joy of being in this place and his absolute dedication to staying alive for as long as possible. Snap. We were soul mates. He was saying what I believed. How could I have possibly got mentally drained, as I had thought the previous evening, when resilience, joy and dedication should always be my companions? There were two of us on the cycle track, but I fancied that my Dad and my other forebears were lurking in the bushes listening to our conversation and nodding sagely.

We shook hands at his turning point and he wished me all the best for the rest of my journey. He had no way of knowing how meaningful our meeting had been for me, or how many of us there were on the track that day.

At mid-morning, I stopped for a coffee and read about the building of Venice. The lagoon in which Venice is floating comprises nearly 120 islands. Ten million wooden poles support from underneath all that beautiful stonework. The poles were sharpened like a pencil and driven into the mud under the surface of the sea until they hit harder ground. The process of positioning them and making the platforms in between, upon which buildings could be built, began after the fall of the Roman Empire and when the invading tribes rode down from the grassland steppes, which ranged from what is now called Hungary in the west, to China in the east. Many people from around the Veneto fled these tribes to live on islands in the lagoon, at the edge of the Adriatic.

Venice became a great sea-going empire, so apart from the oak and pine needed for the stakes and buildings, more wood was needed for ships. They probably began with timber that grew nearby and then sourced it from further afield, across the Adriatic in what is now Slovenia and Croatia. A by-product of harvesting the pine trees was the use of its sap as pitch. This black, sticky goo was used for waterproofing barrels, buckets and of course ships.

This is where the River Adige came in handy. Putting logs into the water near where I was drinking my coffee and steering them downstream, would eventually bring the timber to the mouth of the river at the southern end of the Venetian lagoon. This area is an important location in Italy because the largest river, the River Po, also spills into the sea at this point. Geographically, the region is called the Delta del Po, which is a bit of a slight on the poor old Adige, which merely gets a silver medal in the most important river contest.

As I walked on, I totted up why I was feeling brighter, more positive about the walk and life in general. Of course, the return of the fine weather helped, as did meeting that man this morning, but an underlying reason hit me out of the blue. I was walking directly south.

Once I had turned the bend in the river at the castle after breakfast, I had turned south.

For many days, I had been walking in an easterly direction, with only a slight feeling that I was making much of an inroad on my ambitions for heading down the length of Italy. Now I was – and that made a huge difference. Then there was the fact that it was 15 June, which was my parents' wedding anniversary. They were married in 1935 and both worked in London, he as a compositor in Fleet Street and she as a shorthand typist. To become a compositor William had attended evening classes for many years. Once married, they were the first in their families to buy a house and the first to move out of London. They had a mortgage on a brand new mock Tudor house on an estate in what was then the countryside to the south of London. They were working class with aspirations. When my father died, it was my mother's sheer hard work, resilience and love in looking after my disabled sister and me, which must have seeped into my whole being and given me the determination to survive hardship at all costs.

I was so happy walking along in the sunshine that I burst into one of my busking songs called 'Rolling Home' by John Tams. Cyclists began passing me; they looked somewhat surprised to see someone singing at the top of their voice while hiking along with a rucksack. Especially the straight faced ones that looked like Ofsted inspectors on their holidays. They tended not to be decked out in the blue Italia kit but wore grey shorts and tee shirts with a matching helmet perched on their heads. They sat bolt upright in the saddle and sailed along looking purposeful but clueless – just like a schools' inspector, some of my teacher friends would say, cruelly.

Just then a long-haired man on a mountain bike came up next to me. He was not wearing a helmet nor was he holding on to his handlebars. His arms were folded across his chest. He could see where he was going because he had one of those rigid plastic hair bands holding back his tangled locks. In bright red kit, he looked like a student who had never quite settled down. He glided past me in full voice, singing an Italian operatic love song. There we were, me singing about farm workers rolling home after work and loathing their masters; he giving a dramatic love song his all. The Ofsted inspectors stared straight ahead as if we were an embarrassing smell under their noses.

I don't know what came over me, but a combination of Alice and William's wedding anniversary, turning south, singing for the hell of it, meeting a soul mate that spoke Ladin, and missing home – it all got too much for me. I sat down on a bench and sobbed deeply, silently and unnoticed, until some more cyclists headed my way and I turned around as if looking for wild flowers in the banking.

I stayed in a small place called Laghetti that night in a recently established B&B, which was comfortable and provided great food in the evening. Basically, I arrived, ate, slept and left. I was on my way to Trento so that was all I needed. The view from my bedroom window looked out over the meadows to the high riverbank path on which I had arrived and by which I would leave the next morning. It was really the walkers' equivalent of a hotel on a motorway service area, perfectly situated.

The friendly host at the Pension Dolomiten told me over breakfast that after a village called Salorno I would not hear German being spoken again. 'That is where the real Italy begins,' she exclaimed with authority. I worked out that by then I would be in the Province of Trento rather the Province of Bolzano.

My host was right. The fields I could see that morning were less regimented. Pear trees were mixed with the apple trees. There were trellises of grapes in some fields and the gaps in between them were planted with potatoes and lettuces: no space was wasted in growing, hoeing and garnering food for the table. On one scrap of spare land beside a roundabout, a small allotment had been created in which fennel and artichokes were growing to the sound of the cars and lorries as they changed gear noisily to negotiate the roundabout at speed. As I walked down an avenue with houses either side, the hedgerows of jasmine were hypnotic. I drank in their perfume and felt woozy. They were so intoxicating.

I saw my first Italian style Eurospin supermarket, a driver tried to run me down at a pedestrian crossing and every driver that passed me was talking on their mobile phone. I had arrived in Italy for real. Here began the beauty and the chaos that I had walked all this way for.

Later, when I was back on the cycle track, a middle-aged woman with a rucksack protected with a red rain cover like mine stormed past me at double my walking speed. She took no interest in me at all. I took that badly because by the evening I would have walked 900 miles and she was the only walker I had come across on the whole of my journey. Not to have a conversation amounted to walkers' heresy. So I sped up and in a couple of 100 yards I was alongside her saying rather breathlessly: 'Hi, where are you going?'

'Florence,' she grunted.

'Where did you start out from?' I tried again.

'Munich to Florence: 10 days so far,' came the extended, but somewhat breathless, answer.

With that I fell back and resumed my normal snail's pace compared with her gargantuan strides.

I whipped out my phone and looked up the distance between those two cities for a walker: 392 miles. 'Huh, a lightweight,' I said out loud, cruelly. I was ashamed of myself immediately.

About an hour later, I saw her sitting on a tree stump, off the path, just resting. It seemed a funny style of walking. To speed off and then stop for recuperation every so often. While I was watching her she swung her rucksack up onto her back and rushed off towards the main road, disappearing in the direction of Trento.

I calculated that she was doing about 20 miles a day, the same as me, but at that speed she would get to her destination for the day just after the middle of the afternoon. The hare to my tortoise — I would rather smell the jasmine on the way. I hoped that our paths did not meet in Trento that night. I was not sure what tortoises had to say to hares.

I suppose I could have told her about the Chimney Sweep Way that she was about to follow into Florence, but it was debatable whether she would have time to listen to such an idle piece of information.

Near Nave San Felice, I stopped for a rather overloaded mixed-meat pizza; that was a bad mistake as it gave me indigestion for the rest of the afternoon. Ten mistakes and the snowball kept rolling. I was forced to adopt a wandering mode of walking for about an hour afterwards, which forced me to 'smell the jasmine' even more. I saw a large mob of house sparrows, which was odd because they have virtually died out back in the UK. I suppose it was because it was my Mum's birthday (had she lived, and not died of cancer at the age of 64, this would have been her 106th) that the sight of house sparrows brought my primary school years flooding back.

Our Mum came home from work, in London, at about 6.30pm, so after school my sister and I stayed at home and waited. When it got near the time of her arrival we often went up to Mum's bedroom.

From the window we could see the length of the road and could spot when she was near so that we could rush down and put the kettle on. While waiting I studied the house sparrows that I imagined lived in the eaves; the way they strutted on the window ledge, flew around or just got on with their own social scene. They became my favourite neighbours. To see them in such large numbers here, in Italy, after so many years became an ornithological treat: the silver lining behind a cloud of indigestion.

5: The Teeth of Trento

The back door entrance to Trento was a bit more welcoming than Koblenz, but still a massive challenge. There was the usual Italian jumbled collection of factories, cafes and offices surrounded by unfinished pavements, potholes and dangerous road junctions. At the end of a long, hard walk I found that uneven surfaces or having to run to avoid dangerous drivers played havoc with my legs, ankles and feet. They weren't used to the sudden, or ungainly, movements involved. But it all became more enjoyable again when I arrived back at the riverside on the final approach to the historic centre of the city.

I was just thinking about the Roman solders, and the apprentice chimney sweep, both of whom might have walked exactly where I was placing my feet, when I glanced to the left and there sitting on a pavement bench reading a newspaper was a man whose legs struck me instantly as being a bit old fashioned. I only saw these crossed legs because the newspaper he was reading masked his entire upper body.

His trousers were in the style of Oxford bags; the matching socks and brogue shoes below them also had a 1930s appearance. As I stopped and stared at him, he lowered his newspaper and beamed a broad smile directly at me. His white shirt set off the colourful tie he was wearing; its small knot matched the rest of his retro outfit. What struck me the most were his glasses. I have a photo of my father wearing some round tortoiseshell glasses, typical of the 1930s. This man's glasses were identical. I suddenly felt elated but uncomfortable; my palms started sweating.

His eyes held mine for long enough for the sheer warmth of his smile to find its mark. Then, without a moment's hesitation, he raised his paper up again; the episode was over. We weren't going to have a conversation. How could we? The traffic flowed like a river between us.

I knew people would say that I imagined it, but this did not stop me from shaking with excitement. My father was waiting for me on that bench. He was there in Trento just wanting to see me arrive safely from the Alps. His smile was one of total pride and approval. I was certainly not a laggard or idle stay-at-home, in his eyes.

I looked back when I had walked on a bit further. The noisy traffic, the school children going home, the cyclists weaving in and out of the cars, all obscured the bench fleetingly as they flickered past in quick succession, but he was gone. I was sure of that.

I spent two nights in Trento. It was planned to be a period of reward, recuperation and reassessment. The first two were easy but the third was more complicated. My ambition was to get across to the coast and then wander down through the seaside resorts to the ancient seaport city of Ancona, where I would turn inland. The problem was that there weren't any easy-to-find, 20 mile-a-day stopping places. I had mapped out a vague itinerary at home not knowing how I would feel when I got to Trento, but now I had arrived I had to buckle down and set goals. The trouble was that having made it through Austria I was losing the will to push on. Half of me wanted to get to Santa Vittoria and the other half wanted to stay where I was.

I did the only thing to do in that situation, which did not involve a bus shelter. I went to the launderette.

After that, I wandered around the town, ate lots of food, and drank copious amounts of Aperol Spritz, relishing its gentian flavouring. Often, I just stared into space. As I was hanging up my washing back in my accommodation, I realised that so far, I hadn't worn shorts; it had been so cold and wet. The TV weather reports for that weekend indicated that I might soon get some welcome sunshine.

I found out that I had arrived on a festival weekend in honour of St. Vigilius, the Patron Saint of Trento. There were funfairs, food stalls, pop-up bars, open-air music venues and street sellers galore. So there was plenty to stare at.

I knew that I was probably the last person in the world to realise this, but when we learned about the Council of Trent in history lessons at school, I naively thought teachers were talking about Trent, near Nottingham. It only dawned on me while wandering around this magnificent city and reading brass plaques beside palace doors that the Council of Trent (Trento) took place here, on and off, over nearly 20 years between 1545 and 1563.

Simplistically, Martin Luther started the Protestant Reformation in 1517 by pinning his 95 objections to ecclesiastical corruption to the door of Wittenberg's Castle Church, in Germany. Then from 1545 onwards the Catholic Church held meetings of bishops and other dignitaries to devise a plan to turn the tide in their favour, and win worshippers back. This was called the Counter Reformation; and it took place here. Quite momentous, when you think that many of the regulations decided here, about divorce, for example, are still adhered to today.

There I was, worried about whether I could carry on and if so, which route I would take and then I got tied up in church history. I suppose the Council of Trent was, for me, a diversion, rather like the zeppelins in Germany with about as much gas and hot air.

My saviour, in terms of motivation and routes, came in the form of a knowledgeable seller of travel books and maps in a specialist shop near the Cathedral. He knew a lot about local minor roads and paths over the mountains, so with his help I mapped out a way to get to the coast without following the course of the Adige past Verona. It would mean that I would have to leave early because there was a mountain to climb over before 11am. I had to go over this mountain because the busy, main road around it had some more impassable tunnels, for a walker that is. A long hike alongside the River Brenta to a small town called Roncegno Terme, famed for its thermal springs, would follow this. After that, I would walk down in the following days to a town called Bassano del Grappa, at which the plains of the Veneto really begin.

On my last night in Trento, I wanted to be in bed early. So, I found a tiny, family-run restaurant that served food from the Trentino area, which was empty at the time. There, I feasted on pasta ragu and after that, stewed meat served with polenta flecked with herbs and mixed grains. One of the older family members in the kitchen frequently stepped outside to smoke. On my way out of the restaurant, I struck up a conversation with him. He had a florid face and a scarcity of teeth. The three teeth, on show at the front, were spaced out across his mouth.

I was far too polite to bring up the subject of what Trento was called by the Romans - Tridentum which in Latin means a city with three teeth. These three 'teeth' are sizeable hills standing around the city.

Here was a man, I thought wickedly, who was a walking emblem: as long as he smiled, visitors would be confronted with the city's history.

We chatted, in faltering Italian on my part, about my walk and the fact that as a chain smoker of small cigars he didn't walk much beyond the distance from the kitchen to the restaurant's backdoor. He asked me how old I was and when I told him he laughed loudly. Of us, he was the younger by nine months. 'You are my younger brother,' I joked. He loved this comment, so much so that we hugged.

As I walked back to my room, I would have put money on the fact that I was the only tourist in Trento who had been hugged by a 'homo tridentem in Tridentum.'

In the end the town played a joke on me. I was staying at a beautiful development of ultra-modern apartments situated on the site of the old Michelin tyre factory, just outside the centre of town. The landscaped parklands around the buildings were the venue for several bands that were booked to help locals celebrate St. Vigilius' day. It was an open-air concert, but no-one had warned me when I booked that the music went on all night.

By 6am the next day I had not really slept at all, only dozed at most. Up at 5am, I had washed, dressed and packed to the thumping sound of 'Born in the USA' and three other early-morning reveilles. I slipped out of my front door and made my way out of the city on a steep road to the village of Povo that lies in the lee of Sant' Agata, one of the teeth.

On my way up, the scene was one of battlefield proportions. People were lying in doorways (not homeless but incapacitated), groups of friends were still sitting outside cafes even though they were shut, and the ambulant were weaving their way to destinations that kept changing as they lurched from one side of the road to the other. One group of young people swarmed about me and wanted to know what I was doing, apart from walking straight – I guessed. When I told them I got a round of applause, patted on the back (rucksack) and cheered as I walked away. It all seemed so friendly; nothing like the youths I met in Hull. But the betting was on that they would have no memory of our meeting after a sleep.

The air on my way to Povo to take breakfast in a café was laden with the scent of jasmine. On the final approach to the café, that of freshly baked brioche complemented the glorious jasmine. I was in heaven – hoping to meet St. Vigilius to forgive him the all-night music inflicted in his name.

Breakfast fortified me enough to get to the top of the mountain, from where I could enjoy a panoramic view of the valley below, through which the River Brenta flowed. Far down to my left, like ants, cars were emerging from the long tunnels, which I had avoided by climbing the mountain range that now loomed behind me. Lined up on the lower slopes opposite were spa towns of almost equal fame to Merano beginning with Levico Terme. Empress Sissi took the waters there too. She was such an aficionado of fitness regimes it was here that she wanted rooms in which apparatus like ropes and rings had been fitted to the ceiling, so that she could work out before breakfast.

In between Levico and me was a large lake on which I fixed my sights, so that my descent had a purpose. I reached the water's edge in a couple of hours by which time I was hungry again. Walking past a rather grand hotel, I saw a pop-up bar in the grounds, where holidaymakers were already sitting drinking aperitivos and indulging in some elaborate nibbles. I decided to join them and ordered a coffee, for which no one seemed willing to take payment.

Although I stood out like an eccentric uncle at a party, everyone seemed very friendly. Determined to spend some money, I ordered a beer. It was then that a waiter sidled up to me and, very quietly in my ear, said, in Italian, 'I am sorry sir, but your order for a drink is not possible, because it is certain that you are not on the wedding guest list. Please accept the coffee with our compliments.'

I mumbled in English something like 'Gosh, trust me to make such a faux pas. I am so sorry: I will drown myself in the lake if that would help.' He smiled, sympathetically, as if to say, 'if that would please you…'

With that, I grabbed my rucksack and left immediately, as if asked to perform in charades the definition of the verb 'to slink.'

It was not until about two miles further on that I was able to forget the shame and see the funny side of such an embarrassing incident. Shortly, I came to a place called the Hotel Energy, which was an ironic spot because I had none. Outside was lined up a phalanx of Swiss-registered Harley Davidson motorbikes and inside the their owners were sitting waiting to be fed. At the bar, I politely asked how long I would have to wait to have lunch and knew from the look of panic in the eyes of the waiter that there was no chance before these Hell's Angels had all been served.

I left, wondering where on earth I might get some food in this valley on a Sunday.

After the lake, I met a woman walking her dog and she asked me kindly where I was going and if I had eaten. She pointed across some fields to a pizza restaurant saying that this was my best bet. I did not like to spurn her suggestion, so I started to walk in that direction hoping that she would veer off and I could resume my original path.

I was worried that it might be closed and besides, I had found out to my cost that pizza at lunchtime could lie very heavy causing indigestion. When the woman had disappeared round a bend, I doubled back and followed her at a distance. About 10 minutes later I saw her scrumping cherries from an orchard that lined the track on both sides. Realising that I had not been anywhere near the pizza place, she came over and asked me to hold out my hands.

In an act of extreme generosity she piled me high with virtually all of her stolen cherries. What an act of selflessness, I thought. Realising that my need was greater than hers, she gave me her spoils to stave off my hunger pangs. After gorging myself, while continuing to walk through the orchard, my second-hand villainy could be easily evidenced by the cherry stains all over my hands and around my mouth.

Feeling deliciously guilty, I kept an eye out for the main course.

Luckily, there was a Bici-Grill ahead of me, on the cycle path. I was welcomed in by a rather tired-looking student who informed me that St. Vigilius was to blame for her downbeat service that day. Speaking quietly so as not to make matters worse, I chose a mammoth roast pork and vegetable bap. It disappeared in less than a minute.

Studying the map, I concluded that Padua would be an ideal spot to put down my hat for busking. It had to be be sunny by then and anyway time was running out as I had already been on the road for 60 days, covering just over 900 miles. If I was going to become a famous street singer, it had to be soon.

The afternoon was a long one. The total distance to cover before bed was 25 miles and I still had 10 miles to go. As the weather clouded over, the mountains on either side of the wide valley increasingly looked bare, grey and forlorn. Their worn limestone sides were razor-sharp against the bulging grey clouds that balanced precariously on top, though not yet punctured enough to shed their waters. It was like this all the way down to Roncegno, except that as I turned off the main track to climb up to the town, it began to rain in earnest.

The Albergo Villa Rosa was situated right in the centre of this small, quiet town. The hotel blushed demurely, behind a fan of wisteria, proud but not overtly boastful about its former glory as a spa retreat for eminent city folk. A small flight of stone steps led up to a tiled, arched-fronted veranda. From there an open dark-oak front door revealed an elegant hallway set off by Turkish carpets and antique armchairs. Above the front veranda were the balconies belonging to the upstairs bedrooms. Mine was the central one above the front door. From a cane settee, stuffed plentifully with plump cushions, I sat and watched the evening sunlight sliding off the bald patches of the mountains opposite while a single, green bell rang dolefully on top of the yellow painted church in front of me: mourning the passing of the day.

6: A Seagull over the Veneto

Early the next morning, I was walking through a town called Borgo Valsugana when it struck me that I was still on the Via Claudia Augusta.

The day was bright; warm but not hot, perfect for walking along a river route. My footsteps led me through places of boundless peace. I read signs that told me that these stretches of the river were designated as a nature reserve. Before some turbulent tributaries joined the Brenta further downstream, bends, boulders and shallow beds forced the water to dawdle. Occasional rock pools spawned a host of common plants, which looked exotic growing together in profusion. The palette of vibrant green created by these plants made me stop and gaze for a dangerously long time: my leg muscles stiffened as I lingered over this spectacular array of ferns, grasses, mosses and white-button flowers with matchstick-slim, green stems.

The feeling of peace brought on by this scene was accompanied by a halo of anxiety. I worried that I was missing something. A nagging voice told me that tragedy was just around the bend. In this case, a symbol that proved my instinct correct stood in the river on a little island encircled by eddies and swirling fronds of water-weeds. It was a large seagull. He was strutting about as if he owned the place. He seemed like he was taking no prisoners, when staking out his piece of land.

Here the river was crystal-clear and the chance of plentiful fish was guaranteed. No wonder the seagull had made such a relatively short journey from its more regular habitat.

A quick calculation on my phone maps proved that the seagull and I were about 75 miles from Venice: a day out upstream for the seagull. That was the point. The sparkle and temptations of Venice were so close, but also the valley, as a gateway to other lands and riches, possessed a glister all of its own. The Romans, Napoleon and the Austro-Hungarian Empire had all claimed these rivers, valleys, plains and coastal towns as theirs. They knew the cultural splendours, fertile land and valley routes represented life in all its forms for them. Somehow, for me, the cocky, self-assured seagull that was claiming this stretch of river, and the fish therein stood for this base territorial desire, common to all animals including us.

I had read about the World War One battles that had taken place in the Alps and often wondered how near to me the fighting had been. The Italians wanted these lands back from the Austro-Hungarian Empire, and this caused them to enter a pact with the allies on the promise of regaining these jewels. A united Italy, which was less than 60 years old in 1915, ditched old allies and fought them to regain lost lands.

I didn't know it then, but the conflicts that happened nearby were to fuel my feelings of anxiety with a flame to keep them burning for a long time. In fact, I only had a day before the fire would burn to a crisp the peace that the ferns, grasses and flowers had given me.

Meanwhile, still in a tranquil mood, I ambled on. I got a sandwich in a village café, spoke to a woman at a bus stop who listened longingly to my tale and wanted to abandon her trip to town and come with me; and I chatted to a man who was pushing his bike. He spoke like a retired mountain farmer. Love for his homeland oozed from his pores.

Just before I reached my destination for the night: the Albergo Ristorante Valsugana, I passed a sign that told me I was leaving Trentino and stepping into the Veneto. So, the seagull had even gone beyond its own neighbourhood on its day trip. At the bar, after I had checked in, I asked for a beer and totted up my mileages so far. I was closing in on the much-anticipated 1000-mile mark. That night, at the end of Day 61, I had covered 947miles.

The Albergo had a fabulous deal for dinner, bed and breakfast, even though my single room was more like a monk's cell. The dinner was fabulous. No menu but food just kept coming to the table: piled high on plates in quantities that easily replenished my lost calories. To counterbalance the plentiful supply of food at night-time, breakfast was sparse, so I started my walk early on the lookout for a suitable place for a second breakfast.

I was walking towards Bassano del Grappa, which was reputed to be a beautiful town on the banks of the Brenta full of Palladian-style buildings. I dreamed of swapping a monk's cell for a room with a bath.

At about 11am I saw a glut of cyclists on the path, near what looked like a café. My taste buds started going into overdrive. Unfortunately for all of us, the café never opened. It was easy for the cyclists; they just took off at speed in the direction of another village, but I had to plod on to a place called Valstagna, which on the map looked big enough to have cafes and restaurants. By the time I got there, it would have to be lunch and a second breakfast rolled into one.

As I was dawdling around the wooded area besides the closed café getting motivated to push on, I spotted something intriguing among the weeds. A gravestone, at the top of which was the Star of David. Below the star was some script in what looked like Hebrew, and then right at the bottom was a little sign in Italian that read:

'Eli Vogel: 26 Agosto 1918 Primo Conflitto Mondiale.'

This set me thinking. Why was this grave of a lone soldier here in this spot? Which side did he fight for? Where could I find out more about him? Did the Hebrew contain any hint that antisemitism had been the cause of his death?

A few yards further on was a poem in Italian typed on a laminated page tied to a tree trunk. I hoped that the Internet could provide a translation and some answers to my questions. Food for thought, which would take my mind off the need for actual food for a while.

I knew that there had been some World War One conflicts here-abouts, but I was in the dark about what had taken place, exactly. I would not begin to know any more about Eli Vogel until I got to Bassano, so I dug in and headed for Valstagna.

When I got close to town the valley opened out, the river widened and the waterfront was busy with people shopping, getting canoes ready for the Olympic standard slalom course, or just eating ice creams while strolling idly beside the water.

The town hugged the sweeping bend of the river. Despite some of the waterside buildings being four storeys high, the cliffs behind them were 10 times taller. There were yellow, cream and faded pink houses, as far as the eye could see. I ate a huge pile of sandwiches and some Edelweiss-flavoured ice cream, while chatting to the woman who served me. She showed me some photos of her family at the beach in the summertime, just to prove how close the Venice Lido was from Valstagna. She asked me if I had heard about the tobacco smuggling that went on in this valley, mostly from this town, hundreds of years ago. When I confessed my ignorance, she told me the story.

Apparently, some enterprising monks brought tobacco seeds back from the Americas in the 17th century and Venice gave the town a concession to grow the plants. Obviously, the city's smokers created a great demand for the dried leaves. It was big business; there was much money to be made by the authorities in way of tax.

The monks saw to the construction of stepped beds on the steep slopes that rose up from the town. There tobacco was grown plentifully. Inevitably, some growers found ways to evade the stringent taxes by distributing their tobacco surreptitiously round the Republic especially among the wealthy folk, many of whom had built luxurious houses along the Brenta Canal, which ran from Padua to the coast. Of course, this kind of illegality was not without its risks; if caught a smuggler could be sentenced to three years on the galleys.

Valstagna became a prosperous outpost of the Republic because it also provided Venice with wood, which was rafted down the river or carried over the mountain tracks on specially made paths. These paths doubled up as rat runs for the tobacco smugglers.

One of the things that I enjoyed so much about my walk was the opportunity to sit and listen to people's stories. It's not often that, while savouring an Edelweiss ice cream, one learns about the risks of smuggling tobacco on the slopes above the café in which you are taking lunch. But there was more to come, as I was to discover when I researched what happened to Eli Vogel.

Later that afternoon, I met a woman with her three young daughters on the road. They had bikes but were huddled together on the pavement eating ice cream, This, I discovered, was proving to be one of the most popular Italian pastimes. They wanted to show me a riverside shortcut to Bassano, which was not on my map. Not only that but they volunteered to guide me. They set off, keeping me in sight behind them, and waited every time they edged ahead. By this cat and mouse method we got to within a mile of the town, and pointing ahead, they turned off to go home.

I was left walking alone into what turned out to be one of the most beautiful small towns I had ever seen. A secluded, woodland path suddenly opened out to reveal a broad view of the river, with – on the other side – some magnificent faded pink, four-storey houses. In the distance I could just about make out the bridge that I would use to cross the river; it looked like it was made entirely of wood. At this point the Brenta was wide and shallow; islands of warm, sandy-coloured rock on which crowds of young people were sunning themselves interrupted its flow. Occasionally, they flopped into the water like seals.

It only took me a matter of seconds to realise that I was beginning a process of re-birth. It felt like I had been washed up in Illyria, like a Shakespearean character in Twelfth Night.

Here were strange and wondrous people, sun bathing and relaxing surrounded by, and living in, buildings that echoed a Palladian musical rhythm in their design. Andrea Palladio is the world-famous architect who was born near here in 1508. His style based on Greek and Roman temples, with rooms constructed using the mathematics of musical harmony, spread across the world because people felt so uplifted by living and working in them.

Behind me, the mountains were disappearing from sight with every step I took toward the town, and in front a view of civilisation bedazzled.

When I arrived at the town, the wooden bridge that I had seen from afar was wide enough to march an army through, which is actually what happened during World War One. It is nicknamed the wooden Ponte Vecchio after a similar stone-built bridge in Florence.

What I loved about the bridge was the sense of community that one felt while walking across it – many other people shared in marvelling at the simple process of crossing a river on a beautiful structure. Inevitably, at some stage in our crossing, we all stood and gazed from the relative darkness of the bridge's portico across at the old town rising up, in yellow, pink and cream strata, from the river bank below.

The afternoon was fading and so was I. The belt on my trousers had been tightened progressively over the weeks. Whatever I ate in one day, I was still losing weight. I probably needed to stay in Bassano del Grappa for a few days to feed myself up like the sunbathing 'seals' that I looked down upon from the bridge, but my timetable meant that I had to move on the next day. So, when I found my room with a bath, and while having a long soak to take my mind off food, I started to look up Eli Vogel.

His Hebrew epitaph read 'May his soul be bound among the living.'

This was an apt wish, because a wayside-grave such as his was likely to arouse the curiosity in many people, like me. We would inevitable carry his soul with us wherever we went. He was a Sergeant in the 9th Galician Infantry Regiment, which probably meant that he was a Jewish soldier from what was then the Polish/Ukrainian part of the Austria-Hungarian Empire. During World War One, this honourable regiment, which dates back to the 1700s, was joined with the 5th Infantry Division that, in turn, was part of the 11th Army Reserves. In 1918, the year of Eli's death, the 11th Army was dug in to fight the Second Battle of the Piave River. Their section of the enemy was the 6th Italian Army. The battle lasted from Saturday 15 June to Sunday 23 June.

These facts were all very interesting and easy to reflect upon while lying in a warm bath, but the horrors of the war lay in the details. The soldiers of the Austro-Hungarian Empire held the high ground of the mountains and valleys, while the Italians, British and French were trying to break through their lines and take back land all the way to Trento and beyond. What is more, I was lying in the bath reading about this on 21 June 2016: 98 years to the day after this battle was in full spate.

By 1918, the soldiers in the mountains were exhausted. Who knows where Eli had been before then? It is likely that he had come from the Eastern Front where he had been fighting Russia before it dropped out from the war in October 1917, following the Russian Revolution. The chances are that he had marched along the same route as me, down the Brenta valley to reach the Veneto. The carnage that he would have witnessed there, and along the way, was enough to pollute the peace of this beautiful place forever.

Military experts suggest that, in the mountains, soldiers need to consume at least 3400 calories every day to maintain their energy for travelling and fighting. That was something I knew about, only too well. Food dumps had to be planted in advance of a push forward, as men soon became listless and demoralised if their energy levels fell too low.

What we do know is that Eli survived the battle because he did not die until 26 August, but what he did between 23 June and the day he died is unknown. He was on the losing side and after the battle was over, there must have been groups of Empire soldiers wandering around: lost in every interpretation of the word. They were behind their line, but it was a flimsy front that had been broken in very many places.

This battle was a complete disaster for the Empire and marked the beginning of the end. On the morning that the Second Battle of the Piave River started, at least 20,000 soldiers from the Empire died. They were trying to cross over to the east side of the river and were killed by swollen floodwaters and heavy fire from the Italians and their allies. Fire with which the Italians had started battering the soldiers of the Empire, on the same day, at 2.30am.

As he forced some breakfast down in a trench somewhere on the mountains near the village of Enego close to where his gravestone now lies among the weeds, Eli Vogel didn't realise it that, like his own, the Empire's day were numbered.

While in my bath, I translated the poem by Nico Bertoncello from Bassano del Grappa, which I has seen hanging from a tree beside the gravestone. A verse from this poem reads:

'Fatigue and sweat in the height of summer
Of a hard war and dying
That would end in November
But they did not leave you time
To see peace bloom
Because hate knows no secrets
And strikes with eagle claws'

This was so true: Eli missed seeing 'peace bloom' by only two months. Fighting ended on 4 November 1918. There were 400,000 deaths on the Austro-Hungarian side with 1,200,000 wounded, in these mountains and on the Veneto. For Italy and its allies, there were 650,000 dead and 950,000 wounded.

Eli Vogel was just one of the nearly half a million soldiers who died trying to keep those mountains and valleys within the Empire. Of that number, about 40,000 Jewish soldiers died fighting for their country, a place where they were held in high esteem. So much so that there were 76 Rabbis in the army, with a rank of captain, and Jewish soldiers were allowed to mark their High Holidays in prayers held on the battlefield before they went on to fight.

Just as the story of Dana T. Mudd, the glider pilot whose picture I saw in Groesbeek, is imprinted on my mind; so now, for me, Eli Vogel will never be forgotten.

Did locals, who felt the need to finish what the battle didn't quite do, shoot him? Were there formal skirmishes led by Italian regiments that were designed to eliminate stragglers? Why wasn't he taken as a prisoner of war? Who erected his gravestone? Did he die alone without his squad around him? Where was his nearest Rabbi when he needed him? Did his parents receive news of his death? How old was he? Was he married? My questions are endless, but I am glad I came across his grave. Finding out about him helped me understand more about the war that had raged in this beautiful place.

Wandering round after one of the bloodiest battles on the Italian Front, exhausted, and with his belt being tightened by the day, I only hope that, near the end, he had other people with whom to speak Yiddish, and that along with the other 9 million military deaths in World War One their souls will always be 'bound among the living.'

It may be perverse to mention that had he survived he might have ended up with a recognised pathology like 'shell shock', 'explosion shock', 'gas shock' or 'burial shock.' All of which were the result of the new forms of warfare used in or introduced by that most terrible of wars.

Sadly, for Italy, their allies reneged on many of their promises when the war was over, leaving them with far fewer spoils than expected. This, in part, caused Italy to side with Germany in the next war. The Italians had also suffered massive losses in the belief that 'It is better to live one single day as a lion than 100 years as a sheep.' This piece of graffito is preserved, even today, on a wall surrounded by rubble in the battle zone of the Italian Front as a reminder of the bravery displayed by the foot soldiers, despite some of the most disastrous leadership imaginable.

7: The Night Before Busking

The next morning, I left Bassano del Grappa with a heavy heart. From my hotel at the top of the town, I looked back longingly on the mountains that had been my home for many days. I also knew, after my bath-time reading, that Eli Vogel's grave was a reminder of what horrors took place up there.

Now, everything had changed. There was flat land in front of me and the sun was out. The carnage of a far-off war would still be echoing around the rest of the Veneto, but somehow I imagined that the sun might make it easier to bear. That was wishful thinking; I had to face up to it and move on. I was heading south and the end was in sight, if only I could keep my mind strong.

This was the first day that I had been encouraged by the weather forecast to wear shorts. Crossing the wooden Ponte Vecchio one more time, I felt another wrench as I turned left at the end and headed south. Just then I bumped into a cyclist who was waiting for his friends. We had the usual conversation about where I was going and what I was doing, but then he asked me why I was walking all that way. The reasons that I gave in Germany about my heart, retirement, general health and charity did not wash with him at all. His face remained blank. Searching for a way to sum up my intensions that would mean something to him, I edged the conversation towards my love of Italy, especially the town of Santa Vittoria, in Le Marche. Suddenly, his face lit up and he gestured to his heart. 'Ah, you love the place and the people, that is why you are walking all that way,' he said, with tears welling up in his eyes.

That was the breakthrough I needed to make him appreciate what I was doing. His hand gestures told me his feelings. Crossing his body with his right arm, he tapped his heart with a clenched fist and then, immediately afterwards, he cut the air with his right hand as if karate chopping some invisible wood or shuffling a deck of cards on to the floor. As he chopped the air with one hand, he placed the other firmly on my shoulder. I felt the electricity of his passion for my journey. Reading his gestures, I assumed they meant 'For the love of our land and its people, you are walking a very long way.' I couldn't have summed it up better myself. This gave me a renewed energy and sense of purpose. He had helped me start a new phase of my adventure. I was on my way again.

I walked beside roads that day because, if there were cycle tracks, the signs and directions to them were missing. In the Trentino it was all so easy: the tracks were of a high quality and the signposts were easy to follow, but here it was as if cyclists had to keep to the roads. It was noisy, but it did give me a chance to see more of the life in villages and towns. On one billboard I saw a poster for Procol Harum, a favourite band of mine from the 1960s. They were soon to play in concert at Padua. I wondered whether I should have included A Whiter Shade of Pale in my busking song list. Anyway, it got me humming it for a few miles, which staved off the hunger pains at about 11am.

My original intention was to stop that night at Cittadella, but since I wanted to do some busking at Padua, I calculated that if I could make this a very long day (25 miles) I could get to Piazzola Sul Brenta, which would leave only 13 miles to cover the next day into Padua. I could then have a sleep and a rehearsal before I hit the streets to sing my songs. With that in mind, I cancelled my booking at Cittadella and made another one at Casarosa Farmhouse B& B, on the Padua side of Piazzola Sul Brenta. All this was decided while I stopped for coffee in the village of Cartigliano where I was served some oozingly fresh triangles of pizza with my coffee. Of course, when I took a few more for the road, I only had in mind the 3400 calories a day that I needed to consume.

Now in the open countryside, I seemed to spend hours walking along roads that were either flanked by jasmine hedges or fields of maize (sweetcorn), as high as me. The maize plants were different shades of green, depending on the way that the light shone on them. At their tip the fronds were blood red, waving in the breeze. Sometime after Tezze Sul Brenta, I stopped for lunch in a roadside restaurant that was packed with business people. I chose a typical risotto-type dish from the Veneto, which consisted of black rice cooked in a savoury stock, flecked with pieces of feta-style cheese and mint leaves. It was delicious and was quickly added to my list of favourite dishes of the journey. The TV in the restaurant was showing Sky News and it teleported me back into reality. Enough of World War One, apples, eagles and marmots: tomorrow was the UK referendum concerning the possibility of leaving the EU. I felt a sudden bolt of panic shoot through me.

I toggled my attention between the TV screen and my phone, on which I caught up with the goings on while I had been in the mountains. I noticed that Nigel Farage had said recently to Kevin Maguire of the Mirror that: 'a 52-48 referendum would be unfinished business by a long way. If the Remain campaign wins two-thirds to one-third that ends it.' This gave me hope that in a close-run result it was accepted that the loser would want another attempt at convincing the public of their case. A few little hints and comments that I picked up along the way in the Veneto led me to believe that some people in Italy were slightly envious of the Leave campaign's attempt to break free from the EU, but I convinced myself that I was picking up the wrong vibes or that something was getting lost in translation.

On the TV news, with the sound turned down as is usual in Italian restaurants, correspondents seemed to be discussing the poster that read 'Breaking Point – the EU has failed us all.' It showed Nigel Farage standing in front of a picture of thousands of hopeful, male immigrants heading in the direction of the UK from Europe. My stomach sank at this hateful poster, but I wondered how it was being received at home as my Facebook feed seemed to be packed with friends and their friends who backed this kind of closed door, enough is enough, message. It was all part of the 'Make Britain Great Again' campaign led by the barking dogs of UKIP and the other Leave organisations.

On that day, 22 June 2016, I was watching a restaurant TV, on which Farage was ending his campaign with a final battle cry: 'The people versus the Establishment.' It was all very convincing, if you accepted his logic. Have a dig at the out-of-touch lads from Eton that ran our country, and the stream of politicians before them, who had left people feeling that no one had their interests at heart. If that was you, all you had to do was 'vote leave.' So convinced was he that people harkened to his rallying call that he proclaimed: 'Brexit voters would, "crawl over broken glass" to get down to that poll.' He called on those who had never voted before to grasp the opportunity to make a difference.

I left the restaurant worried about the vote but feeling that somehow even if it was a close-run thing the debate would go on. Meanwhile, I had a more pressing problem. I still had about five hours more walking to do and it was getting hotter. At 12 noon, it was already 30 degrees. I was beginning to ask myself if I should pray for rain again.

The afternoon's walk was a real feat of endurance. Much of the way, I was beside the main road but towards Piazzola I turned off towards the River Brenta again. The surface of the water was quite still and I could see reflected in it the darkening blue, late afternoon, sky which was only slightly splintered by thin wisps of white cloud. The landscape was entirely flat with a tree line that came right down to the river's edge on the west bank. A calm pastoral scene as befitted an evening in early summer.

As I came near to Piazzola Sul Brenta, I could see the church spire at Campo San Martino, high above the tallest trees. It was 6pm and I still had some way to go before I reached Casarosa, but I felt near enough to start looking forward to a big meal. However, as I turned right to cross over the Brenta on quite a busy bridge, the energy started to ebb away from my legs and my journey was reduced to a snail's pace. It was 7.30pm by the time I had walked the final three miles. At any other time of the day it would have taken about an hour, or less, to walk that far, but in my condition it took another 30 minutes on top of that.

Casarosa really was a pink farmhouse. As I walked up the drive the sun was fading fast, the edges of the sky were turning pink and the hay bailer was working at full speed in the field beside me. Dogs from the farm were trying to round me up; I was too jaded to even rebuke their advances of treating me like a sheep. Twenty-five miles was about my limit for a day with the pack that I was carrying, especially since by mid-afternoon it had made my shoulders feel as if they had been pummelled by a giant.

Apparently, the chance of finding anywhere to eat nearby was nil, but my host was kind enough to produce some bread, cheese and a drink of juice. Slim pickings but welcome enough, as I was too tired to eat a bigger meal. By half past eight, I had eaten, washed and was in bed ready to sleep. As I drifted off, I was consoled by the fact that I only had to walk 13 miles the next day, the UK referendum tomorrow was surely going to be a success for Remain, I would probably become nominated for International Busker of the Year 2016 – 'I maiali potrebbero volare,' (If pigs could fly) as no Italian would say.

8: Padua and the EU referendum

On 23 June 2016, at six minutes to one, I reached the 1000-mile (1600km) point. Two days south of Bassano del Grappa, I stood in an ordinary road on the outskirts of Padua in about 35 degrees heat. Checking my phone for the exact distance, I found a bollard that marked the spot, just beyond a warning triangle for motorists to inform them that there was a strong chance that an older school boy with a brief case would shortly be leading a small girl with her own bag, out onto the road, and that in every likelihood they would be running. Funny that in England the same kind of school warning sign depicts an older girl (or mother) leading a small boy: the female walking and the boy running to a standstill behind her. Neither is carrying a bag of schoolbooks.

Wanting to shout out to every passer-by that I had just walked 1000 miles from England and that this spot marked the achievement, I was forced to spend a moment in quiet reflection because, as dictated by the Italian lunchtime rules, there were almost no passers-by. A solitary man on a bicycle kindly took my photograph and quickly left me to my revelry.

When I told people before I had started my walk that I planned to busk along the way, I got replies that revealed their disbelief. 'I didn't know you could sing?' 'Have you had singing lessons?' They always tried to make these questions sound as casual and non-threatening as possible, but I knew just what they meant.

To begin with, even I thought I was biting off more than I could chew, but as 21 April approached, I developed the opposite view that not having done something before was the very reason to do it now.

'You're a long time dead,' had been a favourite catch phrase of my Mum's, but now my Buddhist beliefs kicked in. I began rehearsing a reply about having an unfailing faith in my capacity to do anything, regardless of my past. I looked forward to delivering this homily if conversations along these lines ever went beyond the first base. Instead, they usually ended in polite laughter about the fact that crowds on the pavement would be more likely to pay me to go away than stay and listen.

The flames of this idea were fanned one night when, walking back home from Hebden Bridge station, after being away in Sheffield for work, I saw a young man juggling in the park. He introduced himself as Hutch. Falling into a conversation, he told me that he was a professional street artist, busker mainly, but now he was broadening his repertoire by learning how to juggle and that he needed to be outside to practise reaching the heights required to attract a bigger audience. The fact that it was dusk gave everything an added sense of magic, because his clubs lit up as they soared above the trees near the edge of the park. Also, I noted this piece of practical advice: 'Always busk at lunchtime because people in the street are likely to have time to stand around, unlike in the early evening when they are rushing home to see their families.'

I conjured up a picture of me singing passionately to a small crowd of polite pedestrians (typically Dutch, Germans or Austrians) who, while munching on hearty granary rolls, would be listening intently to my songs while simultaneously reading the cards that stood up around my hat, brimming with Euros. These cards told them about my walk and the charities to which they could donate.

After this divinely apposite meeting with the juggler, who I believed, rather fancifully, to have been placed there for my benefit, I bought a ukulele - handmade in Hebden Bridge by a craftsman and absolute enthusiast - and set about choosing the songs to sing.

I vowed to be positive about this somewhat tangential plan that grew out of and obscured my original objective. It ran alongside 'the walk project', like a small boy on the pavement chasing his relatives who were in their car beginning to drive home after Christmas. The running boy waved, laughed, gurned and generally refused to be ignored.

After weeks of dipping into Spotify playlists, I settled on a clutch of songs themed around leaving home, travelling, walking and arriving, and with an 'on the road' appeal (mainly for me, I have to admit), such as Roy Bailey's version of a John Tams song, 'Rolling Home' or more famous ones that mirrored my era and general preoccupations such as Bob Dylan's 'My Back Pages.'

From then on, my walk preparations were notched up a gear. There were certainly 'crimson flames tied through my ears,' as I spent my planning time 'using ideas for my maps.' Eagerly, I wrote out the words, learned the ukulele chords and practised them in solitary confinement. It was during this time that I found a wonderfully enthusiastic singing teacher, in Hebden Bridge, called Rebecca who seemed to appreciate what I was trying to do. In the limited time available between her performances in cabarets onboard cruise ships, she tutored me in street performance. I learned how to project my voice and the key to sing in if I wanted to attract an audience in the open air. In the end, about a week before leaving home, I was still nervous but dedicated to giving it my best.

In my darker moments, I wanted to back out of the singing project, but I had told so many people about it, the small boy on the pavement kept waving. I couldn't let the nagging voices in my head take centre stage. They told me in loud tones several times a day: 'You are soooo not ready,' 'No one will like your songs', 'You're just an old guy with a silly dream of busking through Europe – get a life!' 'Fool, stick to the main job of walking: for your age – that's enough to worry about.'

It was only in the week before I left that the main balloon of my foolishness inflated to its full size. The ukulele was not going to fit in, or on top of, my rucksack! There it lay on the floor in its hard, black case refusing to behave. I tried everything but the cold fact was that, with all that I needed to take, which amounted to 18kg of necessary equipment, I was not going to be able to carry my own accompaniment.

'Why did it take me so long to realise? How was I going to explain this to friends and family? How could I deflate this ever-expanding balloon of stupidity?' The lucky thing was that no one really bothered.

My paranoid mind was convinced that anyone's disbelief about me walking to Italy would easily extend to their scepticism about me singing through Europe. I'm sure that they might also have imagined that I could present the very reason for people abroad to welcome Brexit (or Britex as, in my solitary state, I erroneously referred to it while walking – sounding a bit like a new material for men's underpants made of a mixture of Bri-nylon and Airtex) on the basis that if this was what the UK had to offer; it might be better to be rid of them as soon as possible. The only person who felt my pain was Kate, but at this stage she just seemed to want me to make a start in the best possible shape and if that meant jettisoning the ukulele, then, sadly, so be it.

I promised myself that even without my instrument, I would find the opportunity to entertain my fellow Europeans with a small collection of pure unaccompanied delights. They would realise in an instant all that I stood for, was doing and had prepared for them. It would be the singing equivalent of the juggler's clubs rotating gracefully in the air, lighting up the sky above the trees at dusk.

But now I was here and by dusk, I planned to be in Padua to begin my busking career. I had walked 10 miles to reach the 1000-mile mark and I was now on the last stretch into the city centre.

All day, I had been thinking about the EU referendum: how it was going and what last-minute enticing offers, on both sides, were being announced from the steps of the battle buses. I was possessed by a twin-fold sense of dread: I was panicked that between warming up my voice in the shower, as recommended by my singing teacher, and the short walk to find my busking spot, my voice might disappear altogether; and that the sense of camaraderie with my fellow Europeans, which I had enjoyed so much, might be ruined by the outcome of voting taking place today. There was a palpable ache in the pit of my stomach.

The fact that I was only just about to begin my street singing life was due to the almost daily rain, and the absolute lack of people around at lunchtime in all of the places I had walked through – not for a lack of desire. The trainee juggler's advice about lunchtime gigs was, in reality, only relevant to the kind of singers who turn up in city squares with speakers and microphones. Not for the rain-soaked, solitary footpads, like me, whose only thoughts at lunchtime were of food and a rest after four to five hours of walking.

After finding my vastly discounted room at The Plaza Hotel, I showered, changed, and gathered my hat, information cards and pad of lyrics ready for the short walk to the Piazza dei Signori. I chose this square – apart from it being for gentlemen – because, in the early evening, it was likely to have plenty of folk strolling around and sitting down for aperitifs before their meal.

Walking through the streets of Padua in June, the evening's assault on my senses did little to calm my nerves. The shrill buzz of scooters, the insistence of car horns, the slap of warm summer air on my face and the snatched aroma of pizza seemed to both slacken my resolve and tighten my vocal cords. To keep buoyant, I kept telling myself that a man, albeit without a ukulele, but with the well-rehearsed opening notes from Steve Ashley's song called 'Best Wishes' was bound to command the attention of the after-work drinkers and relaxed tourists.

Soon Via Nicolo turned into Via Dante Alighieri and then in a few more metres I looked left at the enormity of the Piazza dei Signori with its hordes of already well-oiled tourists. In all directions, people seemed to belong; they were nesting cosily in bars and restaurants in a way which suggested that a lone traveller with a song would be shooed away at the first opportunity for interrupting their night out.

Instantaneously, I felt the blood drain from my limbs and the sensation of my internal organs shrivelling caused me to stand dumfounded. Sadly, I realised that my vaulted ambitions had led me astray so badly that if I didn't get a grip on the situation, I was going to end up like a spent matchstick underfoot on the pavement.

I quickly formed a plan. I was going to tour the Piazza's perimeter to look for nooks and crannies in which to perform to a more modest-sized crowd. Then after staking my claim to a piece of pavement, I would sing one or two songs to see how I got on. If it went well, I might move to a smaller square, somewhere else, to make a more confident entrance. Unfortunately, very professional looking outfits with trendy clothing, instruments, speakers and microphones had already bagged all the available performance spaces. My lightweight mufti, to be worn every evening for three months, was no match in these X Factor stakes.

At last I stood nearly directly under the Clock Tower at one end of the piazza, outside what is now the City Hall, looking all the way down its vast expanse. I got myself ready by placing my hat on the pavement, arranging my cards around it and easing my way into a comfortable standing position. If I had known then that I had pitched up in such a fabulously historic spot I might have slunk away without emitting a sound. The blue-faced astronomical clock above me chimed the hours 1 to 24, showed the phases of the moon and the place of the sun in the zodiac. The original clock was erected in 1344 but marauding soldiers from Milan destroyed it when they stormed the city. The replica above me was positioned in 1428.

The opening notes of my first song, 'Best Wishes', were delivered with all the confidence of a snail crossing a motorway. Thankfully, they were drowned out the moment they were uttered by an unexpected rush of traffic from my right. Coughing and pretending that I was just warming up, I began again with slightly more gusto than before. I struggled through to the end feeling bruised. People were walking past, crossing the road, or generally ambling around but none, it seemed, took a blind bit of notice of me. What about, I asked myself, 'the tender lyrics, the rousing chorus and the beautiful images that lay like golden nuggets amongst the verses?' My education in busking inflated in those few moments like a universe expanding from its singularity. The noisy echoes of the Milanese horsemen had faded into an aimless hubbub of indifference.

The teenage son of a friend had given me some advice about busking some months before I left, which came to mind at that moment: 'remember to sing as if you were talking to yourself. Just get on with it regardless.' So not daunted (too much), I began to sing 'Rolling Home', giving it all the passion of someone who was yearning for home. Nothing. Not even a quizzical stare. People on the move kept on moving as if Brexit had already happened and a cold shoulder was going to be the response whenever the English tongue was voiced.

There was only one thing for it: Solsbury Hill. I had seen a singer try this in Manchester in March and people were drawn by the rhythm and energy of the lyrics. Admittedly, he was a good guitarist and had a pre-amp, speakers and a mic, but as the sun was fading in one of the most spiritual and romantics squares possible, I had nothing more to lose. Just as I got to the bit where I was walking out of the machinery and my heart was going boom, boom, boom and before that marvellous moment when the eagle says (for the second time) 'grab your things I've come to take you home': a great gust of wind whistled down the length of Via Monte di Pieta and blew all of my information cards high up into the air.

Instinctively, I stopped singing and dashed to gather them up by diving in amongst the legs of passing pedestrians before they were trodden underfoot. My bubble burst, my throat closed up in frustration and my resolve disappeared down a nearby drain. Above me, the Astral Clock on the clock tower struck the hour at 7pm and I almost felt its metal full moon swing out into view. I knew it was a full moon because the real one had entranced me the previous night: in pink majesty, on the horizon, above the fields.

My degree of insignificance was sealed absolutely when a passing Italian woman of about my age stooped down to help me pick up my cards. Standing to read the one in Italian, and before handing it back to me, she said sensitively 'There you are dear. Oh, I see – you were singing. I'm sorry but I didn't hear you.' I curbed myself from saying 'No. Neither did anyone else.'

It wasn't long before I was seated at a table outside a café called Il Gancino, facing the Piazza Duomo, only a stone's throw from the scene of my busking, but far enough away for me to reflect on my voyage of undoing. I nursed my ego with an aperitivo of Aperol Spritz and a plate of wonderful snacks. I realised that to expect people to listen to an unaccompanied singer, the performer has to be of an almost operatic standard and dressed the part. Alternatively, you need an instrument and a batch of songs that people of all nationalities will recognise.

In fact, you have to do and be all the things that I was not, which is why I collected nothing by way of donations for my causes. Failure on such a grand scale – here in the one of the oldest cities in Italy, the setting for Shakespeare's 'Taming of The Shrew,' the home of the University at which Galileo lectured and the place that once hosted an audience of 300,000 to listen to Mussolini in the Prato della Valle – was truly humbling.

'Oh well,' I told myself, 'At least there were no rotten tomatoes thrown or keys to the local stocks rattled.' After a second Aperol and another chime of the Astral Clock, I was resigned to the fact that busking could be ticked off on the bucket list but only with an IKEA-sized pencil. With that I found the nearest restaurant, the Osteria dal Capo, which as luck would have it, was wonderful. I rewarded myself with wild boar prosciutto, pasta and beans, and a beef stew. My tight throat relaxed again, quite quickly, after a liberal dose of red wine taken, of course, mainly for its medicinal properties. Over my meal, I debated (with myself, of course) which would prove to be the greatest failure: my singing or the UK referendum on EU membership? Only time would tell, and I didn't have very long to wait for the answer.

9: Everything changed

Kate telephoned me before 6am in the morning to tell me the news. The Leave vote had won 51.9% to 48.1%. Bleary-eyed and brimful of anxiety, I recalled what Nigel Farage had said about the same sort of figures, but the other way around, 'a 52-48 referendum would be unfinished business by a long way.' I wondered if he would still be saying that today?

Shell-shocked and trying to focus on getting ready for a 25 mile walk, bearing in mind that mine was a largely sleepless night owing to the fact that the air conditioning was broken and the forecast was for another very hot day, I said goodbye and packed up ready to leave. I wanted to cover; at least, the first 10 miles before the heat became unbearable.

It seemed, on that historic morning, that it took as long for me to get packed up as it did for David Cameron to resign and Nigel Farage to say that it was a mistake for the Leave campaign to promise to spend 350 million pounds extra a week on the NHS. Events were moving fast. Whatever happened from now on, it began to dawn on me that nothing would ever be the same again. What would people's reaction be in Italy, I wondered? It did not take me long to find out.

I left my room at 6.15am and went straight to the reception desk to complain about the broken air conditioning. The disgruntled night porter said that 'this has been an ongoing problem,' and that after last night when he had only managed about two hours' sleep and despite that fact he had gone to a storeroom and found an electric fan to keep him cool, 'they would have to sort it out, now.' Selfishly I thought, he judged that the management would have to mend the broken air conditioning because he had been inconvenienced, not because dozens of guests like me had had sleepless nights.

'Anyway,' he said by way of lightening an awkward situation, 'what are you still doing here. I thought Britain had left Europe?' I left him laughing at his own funny quip and went outside looking for breakfast and the fastest route away from Padua.

I passed my busking spot (there was absolutely no-one around except for a rather noisy road sweeping van) and shortly after, the restaurant from last night. Everything came flooding back: the feelings of being a backwoods' boy singing before a clean, spruced-up, civilised populace, or a children's entertainer who had been booked for the wrong audience. After standing at the counter in a backstreet bar for a cappuccino and two brioches, I walked into the Prato della Valle, in which Mussolini had addressed the masses. It was deserted and covered in shadows, as the sun had not yet risen high enough to make a day of it. Then I followed the SS516 out of town.

My plan was to reach Legnaro before the rush hour traffic built up, and the heat made staying on the busy main road impossible. I planned to take a cross-country route on minor roads and tracks, thereafter. After Legnaro when I couldn't stand the constant noise and commotion of the traffic heading for Padua anymore, I turned left into the Via Ardoneghe.

Ahead of me lay nothing but fields, villages and small towns, all of which were beginning to shimmer in the heat - it seemed to deaden every noise around me, as if the sound waves were dancing in slow motion. It was over 30 degrees and rising. To keep the sun off my head, I was forced to wear my Tarp hat, but its material was far too thick, which meant that I was sweltering. In shady spots I could take my hat off and let the air get to my dripping head, but these cooler moments were rare. Experience helped me to calculate that I needed at least a litre of water every two hours just to keep going.

I had run out of water by about 11am and was desperate to find something to drink. Stumbling across a small village grocer's shop, I was waved over to the concrete apron outside it by two men who were simply chatting together in the shade. I was drawn to them partly because I wanted to remember what it felt like to just sit and pass the time of day.

Joining them was like emerging from a sauna and stepping into the relatively cool veranda of a roadside café. It was in fact a ramshackle grocer's shop, on the ground floor of a plain building where every other window or door was shuttered to keep the heat out. It had no sign to denote a shop, as if someone had decided to hold a garage sale and gone to the wholesalers to buy things to sell. None of that worried me at all, because it was just bliss to stop, rest in the shade and talk to someone.

The younger man, Diego, spoke English, but the shopkeeper, Giuseppe, talked in Italian only. They wanted me to take my rucksack off, sit down with them and drink a couple of cans of pop that Giuseppe had discovered after rummaging around in his store for a couple of minutes. Despite being soaked with sweat, suffering with sore, roasting hot feet and nervous about walking any more that day in the scorching heat, I found my break at the grocer's shop an idyllic diversion. Here were two men who seemed genuinely interested in what I was doing as opposed to the silent passers-by in Padua, for whom I was nothing but nondescript wallpaper.

After a brief, humorous interlude about my presence in mainland Europe after yesterday's vote, Giuseppe wanted to know how I had managed to afford this journey. I got the feeling that he would like to have done something adventurous with his life if only the funds had been there. He was momentarily deflated when I said that 'I worked on for three more years after I was due my state pension, so I saved that pot of money for this project.' He replied, quietly under his breath, 'you must get big pensions in the UK.'

As a relief, the rest of our conversation was about the route ahead and how I should manage with the heat. Underneath, though, I was suffering from the realisation that compared to pensioners in Italy, I seemed like a plutocrat. There was the UK, as a wealthy nation, striding around on the international stage, in a seemingly cavalier manner, casting ourselves off from our fellow Europeans to seek our fortunes across the world. Any semblance of loyalty to a common cause, which the UK might have had with the other 27 countries of the EU, seemed to Giuseppe to have evaporated in front of his eyes in the scorching heat of Brexit fever: those same eyes which told me that the Italian economy was precarious enough without us causing them to be even worse off.

Meanwhile, Diego's charming manner rescued me from my doldrums about the Leave vote; his conversation was filled with optimism and warmth. At first, he called me 'a crazy man,' but when that did not quite crystallise his feelings he changed it to 'the strong crazy man of England.' I felt forgiven. We may have voted out but I was in Italy, I was crazy and I was chatting with them; that was all that mattered in the mid-day, melting heat.

With their support, I plucked up the courage to begin walking again by taking a route that would mean even fewer cars and some stretches of trees that might shield me from the blistering afternoon sun. Diego made me his friend on Facebook, we posed for a selfie together, and then we all shook hands manfully as if to say: 'at least we want to maintain solidarity across Europe.' Sadly, by the time I had eaten my lunch even that was looking an impossible fantasy.

After another hour or so, I had to stop for some food. I decided to have an extended lunch break, hoping that it would be cooling down when I started walking again. The heat depressed me. I imagined being beaten by the weather. There were not enough places to get water and I couldn't carry all that I might need. Meanwhile, the atmosphere was constantly oppressive. The air closed in on me like a warm unwelcome blanket trying to smother me in kindness to make up for the weeks of rain that I had suffered. This hot, nurturing cloak was sapping my strength and killing my spirit.

I dived into a restaurant, which was still feeding a handful of people gathered near the TV, and asked for some food typical of the Veneto and lots of it, in a desperate tone that suggested it had to last for a couple of hours at least.

As I ate my way through the entire breadbasket topped with thin slices of salami, the silent but flickering TV on the wall opposite told a fascinating version of the Brexit Saga. It was like a silent movie, but without a Charlie Chaplin figure, with a derby on his head, and swinging a cane on his arm, appearing in shot. The newscast consisted of politicians in Germany, Italy and Spain looking worried and concerned in their separate countries. They were getting in and out of cars, walking quickly up and down steps in front of impressive buildings and speaking expressively into large microphones to squads of reporters who were waving big fluffy microphones around and recording what was said on their mobiles.

I was halfway through my seafood risotto when it dawned on me what they were saying: their gestures told me that they were appealing for calm. They were trying to do their best to staunch the flow of events, which might, if left alone, cause a domino effect across Europe. It was as if an amoeba in a petri dish had been lanced with a sharp implement and, in shock, was desperate to seal its single-celled membrane to preserve its insides. We had spilled out of its skin and were now looking in from the outside. Even if we tried to get back in at a later stage, we would always be the ones that caused the rupture. Although the political puppets on the silent TV soldiered on, I could hear the low thunderous growl of big dogs waking up.

When Italy's prime minister Matteo Renzi started to speak at last, someone near the screen turned up the sound. He spoke about the failing economy in the country and tried to convince the viewers that staying in the EU was the country's chance to become financially stable. He wasn't given an opportunity to finish his little homily before someone else switched the TV back to silent and a wave of cynicism and mutterings about Italy voting out, in the footsteps of the UK, swirled round the room.

By the time I had started on my horsemeat steak (another delicacy of the Veneto), the TV had turned its attention to the Euros. I noted, when I had finished the meat course and was spooning up a panna cotta, the attention given to football was greater than that to Brexit. This proved that, in Italy at least, Farage, Johnson and Gove (important as they considered themselves to be) would always have to give way to football. I paid my bill feeling bloated but in the knowledge that the sun would, by now, have slipped down behind the tree tops, which, ironically, was a bit like how I felt after watching the politicians struggling to stop the dominoes from falling over.

The road to Correzzola was long and straight, in true Roman style, and my plan worked beautifully. I was able to escape the direct blare of the sun by walking on the tree side of the road. At one point, coming out from under the trees, I crossed the River Bacchiglione, near Pontelongo, which at that stage of its life had been made into a canal, before its waters spilled out into the lagoon near Venice. This was the river that I had last seen running though Padua. I loved it when I saw friends again.

While on the move in the morning, I had booked dinner, bed and breakfast at the Agriturismo Fondo San Benedetto (an Agriturismo in Italy is basically a B&B on a working farm) and the lure of the homemade food it advertised beckoned me down the road like a siren. I could feel myself getting sucked into a world where food and water were the only things that mattered. My body was a machine that needed those things to keep it moving forward. These two elements had to be present in the correct proportions for me to survive. Having had a large meal at lunchtime made no difference: I was ready for more to eat by the time I stumbled into the Fondo at about 7pm.

Despite being mentally drained by the heat, I was happy to remember that I only had to walk about 12 miles the next day to reach a town called Adria. I had not had a day's rest since Trento and did not plan to take another one until I reached Ravenna, so this short walk to Adria was the next best thing. Anyway, I liked the sound of the town because despite being inland by about 14 miles, it was once an important seaport. Greek and Etruscan traders helped to change a small farming village into one of the most important ports on the east side of what we now call Italy. In fact, the town boasts that the Adriatic Sea is named after it. Sadly, for the town, over the decades, the silt deposited by the River Po gradually created a stretch of land that cut the town off from the coast.

10: Venice beckons

The following day's journey to Adria was a very difficult one. The narrow space allowed for walking alongside the road was perilous. The volume of cars coming towards me was frightening. I began to perfect a series of Italian hand gestures to show my appreciation for them not actually maiming me. Firstly, I tried the fist across the heart sign, which was designed to show my love for them; it finished with a flourish, as my fist came away from my heart it opened out into a flat palm of peace offered to them as they sped past. One or two smiles from drivers proved that they liked this one.

My second Italian gesture was the zipped mouth one to show an ultimate liking for something. In this case, my slowly, pressed-together fingers were drawn across my mouth to indicate how supremely kind they were not to commit violence on me. With these handmade talismans, I made my way towards Adria gingerly, step by step.

The trouble is that Italy has no joined-up thinking about pedestrians or cyclists. There are some good cycle tracks beyond Trentino, but they are few and far between. The Italians venerate the kind of cyclists who are mostly men in tight, brightly coloured Lycra. They race proudly along roads with no need of a cycle track because cars give them the space they command, but the casual, going-to-see-your-mum, cyclist or shopping-trip cyclist has to risk their lives on a daily basis. They often cycle against the flow of the traffic just to make their presence felt in quite a dramatic way.

In Germany, you can just hear the planning department conversation when the building of a new road is being discussed. 'Ah, so you want to build a road from A to B. Very good. Will the cycle track be beside the road or set back among the fields for maximum enjoyment?' 'What, you haven't drawn a cycle track on your plan? Then we are sorry; these plans are not going to be passed until you have. Good morning.'

By contrast, it is the wonderful, unplanned, chaos of Italy that I love. My only hope on the walk was to stay alive long enough to enjoy it. Strange, but at a local level, Italy can produce an unbelievable level of perfection. In Reggio Emilia, for example, there is a school system for young children, founded by Loris Malaguzzi, which is world-famous for helping youngsters reach their potential through creativity and the arts. Unfortunately, across the rest of Italy children's early education rarely reflects this trail-blazing initiative.

Even in my accommodation, at the Fondo San Benedetto, the homemade food was magnificent: smoothies of apple, grapefruit and mint, fresh creamy yogurt, just baked bread and fig jam, and exceptional cakes made breakfast a heavenly experience. What is more, the air conditioning was in good working order: all proving that high quality can be achieved at a local level. It is just when projects require a wider consensus, collaboration and cooperation that things tend to fall apart a little.

My short walk to Adria the next day could have been my last. Sometimes, when faced with less than 20 miles to walk, I found that I lost momentum. It was hard to get going after the splendid breakfast and it was already nearly 30 degrees by the time I set off. Added to that, the sight of my boots was a constant reminder of how things (including me) were wearing down, as time passed. It would not be long, I was sure, before I got out the duct tape.

My journey consisted of hopping between watering holes and food stops, trying to keep out of the sun as much as I could. My first break was at a small town called Pegolotte with a very lively bar called The Wall (after the song by Pink Floyd), which I hoped was not an omen for me, metaphorically *hitting the wall* or after Brexit, *building the wall*. I could not bring myself to stop there but I had coffee opposite in the shade, just contemplating my next few hours in the Veneto cauldron.

Fortunately, by 11.30am, at Cavarzere, I came across the River Adige again. I recalled the days we had spent together in the Trentino. In fact, I had almost been at its birth as I came over the Reschia Pass into Italy from Austria. Now it was full, broad and slow: swaggering down to the sea, old and heavy with silt. My body told me it was time to take a long lunch break, so I found a café, with a veranda, on a quiet road, and lodged myself there for a couple of hours: drinking water and eating Panini. Every 20 minutes or so, a bus pulled up close to where I was sitting. It was a local shuttle, going to Venice.

My eyes glazed over every time a bus stopped. I wanted to abandon my walk, hop on the bus, see the American professor and his students, and then take an extended break wandering in the winding alleys on the main island. Had I not done enough to prove myself? Surely people would understand that the heat was impossible? Was this good for my heart? Wouldn't William Albert and all my other spirit followers appreciate a stay over in Venice?

One of the main things that made me want to abort was the ever-looming intended finishing date of 10 July (still 15 days away). Every plan I made had to fit in with that. It was a millstone round my neck. I reflected that the date was only set to make it easy for people to grasp the idea of what I was doing and arrange to meet me at the end. What was it to be – an extended trip to Venice with a chance to end it there, or not getting on the bus and carrying on with the plan?

It was 35 degrees by the digital clock on the Farmacia at 1.30pm, when I walked out of Cavarzere. My head was full of my mother's advice about everything – 'do your best, stick at it, and finish what you start.' Kate had also said at breakfast, standing on the towpath on the day that I left, jokingly (I hoped), 'don't come back if you don't finish.' Also, while sitting on my bus-stop veranda, I re-read all the encouraging emails, texts, messages and tweets that friends had sent me along the way saying what an inspiration I was and how they had decided to do something adventurous when they retired or how they wanted to raise money for their favourite charity by doing something like me. Tired, hot, heavy with the silt of old age, I decided to keep moving forward like the Adige. It was 5pm when I loped into Adria. It was still 35 degrees and I was reduced to drinking half of my water bottle and pouring the rest over my head.

After sleeping for a couple of hours, I sauntered into town for an Aperol Spritz and a large bowl of spaghetti with squid cooked in its own ink. I was eating at a table tucked into a little side alley that was bathed in the yellow light of street lamps, tinged by the glow of the dying sun.

I thought back to the struggles I had suffered just to walk to Adria that afternoon and the way that I had been helped greatly by the kindness of strangers. A university professor, who worked at Padua, was standing lookout at his front gate for children coming to his son's fifth birthday party. As soon as he saw me, he ran into his house and brought me out a litre bottle of cold spring water. We chatted and he hugged me in respect for what I was doing. Later, I stopped at a small market garden beside the road and asked if they sold drinks. The owner took me to the drinks machine, unlocked it and asked me to take whatever I wanted, 'free of charge, of course.' To them I was like a pilgrim. This helped me resurrect that way of thinking again. I had been trapped in the machine mindset with the sole ambition of delivering myself on a certain date. They helped me come back from that cul-de-sac and live more for the here and now.

In two days' time I would reach the Adriatic Sea. This magnificent corner of the Mediterranean had witnessed the comings and goings of the Venetian Empire for centuries and from whose waves characters from Homer and Shakespeare had been cast up on the sands of Illyria. From then on I would be walking along the Adriatic coast, through holiday resorts, all the way down to Ancona. I would be able to get all the water and food I needed, whenever I wanted it.

I went to bed convinced that seeing The Wall at Pegolotte had not been an omen for me; I had not hit it; though I was still not sure about Brexit and the wall Farage might need between him and all the men queuing up to come to the UK.

11: The Po Valley

There was a soft, light breeze stroking my face as I approached the River Po early the next morning. This was a moment of boundaries. The Po, the longest river in Italy, almost slices the country in two. Above it one could talk about being in the north of Italy, but after crossing it into Emilia-Romagna you were verging on the middle region that includes Le Marche. I was not aware of an actual North/South line but the crossing ahead of me felt significant. I guessed it was like the debate in England about whether the North began at the Watford Gap. Almost on cue, I spotted my first stork since I was on the outskirts of Heidelberg. It was circling, in long sweeps, above the warm wetlands around the River Po: a good place to stop after flying to the north of Italy from Africa.

It was Sunday morning on the 26 June and I was aiming for a town called Codigoro and an Agriturismo called Il Dosso. I was faced with a distance of nearly 25 miles, which gave me no time for an anxiety attack such as the one that welled up in me yesterday.

At its widest, the River Po is about 500m across. I guess that the bridge on which I walked was about 300m long. I was just doing some mental arithmetic about the bridge and its length, when a small Fiat car pulled up and the passenger in the front seat wound her window down. An attractive, fully inked, young Italian woman with lots of piercings – notably on her tongue and upper lip - called out: 'can we give you a lift?'

I bent down to see who 'we' meant. A young man with a full red beard was driving and behind, in a child-seat, was a baby who was gurgling away quite happily. If I was not, on principle, taking lifts, the thought of some lively company appealed to me. After I had explained why I was refusing her offer, she continued, 'well, can we give you some food?'

'That's very kind of you, but I have not long since had breakfast,' I said, then immediately regretted my choice of words - 'long since' was far too complicated for someone who was trying hard at her English.

'What about a lift to the end of the bridge?'

With every refusal she seemed more determined to be helpful. I began to feel that I should accept their next offer whatever it was. Luckily, she smiled enthusiastically and wished me all the luck in the world. As the Fiat sped off so as not to block the traffic, I calculated that it had only taken two days for the Brexit vote to drop out of any roadside conversation. I had just encountered unprompted, open-handed, love-filled European comradeship.

As soon as I came off the bridge, onto the tarmac proper, and made for Ariano Nel Polesine where I hoped to find a place open for lunch, the breeze became intermittent, the sun found its full strength and finding water became a priority. The only trouble in that was the scarcity of houses. Vast fields of maize and rice surrounded me, but I felt uneasy because I had very little chance of bumping into someone who could help me. There were some isolated trees at the side of the fields that I could head for when I wanted a rest, but that was about it in terms of respite. In the next hour, when walking became really difficult because of the incessant heat, I just set my sights on a shady tree. That was all I was doing: making for the tree to have a rest. In that way I covered a few miles until I saw a woman disappearing into a farm outbuilding. I called out to her for help and she was glad of a chat. Since she only spoke Italian, I did my best to tell her my story and ask for water. She went into her house and came back with a 1.5 litre bottle of cold water. It was like a miracle. I drank half of it standing beside her. She smiled.

I told her that I could spot the rice fields (the tall grassy leaves of the rice plant were by now a familiar iridescent green) and there were the thin canals criss-crossing the fields, which delivered the large volume of water needed for the rice plants to flourish. The other main crop confused me a little. I took it to be spinach but there was something not quite right with that theory. 'What was it?' I asked. She told me it was soya beans. Standing beside her, glugging my water and surveying rice and soya beans as far as the eye could see, I felt suddenly at home and content. It was one of those moments of feeling at one with the environment: a pilgrim's waypoint of sorts. On a quiet Sunday in June, with no one around except an immensely kind farmer, I was peacefully in the middle of endless fields containing millions of soya bean and rice plants. It was surreal but satisfying.

For the last two days, while walking near the rivers Adige and Po, I had been looking down at a different kind of pavement friend, or roadkill as some might call it. I had yet to see the dead creature in its entirety, I only came across bits of its remains strewn along the roadside or drying like cowpats in the middle of the road where the animal had been crushed under a car's wheel and its guts were still being picked over by carrion crows. When all of the soft-meat gizzards had been eaten, there was left a thick, leathery skin covered with gingery fur. Finally, there was always the tail looking like a thick, battered elasticated band. I just could not work out what it was. They were the size of a cat or small dog; too big to be a rat. Then, as I rested on the roadside under a walnut tree, Google gave me the answer.

They were the sun-dried remains of coypu. Italy had declared war on them. Farms were opened in Europe in the 1920s after coypu were imported from South America to breed for their fur. The demand for this kind of luxury dropped off in the era of the Great Depression and the coypu escaped from the dilapidated farms to spread over the whole of Italy and further afield into Europe. The landowners and farmers in the Veneto and Emilia-Romagna now hate coypu because they destroy riverbanks and canal sides with their extensive den digging, and they eat many of the valuable crops growing close by, such as maize. What is more, they cause massive problems in the rice paddy fields near the River Po. In South America alligators, large snakes and eagles eat them, but in the Po valley, without such predators, they have to be culled by traps, shotgun, and passing cars.

These cute-looking rodents multiply very quickly, with the females able to produce a litter of up to 12 young at a time. Confronted with this, my surreal experience of gazing out over peaceful soya and rice fields took on a different perspective. I discovered there are roughly 4.5 million people in Emilia-Romagna who live alongside over 1 million coypu, which are digging away in and around the waterways that cover most of this beautiful territory. The orangey-yellow incisors of these creatures from South America were slowly undermining the peaceful landscape, which I was observing on that glorious Sunday morning in June.

After an hour's lunch break in Ariano Nel Polesine, which on this Sunday was empty except for two men in the only café I could find open. This seemingly deserted town was situated alongside a tributary of the Po. As I approached the café I could see the banks of the river rising to a few meters above the road. It was as if, over the years, people had banked up the waterway right along its course. They must always be guarding against the degradation of the banking caused by the coypu in an attempt to stop the town being flooded. Life must be a constant battle against the rodent, possible flooding, and the need to siphon off enough water to irrigate the fields. No wonder then that regional targets are set for killing the animals. I read that a target to kill 300,000 coypu in 2016 was fairly typical for that area. In a small way, the 10 which I saw, squashed on the road, would have helped to meet the target.

The road to Codigoro was long, hot and unyielding. When I was about two-thirds along, I had to find some shelter, because I was feeling faint with the 35-degree heat. I even thought of breaking into an outhouse to get some shade, but instead I found a church with a large hall next to it. At the back was a small garden, which the sun could not reach in the afternoon. I settled down on a stone bench to have a nap. With my rucksack beside me, but looped over my wrist, I lay down, with some spare clothing for a pillow, feeling like a homeless person, a vagrant, or a tramp rather than a pilgrim. I was beyond caring. I knew when I started out again that I would need to knock on someone's door for water, but in that moment I was safe, shaded and at rest. On waking, I rang Kate for a much-needed pep talk and moral support, and then set off to find water.

A woman in a large house was sunbathing in her garden. I thought of leaving her alone but, looking up and down the road, there was no other house in sight. It took me some time to convince her, from the other side of a tall, fortified fence, to leave her sunbathing and fill my water bottles, but in the end she put on a robe on and fetched me a litre bottle from her refrigerator instead of filling my bottles from her tap. I felt like a real outsider when she handed me the bottle through the fence, as if I was a beggar at the gate (which in a way I was), and she was a bountiful lady.

I found that, subconsciously, my body always started to relax when my destination was close by. Thus, it was when approaching Codigoro. On entering the town, in the late afternoon, I began winding down. I felt successful in having survived another scorching day in the flat lands of the Po delta. There had been a car crash right in the middle of the main crossroads at the town's centre. I felt sorry for the unlucky participants in that accident because they were probably the only two cars to be using the road at that time; so quiet was the whole place on a Sunday afternoon. Just by way of checking, I asked a policeman, who was standing watch over the crashed vehicles, where my Agriturismo was. Unbelievably, he told me that Codigoro stretched a long way and that I wanted Pomposa Sud, which was another 8km away (5 miles). Apart from sitting down in the gutter and weeping, there was nothing to be done but wind myself up again and get moving. It was hard.

As dusk began to roll over the landscape, a silky, purple sheen coated the sky. It silhouetted, sharply, the farmhouses surrounded by conifers on the horizon. Meadows lying fallow were stained with a splattering of blood-red clover interspersed with sprays of tall Rough Hawksbeard that were now furred with seed heads ready to scatter. Rows of soya beans, which had grown thigh-high, being picked by labourers on their last gathering of the day. Many, of these migrant workers were already making their way off the land to get some rest before another backbreaking day on Monday.

At long last I arrived at Il Dosso. I had dinner with an Austrian woman called Anna, who was travelling alone with just a Lonely Planet Guide for company. I took to her immediately thanks to the blocks of purple and orange on her blouse, her shock of orangey-red hair, the purple spectacles on a chain round her neck, the dedication she showed to learning new things on her holiday, and her passion for telling people she met about what she had discovered. She was amazed that I had not planned to see the famous Abbey at Pomposa, which was on my way in the morning. The medieval wall paintings were reckoned to be magnificent. In keeping with my resurrected dedication to living for the moment as opposed to just finishing my walk, I decided to follow her advice as soon as I left the next day.

As she said, the church was a superb. It was a Benedictine Abbey, which dated back to the 9th century. I discovered that it was famous for frescoes depicting hell among other things. It is a treasure trove of documents, books and art from the Carolingian Dynasty, which was led at one time by Charlemagne, who I saw astride his horse in Nijmegen, Holland. One of the Benedictine monks, Guido Di Arezzo, who studied there, is credited with devising the musical notation on a stave of five lines that we still use today.

Nothing of what Anna told me really prepared me for the shock of the artwork depicting hell and The Day of Judgement. It took me some time to find these particular paintings because I failed to realise that they could only be seen on the way out. Of course, it dawned on me slowly. No matter what inspiration a member of the congregation might have received during their time of worship in the main part of the church, they had to walk out by passing the disturbing pictures of hell, just as a final reminder to heed the words of the priest. I had also failed to realise that in early Christian thinking, Jesus descended to hell on the day of judgement to liberate those who should not have been sent there or had repented while wandering around down there. Believers thought that heaven was not a place for humans until Jesus died on the cross, so everyone before that went to one or another level of hell. The ones that really deserved to be in heaven needed rescuing.

It was true the paintings really did imprint themselves on my mind. For many days, I carried with me a vision of a huge, devilish face, horns on its head, with a man and a woman disappearing into its mouth: one on each side of a terrible grin that stretched far wider than the creature's slit eyes. The man was trying to escape with arms outstretched while the woman looked resigned with her hands clasped in an attitude of prayer. I wondered what the artist had in mind when he placed the two characters in such contrasting poses?

All around the abbey were fields of soya beans. Here and there the soil was exposed to show how sandy it was. Of course, I remembered that it was silt deposited by the River Po. It was the same silt that had cut Adria off from the sea and ultimately caused the abbey to be abandoned by the monks because it had lost its contact with the coastline. I had seen this kind of agriculture, on sandy soil, in Holland, only this time there were no seashells intermingled with the grains of sand.

12: The Adriatic Sea and Death Valley

At 3pm precisely on 27 June, I emerged from a belt of woodland and saw the sea for the first time since getting off the P&O Ferry at the Europort in Holland. I had just snatched a quick lunch of mixed seafood and salad at a café on the other side of the trees bordering the beach. When realising the sea was so close I bolted down my food and headed for what was a free beach rather than a paying one with folded-up beds and limp umbrellas.

The Lido di Volano mesmerized me. Instead of a beach ready for the summer, I came across an enormous accumulation of driftwood in the form of whole trees, branches, roots, palm fronds, crafted timber; all intertwined by different types of rope and plastic. This matted tidewrack, which had become trapped following the winter storms in the cul-de-sac of the Adriatic, went south as far as I could see. Beach enthusiasts had even built cabins and BBQ areas out of the driftwood, but even these were abandoned as new layers of wreckage became draped over it all.

It was a different first sighting to the one I had imagined. There was no-one to be seen. The only sounds were the wind off the sea and the cicadas scratching their incessant music in the pine trees. It was beginning to rain. Huge drops of water hit the sand causing a battle-field of pockmarks. Visions of coming off the mountains, crossing the Veneto, walking down the coastline and mingling with all the holi-daymakers were lost among the debris.

I found a sandy footpath heading south and walked quickly on in search of my campsite for the night. In order to make progress, I had to cross two river estuaries along the way, one at Porto Garibaldi and the other at Lido degli Estensi. There were bridges for the traffic, but I chose to pay a Euro and use the traghetto (a small ferry – often winched across the river or canal at that point). It was also interesting to see who was out and about, on bicycles, or on foot like me. Mostly, people seemed to have things to do locally on either side of the estu-ary; at last I was just rubbing shoulders with people getting on with their daily life.

I had arrived at the Adriatic.

When I booked Mare & Pineta, the campsite at Lido di Spina, by telephone, it sounded like a small site set among the pines, near the sea. I was relived to get there at about 6pm, so that I had time to pitch my tent before watching England play Iceland on TV, in the campsite's bar. That was the plan. There was a gatehouse just inside the camp where you could book and pay for the night. Behind it, I could see many tents and mobile homes scattered among the trees. It looked pretty full, so I felt glad to have reserved a place. The computerised booking-in procedure took ages and I was shown my emplacement on a map. It was then that I began to realise the size of the site. 'How many people do you have in tonight?' I enquired casually, so as not to appear overawed.

'There are 3,000 in tonight,' I was told in excellent English by the pleasant assistant.

'So, as a matter of interest,' I went on, 'how many are British?'

'Umm, just a minute,' she replied while bringing up the correct spreadsheet on the screen. 'You are the only one! The others are Ital-ian, Hungarian, Russian, Bosnian, Swedish, Norwegian…is that enough to give you an idea?' She said, smiling at my bewildered gaze.

'Where did you learn such good English?' I asked. 'I am English,' she laughed.

'Then there are two Brits. Not just me in a 3000:1 ratio'

'Yes, but I live in Ravenna, so I don't count,' she said so as not to spoil my mathematics.

My pitch was so far away that she called a ranger with a battery-driven buggy to take me to it. It was a challenge to drive my tent pegs into the dry, root-laced ground, but I managed it, to the accompaniment of the ubiquitous cicadas.

I found a bar with a large screen, ordered the biggest pizza on the menu, a large beer and settled down to wait for the England v Iceland match to begin. The room was packed with what felt like hundreds of football fans, some eating, some drinking and some just standing to watch the game. After the referee whistled to signal the kick off, I felt the chill of a Brexit cold shoulder. I was cheering for England but every other person in the room was rooting for Iceland and that is how it stayed for the whole match. My grin, which I beamed round the room, when Rooney scored in the fourth minute, was well and truly wiped off my face by the following two goals from Iceland. I slunk back to my tent at the end of the match without catching the eye of anyone in the bar. I don't usually watch football matches, but I had the same feeling that night as I have every year when the results are announced in the Eurovision Song Contest. Why was I surprised?

The next morning, I awoke at about 4am. The disco, in a bar near my tent, went on until about 1am, after which there was the usual galumphing and guffawing around that goes with the unzipping and zipping process of going to bed. Then I got some sleep until it was warm enough for the cicadas to begin their reveille. I was quite relaxed about this lack of sleep because I had a free day very soon. I was going to walk to Marina di Ravenna and on the free day after that I proposed to explore the ancient city of Ravenna, which incidentally was another place that was at the coast centuries ago.

I lay in my tent feeling the warmth of the early morning sun soothing my aching limbs. Each group of tents had access to Wi-Fi by virtue of modems being rigged up in the trees at strategic points, so I spent at least an hour replying to all the very supportive emails and comments on Facebook and Twitter posts. It was only later that I realised that I might have woken people up in the UK, when their phone pinged at 3.30am. I blamed it on the cicadas. I dozed after that, building up the energy to decamp and pack my rucksack.

I had breakfast in a café on site, before setting off further down the coast. I noticed again a trait that men displayed when, with their female partners, they asked me what I was doing. My appearance gave me away now that I was in the land of swimming costumes and beach mats. While I was sipping a cappuccino and waiting for the new batch of brioche to be delivered, a couple next to me in the queue asked the inevitable question. Then true to form, while I was replying, the man took a quick look down at my legs. This downward glance had happened constantly along the way, and it was usually men. I can only surmise what they were thinking:

'You would not have thought he could do it with those legs – wow, well if he can do it with those legs so could I – Nice legs, count me out then – I wonder if they were bigger (like mine) when he started? – I wonder if they are knotted and gnarled under those walking trousers?'

Whatever was actually running through his mind, a little voice in my head was replying: 'whatever you think of my legs, they are actually doing it. What is more, if I can do this mammoth walk with these legs, think what you could do with yours?'

When checking out, I discovered talking to the assistants at the gatehouse that there was a problem with my route to Marina di Ravenna. The River Reno that let out into the sea a few miles south of the campsite was one of the few rivers with neither a bridge nor a traghetto near to the coast. There was only one way to go – I had to walk north and then take a main road west until it met with the SS16 running north/south. This panicked me. I had been avoiding this road because of the fast and dangerous-looking lorries which used it daily. Now, I had to take it. I was told that there was a cycle track so I should be safe, but I walked away from the campsite in an anxious state.

If I had been in Holland or Germany the police would have picked me up, even on the fast-moving approach road. By the time I got to the SS16, I was proved right to be worried. Massive lorries of all nationalities were bulldozing their way through the warm air, in both directions. When there was too little space to overtake, the passing vehicle sometimes veered into the cycle track. When this happened going north, I had time to see what was happening and jump into the ditch beside the cycle track but if the passing lorry was going south, it was behind me so the first time I got a warning was when I heard a loud claxon. This stiffened my sinews, without a doubt, causing me to jump aside in less than a nanosecond. After one claxon incident, I emerged from the long grass to see a Carabinieri police car cruising north in the opposite direction. The driver waved cheerfully, as if to say: 'Hey carry on there. Just make sure to stay away from those deadly lorries. We don't want the paperwork that would result from you going under the wheels. Thanks very much.'

With only six miles to complete before I could get back on a beachside path, I had already covered about four when a car pulled up in a lay-by on the other side of the road. I immediately gave thanks for the kind driver who had spotted my plight. He was waiting for me to pull level before winding down the window and offering me a lift to the next junction, or so I thought. I crossed the road behind the car and walked up to it ready to open the back door and fling in my rucksack.

The driver was busy looking at his phone when I bent down to catch his eye. Failing to acknowledge me, he carried on talking intently on his hands-free mobile. He was a very tall African dressed in a beautifully printed, long gown that reached to his ankles. With open-toed sandals and a kufi cap, he looked both aristocratic and formidable.

When he did notice me grinning through his window, I said: 'Thank you so much for stopping. Could you take me to the next junction? The one past the River Reno, which is just up there.' I pointed at the sign that announced the presence of the river, which was just beyond the end of the lay-by.

He was so absorbed in his conversations that he obviously had no idea what I was talking about. It turned out that he was not my saviour and had not seen me walking in fear of my life. Gesturing for me to get in quickly if I wanted a lift, he dialled another number, put the car in gear and took off down the SS16 as fast as any lorry. His conversation seemed full of complicated information. When it all got a little heated, he took both hands off the steering wheel and gesticulated frantically. I gripped the dashboard and blanched.

I worked out that he was probably a Muslim from the way he greeted his friends over the telephone. He never once asked me what I was doing or wanted to know anything about me. Neither did he glance down at my legs, which actually endeared him to me greatly. He dropped me on the approach road to Casalborsetti, which was the first seaside town south of the Reno. I had only travelled a short distance, but my lift had been a lifesaver even though his driving was decidedly erratic at times. However, I was mightily relieved to have been rescued from the dreaded SS16.

To my driver, I seemed just a minor distraction. A fly buzzing around him while he was making his phone calls. Still shaking from the torments of this Death Valley, I sat down under a roadside tree and called Kate to tell her that I was still alive, not that she was worrying – until I rang her.

Casalborsetti turned out to be a great place to have an early lunch. Randomly, I bumped into a group of friends celebrating the birth of the daughter of one of the men in the party. His partner and baby were still in hospital, but he was keen to start the celebrations. Glasses of prosecco were being handed out and the bar had produced a choice range of antipasti. I was invited to join them. They grinned when I told them my SS16 deadly-lorry stories. Apparently, I was the most recent in a long line of travellers to talk of their near-death experiences on that road.

The man who gave me a lift prompted a discussion about the brave boat people who survived the journey from Africa and landed in Sicily. They were registered in Italy, their place of landing, but soon found that there was no work for them. They were forced to earn money by selling things like socks or lighters on the street, for example, and living in the most basic of accommodation. They dreamed of pushing on to countries like Germany or the UK where employment was, in their minds, more available, but borders were being closed. Austria was already turning migrants back at the Brenner Pass.

This discussion kept me absorbed, but it also made me feel uneasy. The reality of the migrants' lives was quite shocking, and I worried that there might be an Italian backlash against them in the future.

When I told the group of my plans to avoid the main roads and walk south of Ravenna near to the coast, they raised their hands in horror. 'This is a forbidden land,' they shouted. I took little notice and just assumed that the prosecco was doing its job.

However, they told me that the Parco del Delta del Po was the closest that Italy got to a top-class national park. Rare birds' eggs, for example, had to be protected. It was impossible to walk through this fabulously scenic area at the moment. I had to stick to the SS16 or its equivalent after Ravenna. There was no other way. As they got merrier, I got more downcast with the news that Death Valley beckoned again. We hugged. I wished the baby well and with much waving I ambled off to cross the bridge and find the coastal path going south. I had one more bridge and a traghetto to go before I reached my out-of-season hotel at Marina di Ravenna.

About halfway along, I saw a shop selling beach ware: inflatables, buckets, spades, and such like. Kate and I love these shops, so out of loyalty to our delight at browsing round them, I stopped for a look. A young assistant was just putting out an Italian flag, presumably for football fans to buy.

I asked casually 'do you have a small Union Jack for my rucksack?'

'No, but you will get one in the next town, I know you will,' he replied helpfully.

'What did you think of the vote in the UK?' he asked out of the blue, but understandably because my flag request probably spurred him on.

'I voted to Remain; I am sorry for the result,' I answered sincerely.

'You should not feel sorry, if we were given the vote, we would want to leave the EU immediately. In this country we are slaves to Germany. We are forced to pay very high taxes just to keep the EU happy. The taxes are crippling our business. This doesn't feel like our own country anymore. We hate the Euro economy; we want to feel proud of Italy again,' he said passionately.

I felt the pain in what he believed. I had received so many opposite responses in northern Europe, but now I was met with a wave of bitterness aimed primarily at Germany. He and his business partner definitely felt that Italy was a poor relation. I am sure that if businesses in the UK had to pay 63% business tax, they might feel as aggrieved.

It was 7pm when I arrived at the strip of bars and hotels that were to be my home for two days. One bar near Hotel Bermuda where I was one of the very few residents, had a large screen on the wall outside, facing the sea. The TG5 channel's news was on. A picture of Matteo Renzi clenched in a firm handshake with Jean-Claude Junker grabbed my attention. This image of EU solidarity, in the face of Brexit, must have done little for the mood of the beach ware sellers, who were manning their shop a few miles up the coast. I guessed that they were rather hoping for the Italian domino to tumble.

13: No Sightseeing in Ravenna

I caught the early morning bus into Ravenna. I was going to explore the city, but first I had to visit the tourist information office and get my route sorted out. They gave a slightly different story about the Parco del Delta del Po. Apparently, their information was that the beach region was closed because the piles of driftwood and tidewrack had made walking along it impossible. They also said that walking inland was not possible owing to a forest fire and the rare birds' eggs, which needed protecting. They tried to telephone their colleagues at Lido di Dante, but it was Wednesday and they were closed. The only thing I could do was check again at the Lido tourist information office in the morning. It was a risk because if they would not allow me to walk through the park I would have to make a massive detour back to a town called Classe to walk on the dreaded SS16. My whole timetable depended on a good result the next morning.

Outside the tourist Information office in Ravenna, I stood, blinking in the sunlight, at the entrance to Piazza San Francesco, thinking how much I needed a cup of coffee. I spotted Café Palumbo further into the Piazza, with tables outside, sheltered under the colonnade running the whole length of the south side. Since it was an extremely hot day, the cool atmosphere in this peaceful corner of the city really appealed to me. It was there, while sipping my macchiato, that I made the decision of the day. I would abandon my plans for sightseeing and sit here for as long as I could. I am sure that all of the famous sights would have been interesting, but I was somehow not prepared for them. My mind, so taken up with worries about my intended route for the next few days, could not concentrate on what they had to offer.

There were two things which I could not dislodge from my thoughts. Firstly, just after I got off the bus that brought me to Ravenna, I had seen a life-size poster for a Joan Baez concert in July. She was one of my favourites in the 1960s, partly because she became involved with Bob Dylan, but also because she sang such hauntingly beautiful songs. In one month's time, she would be singing in Ravenna; it brought it all back – the 1960s and the feelings that things could change and we could have an influence in world affairs. Her version of 'We shall overcome' in 1963 became my favourite. Even seeing her poster before going to the tourist information office was enough to make me want to sit and daydream for a whole day about whether we did overcome. And if not – was there still time?

Secondly, I was also thinking about the nine-year-old boy who fell in love, at a distance, with a nine-year-old girl and how this passionate first love influenced his whole life. This boy's mother died when he was seven. When he was 12, his father and stepmother arranged for him to marry another girl of similar age to him despite the fact he was not in love with her. He was educated well, fought in a war, fathered six children and became a writer. When he was about 37 some political intrigues overtook him and he was banished from his home city. This forced him to move to Ravenna and travel abroad. He died in Ravenna at the age of 56.

This boy was Dante Alighieri. He was, and still is, one of the most famous men in Italy and in the world. 'The Divine Comedy', his poem written in his local Tuscan dialect rather than Latin, is world famous. I needed time to ruminate on his life and accomplishments before trooping off, with all the other tourists, to see his tomb. I wanted to just sit still and stare into space and think about his life, although there is an interesting story attached to the tomb. Apparently, years after Dante's death, the elders in Florence apologised for their cruelty towards him and asked for his bones to be brought back to bury them in their city. The custodians in Ravenna craftily sent an empty coffin back to Florence except for, in all likelihood, some stones inside it. This is why visitors can still pay their respects to Dante's bones at his Mausoleum in Ravenna and do not have to travel to Florence - there is a tomb there to sit beside but, to this day, it is empty.

My coffee break soon turned into lunchtime. I wrote my journal, looked at maps, read more, and day-dreamed about Dante. Lunch started with a glass of local white wine: chilled perfectly, smooth tasting and full of citrus flavours. I asked for a plate of tortelloni dyed green with spinach and stuffed with ricotta cheese and spinach. To accompany that, I ordered an arancino. This large risotto ball (meaning, a little orange) stuffed with meat ragu and deep fried in breadcrumbs stood proudly on my plate among the green parcels of pasta. I was in heaven or should I say Paradiso since I was still reading about Dante on my phone?

The waiter was kind enough to point out the difference between tortelloni and tortellini. They are both the same shape but mine (being tortelloni) were larger, each one able to sit snugly in a serving spoon. Tortelloni are usually stuffed with cheese and spinach, whereas the smaller variety is commonly stuffed with meat, and can be served with a sauce or in a thin soup (brodo). Of course, it all depends on what region you are in. This, I discovered, applies to most things, when it comes to Italy.

My bus journey back to Marina di Ravenna gave me time to plan the next few hours in meticulous detail. I had to collect my washing from the line in the hotel's courtyard, pack, eat, and have a few drinks at the bar to help induce sleep. I wanted an early night, so as to leave at 6am the next morning. Wandering along the sea front before I went to bed, I spoke to the owner of a gift shop, set up in a booth on wheels. He was enthusiastic about my adventure, and was saving up for a similar journey, as yet unplanned. He just knew that he had to do something before 'he was too old.' At that he coughed and asked me 'how old are you, if you don't mind me asking?' When I told him, he visibly relaxed. He probably thought, 'well if he is doing that at his age, I don't need to rush so much after all.'

14: Paradise

It took me three hours to walk to Lido di Dante. As I left my hotel, in the chill of the early morning, the stallholder to whom I spoke at bedtime was just opening his booth. He waved, crossed the road, shook me warmly by the hand and wished me all the luck in the world. I hoped that his best wishes were not because he was withholding some vital information about the Parco del Delta del Po, which I could have done with knowing before setting out. Everyone had their own story about why visitors had to steer clear of it, but none of them made absolute sense. Anyway, there was not a high fence around it to prevent people from going in. As I passed through other Lidos, I became more hopeful of being allowed through. I expected to see notices pinned up along the way, warning tourists to keep out, but there were none.

The strip of pine woodland between the road and the sea was dark, when I began, but it gradually lightened and became alive with older people taking constitutionals, sea bathers, dog walkers and pram pushers. Eventually, sunshine broke through the canopy above us and warmed the dank area in which we humans wandered. It was healing warmth, which promised a beneficial day.

When I arrived at the long-anticipated tourist information office, it was closed.

My heart sank, but I discovered by asking at the café across the road, that it opened at 10am, which gave me time for a second breakfast. The kitchen staff at my hotel had left out my first, but that was nearly four hours ago. All my plans to read more about Dante before I tried to enter the Parco were thwarted by the presence of two puppies next to me in the café. They were delightful, but I spent most of my breakfast time trying to stop them biting my ankles, much to amusement of their owner. Sometimes poetry just has to take second place.

I did manage to snatch a look at an article on the Internet about a famous painting by Sandro Botticelli, called The Banquet in The Pine Forest. It tells the strange story of a man called Nastagio degli Onesti from the 100 stories told in Boccaccio's Decameron. It would be impossible for this story to be given any credence today - its moral is that women should be kind to their suitors, not reject their advances in any way, and try to obey their every wish. If a woman did not respond willingly, the man might get upset and the woman would have to spend her afterlife being chased by vicious dogs and a man on horse-back with a sword, as exemplified in Boccaccio's story and this paint-ing, on a weird kind of episodic loop as a punishment for all eternity.

There were, however, a few things that I liked about the painting. One was the wonderful depiction of the pine trees and the clearing beneath them, where the tables for the banquet had been placed. This was very evocative of my morning's walk that day. In the picture, the trees had typically tall straight trunks, which then burst forth with umbrella spokes of branches that supported a dome of greenery. This dome possessed long, upward reaching candles that bristled with pine needles. I had camped below them, walked through them and chatted beside them. The painting demanded so much of my attention that I missed the opening of the office. I found myself third in the queue, even after waiting for over an hour.

When I got to the front of the queue my worries about not being allowed to walk through the Parco dissolved in an instant. The assis-tant said that there had been a fire but it would not prevent me going through to the far side. She also informed me about the beach area. It was impassable owing to the immense amount of debris brought by the storm. Then she produced a cyclists' map and showed me the best way to go. The soothsayers of doom were correct but their predictions were not game changers. The oracle standing in front of me had spo-ken and I was happy. I was delighted to take her advice, especially since I had read so much about this miraculous sounding place.

I discovered the fire damage about an hour later. On entering the Parco, I saw to my left, on a stretch of land between my track and the beach, a strip of scorched earth and charred tree stumps. It had been fenced off to let plants grow back. Luckily, it was a limited area of damage, as my oracle had told me, and it made no real difference to my plans.

Like many other places along this coastline, if I had arrived any time before 400AD, I would have had to swim because the whole area was a lagoon and the small town of Classe, on what is now the inland edge of the Parco, was once the largest seaport on the eastern side of Italy. There were still rivers, fosses and lakes dotted across the Parco, but when, at last, I reached its boundary I was confronted by a vast expense of open land preserved as a natural habitat for a staggeringly diverse range of plants and animals.

This was a rare experience. No cars were allowed into the Parco, but there were wheel tracks left by the rangers' vehicles and rough white roads on which cyclists raced past me, throwing up clouds of dust behind them. It was exhilarating to feel that you could wander anywhere and that the whole raison d'être was being there rather than getting through it.

One track I walked along disappeared into the distance under a blue sky that was coated with thin furrows of clouds: ploughed, by the wind, running in the same direction as the track. An avenue of pine trees, exactly the same as those painted by Botticelli, stood tall at the edge of the track. The scent from these pine trees, fanned on a light breeze, filled me up entirely. It reminded me of a bar of soap from my childhood. The smell took me straight back there. The sap on the trunks of these pines stuck fast between my fingers leaving its pungent aroma on my skin as a mark of passage. I felt fully alive just walking, absolutely alone, flanked by these pine-tree candelabras.

I imagined Dante wandering along this path. This whole area features in, 'The Divine Comedy.' He set the ending of his Purgatorio in The Garden of Eden (the Parco del Delta del Po). A character called Beatrice (the nine-year-old girl, now grown up) leads Dante (an observer in the poem), into the garden. He is expected to wander through it and report back on what he sees. I could picture him up ahead of me following the scents on the breeze and gazing contemplatively at 'that forest – dense, alive with green, divine.'

Although I tried to keep heading south, I let fancy take me where it liked in this earthly paradise. Emerging from a forest path, I came to the edge of a lake. A bird hide had been positioned so as to get the best view of the lake and the sky above it. Shovelers, moorhens, great crested grebes and pochards busied themselves among the reeds, while marsh harriers and osprey, churned around in the sky, watching and waiting. Beside the man-made canals, fishing huts with spreading nets that bellied close above the water had been erected at regular intervals. In one stretch, I counted a dozen huts each big enough to allow six people to spend the day fishing, eating and sunning themselves

on a private veranda set on stilts above the canal's edge. Whoever designed these nets must have seen what the spiders in the adjacent
woodland had made. The webs had been copied, almost exactly, along
the canals; they waved in the breeze, jolting the spiders awake when
unsuspecting insects flew into their silky catch-nets.

I wandered for over four hours. Finally, I came to fields in which
crops had been sown; the shoots were ankle deep. Just before the field
was a strip of lime trees. When the wind blew, the leaves rustled like
tin foil, making the sound of applause. Dramatically, I bowed to the
noise, turned and walked on. I had just been in Paradise. I had a strong
feeling that if I turned back to look I might be turned into a block of
salt.

During the previous two hours, I had cut diagonally across the
countryside until I came to the Viale dei Lombardi, which ran east-
wards to the Lido di Classe. Adam and Eve had been banished from
their garden, but I left mine voluntarily. Despite the difference in our
fortunes, I too felt a deep sense of sadness at leaving. There is an
evocative fresco in the Brancacci Chapel, in Florence's church of Santa
Maria del Carmine. Painted by Masaccio in 1425, it depicts the couple's anguish in their expulsion. Somehow, I heard them wailing, as I
had seen them do in the painting in the chapel. Then, looking straight
ahead, I found myself on a tarmac road heading towards the sea.

There really was an overbearing sense of finality about leaving
Dante behind. Especially since the Parco del Delta del Po was his undoing. He contracted malaria from mosquitoes in this swampy region
and died of it in 1321.

15: The Seaside in Full Swing

As soon as I reached the Lido my route would be through a series of
thriving holiday resorts all the way down to Ancona. The summer season was beginning to get underway, in earnest.

A few miles along the coast, I glanced inland and caught a glimpse
of the Apennine Mountains in the far distance. I stopped dead. This
was the first indication that I was nearing my destination. Tears welled
up in my eyes. I was on the home run. If my calculations were correct
and if my sore body could keep going, it would take 10 days to arrive

in Santa Vittoria. What bliss lay there; it was too painful to think about. I walked the last leg of the day just chanting to myself: 'I'm on my way home.' It helped me confront, 'The Phantom of the Last Five Miles.'

By the time I reached Cervia and the Hotel Lydia, I was well and truly back in civilisation. The town is a busy and successful holiday resort, and once it was famous for its beds of natural salt. The shallow waters in some lagoons evaporated leaving rich deposits of salt, which meant wealth for anyone that claimed it, including some Popes. I was told that is why bread in some regions of Italy is made without salt – bakers refused to pay the high cost of salt.

This evening, families were streaming off the beach; getting ready for a walk before and after dinner. I had already walked 1137 miles with only a few days to go before I surpassed my original target of 1200 miles. To the beachgoers in flip flops, carrying buckets and spades, I must have seemed a real oddball with my heavy rucksack and dilapidated walking boots, as I dodged round them. My hotel's receptionist was very apologetic, when I signed in, because the communal television was broken so it would be impossible to watch whoever was playing in the Euros that night. After my Icelandic saga at the campsite, I told him that, 'it was absolutely fine by me.'

That night, I partook in my first holiday menu. For 15 Euros, the set meal comprised a buffet-style antipasto, which, apart from the fabulous range of salads, cold meats and cheeses, was wonderful to observe for the queuing habits and politeness of diners who made sure that other guests had their fair share. It really was a communal feast. The starter was followed by a choice of pasta dishes, then a meat course (I had slow-cooked beef stew) and then a pudding such as tiramisu to end. I sat and summoned up a vision of all the hotels along this very long coastline serving their version of a holiday menu every night from early June to the end of September. There might conceivably be an a la carte menu somewhere, for example in the five-star hotels, but the holiday menu reigned supreme in all the places in which I stayed. It was a perfect way to keep a full hotel happy, after a day on the beach, in one very well-managed sitting.

When I left the Lydia, the next morning on 1 July, I received a warm handshake from the very friendly owner, who was ecstatic about the gulps of swallows, which had arrived from Africa that spring. It was a sign that the summer would be a very good one, he believed. Statistics for the number of holiday menus likely to be served were whirring round his brain, I could hear the cogs grinding as I waved goodbye. He seemed content with his lot. No talk of government tax or Brexit. I wonder whether opinions about business were all down to the amount of footfall or covers served, and not the EU?

Just south of Cervia there is a town called Pinarella, which has an abundance of camping sites only a short walk from the sea. What makes this town so special is that for over a mile along the coastline there is a very wide strip of pine woodland. It is a perfect place to cycle, push prams, sit and chat, or just snooze on a bench. All day there is a steady stream of holidaymakers walking across and among the pines. It provides a cool buffer zone after the beach or before the blaze of the sun.

How I envied the families who spent all day in their swimming costumes and all night in their finery. The perfect Italian seaside holiday here was conducted like clockwork: breakfast, pine woodland, beach, coffee, lunch, siesta, beach games, high tea, pine woodland, walk, dinner and more walking were all completed to some kind of circadian rhythm inbuilt in the Italian psyche – all without a tin of beer, or for that matter any alcohol, in sight. Meanwhile, I cut across this peaceful scene like a lumbering goods train chugging through a forest, leaving everything undisturbed, but only after a short clash of cultures, which caused everyone involved to look up, stare confusedly for a moment, and then go back to their well-ordered life.

I recalled the number of times in the Alps when I had to pull my belt in because there was nowhere to buy food at lunchtime. Now I was never short of water or food. When I came to Cesenatico I stopped for lunch, but I would have stopped anyway because it was like being on the film set of Game of Thrones. I wanted to explore.

A canal runs through the town, which, people told me, Leonardo da Vinci designed. According to Wikipedia, however, he probably just surveyed the project and gave advice. Whatever his involvement was, it is not the canal that I found jaw dropping – it was the barges that floated along it. A flotilla of these medieval-looking barges dominated the town as if an invasion from another dimension had taken place. It was the sails that were so otherworldly. The mainsails and the spinnakers were matching in their colourful designs, using blocks of light and dark brown to give a dramatic effect. Heraldic motifs, mostly depicting rearing horses, were embroidered in bold relief. The mainsail spars were set at an angle like a Chinese junk. When at full stretch, both sails bellied forward with regal prowess, making me feel that the barges contained unimaginable riches or kings and queens from the Orient.

I found a café in which to eat a sandwich. This gave me a canal side view of these magnificent boats. I could have stayed for hours, just gazing, instead of the 20 minutes I allowed myself to prevent muscle stiffness.

My next stop for the night should have been Rimini proper, but I was put off by the high prices of the accommodation. While having my break in Cesenatico, I booked a cheap room in Viserba, which is a small seaside town just before Rimini, in the Hotel Stella D'Italia. It was only when I got there that I realised why the room was so cheap. It was 'Pink Night' that very evening. This is a custom throughout Italy, sometimes called 'White Night.' Basically, the town council puts up funfairs, employs discos and DJs, makes sure that all the shops stay open until very late and puts on a firework display to round the whole thing off. Visitors spend lots of money in the town and enjoy themselves royally.

My balcony overlooked the main square of the town and, in the late afternoon, I looked down on the empty fairground. The receptionist said, as I booked in 'you may notice some noise at the end of the evening when the fireworks are lit.' This could probably have been entered for an 'Understatement of The Year Award' and won.

In the end, I did not regret staying there because had I walked on to Rimini I would not have met Tomas and Aneta from Jaromer in the Czech Republic. They sat at the next table, having the holiday menu, and we joined in the fun of the staff all being dressed in pink. One waiter in particular wore a flamboyant pink shirt with a pink tie and had enveloped himself in a pink feather boa: all very jolly. I got the impression that this was risqué in Italy in a way that it might not have been in the UK.

Whatever, the gay implications of a pink night, it was friendly, good humoured and added to the fun of the evening. Tomas and Aneta were so kind and thoughtful about what I was doing and how it reflected on how they – particularly Aneta – were trying to get fit when at home. They told me that Rimini was a great place to come for Czech people. I told them of my camp experience at Lido di Spina. They bet that many of the 3000 would have been Czech.

It should not have surprised me because a quick look on Google Earth proved that Croatia and the Adriatic Riviera were the nearest sunshine, seaside holiday destinations for Czech people, as they were for some Russians, coupled with the fact that there were daily flights into Rimini and Ancona from both countries. Irrespective of the geographical and tourist industry aspects, I loved just bumping into holidaymakers from all over Europe. Our shared concerns about a better world seemed so real and important, especially when they were spoken about over a glass of wine. I hoped that we could still have that sense of togetherness after 2019, but I dreaded that it might fade away, like the scent of pine from my fingers after I left the Garden of Eden.

The funfair and fireworks were exciting to watch, especially from my hotel balcony from which I had a ringside view. The receptionist was correct, I did not get much sleep, but on 'Pink Night' any sleep is a bonus. Anyway, this was my last night in Emilia Romagna; that alone called for fireworks. The next day, after walking through Rimini and Cattolica, I hoped to reach Gabicce Mare, which is the first seaside town in Le Marche.

On my 73rd day away from Yorkshire, I would be in Le Marche, or just Marche, as it is often known. Compared to Yorkshire, it is slightly smaller but equally beautiful, except that it is virtually unheard of by people in England. Mention Tuscany and everyone at home beams and nods sagely. For them, Le Marche could be in France, by the sound of it. Knowing it so well and how enchanting it is, I went to sleep dreaming of days of doing nothing much except taking a stroll down to Bar Centrale for coffee that might turn into an aperitivo before lunch; or driving to Pedaso to eat a seafood lunch at Il Faro and then sleeping it off on one of their sunbeds. Those were dangerous dreams because they tempted me to relax mentally, when I still had roughly another 200 miles to go in temperatures that never seemed to fall below 30 degrees.

I was apprehensive about seeing Rimini, which was only a couple of miles away from the town of Viserbo. In the late 1960s and early 1970s, Rimini was a favourite holiday destination for British people. People wanted more than just British holiday camps and guesthouses at resorts like Blackpool and Great Yarmouth. The package holiday was born and holidaymakers had itchy feet. This coast was advertised as the Italian Riviera and the British came in large numbers. Then Spain became the place to go and I always imagined that when Rimini was abandoned, it fell on hard times with faded hotels, down-at-heel restaurants and unkempt beaches. Nothing could be further from the truth. What I saw was a smart, upmarket holiday resort with plenty to do, thriving restaurants and very lively beaches. If you wanted a luxury break, the five-star Grand Hotel stood shining bright, and ready, in its own neatly clipped gardens and nearby the Federico Fellini Park looked an enticing place for a passeggiata in the evening.

As I walked on, it dawned on me why the British had retreated from this very appealing town – it was it because it did not serve British food like fish and chips and eggs and bacon? The food on offer looked marvellous but it may not have been to the liking of those who prefer 'home cooking' when they go on holiday. There is nothing wrong with wanting that, but Spain must have seen the opportunity to capture this market, while Rimini was looking the other way. The issue of holiday food was probably also accompanied by cheaper airfares to Spain, more appealing entertainment and discount prices at hotels. However, Rimini is now teeming with a host of other nationalities, including Russian, just not us.

Even when one café made a small attempt to appeal to any stray British tourists who had got on the wrong plane, they got it badly wrong. The sign said: 'English Breakfast.' Whereupon, I went in and asked what was in that particular breakfast. Enthusiastically, I was informed that it comprised: an Americano coffee, bread, ham, cheese and hard-boiled eggs. I wondered how many English Breakfasts they served in a day. I thanked them heartily but walked out feeling sad that this was not the way to tempt British holidaymakers back from Spain. Not that they really needed to do that because, being Saturday morning, a cavalcade of coaches was outside hotels loading and unloading hundreds of people, and their cases, in a friendly but military manner.

Apart from the general hubbub of holiday fever, there were signs of an undercurrent in Italian culture that accompanied the amplified directions from the fitness instructors on the beach; the cars cruising around with loudspeakers on their roofs announcing tonight's entertainment; and the high-pitched buzzing of Lambretta-style scooters changing gear.

Outside one general store, I saw bottles of red wine. displayed Only these had labels on, the kind of which I had never seen before. About half showed Mussolini in full military uniform and the others had various shots of Hitler making speeches or just staring ominously at the potential drinkers. Two bottles deviated from the fascist theme: one showed a picture of a naked woman, who looked ill at ease with the company she was keeping, while the other showed Che Guevara – one to keep the Marxists happy, keeping a balance of political extremism through drinking wine. I wondered if I would hear someone on the pavement next to me say: 'I think we'll have a little cheeky Hitler Merlot tonight.' But the few people around me were either oblivious of the labels or stood, like me, with their mouths open in amazement.

Just a little further along the same road I read a poster that was stuck onto a piece of hardboard, which was leaning against a bicycle. It read 'Prima gli Italiani', which translated means something like Italians First, a concept closely related to Donald Trump's 'America First' slogan. This board was placed by the Northern League, which was then quite a small but strong voice in Italian politics.

Presumably, this party appealed to the street sellers to whom I had spoken only days before. Who would have guessed that soon they would drop the word Northern from their name and would have formed a coalition with the Five Star Party in a populist takeover of Italian politics? It was led by Matteo Salvini who at that time never imagined he was about to become a nationally important political figure.

The dominoes were teetering and I guessed that there would have to be a lot more car doors slamming, suited men and women walking forcefully up steps to give speeches, and firm handshakes on podiums to stem any potential flow away from the EU and indeed the Euro.

By way of contrast, placed at regular intervals along the various resorts were large posters advertising a series of conventions taking place over the summer season. These were to draw people's attention to events such as a Symposium about Jewish Mathematicians, an annual Philosophy Workshop Convention, and a Plautus Festival featuring the dramatic works of Titus Maccius Plautus, a Roman playwright who was born about 255 BC. Quite an erudite selection of events for holiday resorts to mount in high season.

I was just thinking that I had seen it all in the space of a couple of hours: bottles of wine depicting Hitler and Mussolini, philosophy workshops at the seaside...and then a car pulled up next to me and the driver got out. He stood still, briefly on the pavement, while he cleaned out the inside of his ears with his car keys. He then wiped the wax off with his fingers before slipping the keys into his pocket. I needed a break.

16: Le Marche – Rolling Home

Between Rimini and Cattolica is a place called Riccioni, which, it seemed, catered mainly for young people. It was half finished, like many places in Italy, with the derelict, cheek-by-jowl, with the opulent. Luckily for me there was a roadside café with a difference for a sandwich and a rest. The difference being that the awning jutting out above the pavement had a spray attachment all along its rim. This meant that if you sat near the perimeter of the awning you were regularly sprayed with a fine mist of cool water. Every other customer sat away from the mist except me who revelled in its cooling effect. I had taken to buying two half-litre bottles of water in shops along the way and using one for pouring over my head. During this lunch break, the awning spray did that job for me. As I was eating, a band of Harley Davidson bikers drew up outside the café. The riders came in for the spray; now other gentlemen of the road surrounded me, but sadly not

Satan's Slaves, for whom I had been searching since leaving the Ferry in Holland.

I walked into Le Marche, on the outskirts of Gabicce Mare at 6pm after 23 miles of very hot and eventful plodding. My original plan was to camp about four miles past Gabicce Mare, but I could not face a marathon distance in a day in the kind of weather conditions I was experiencing. Since I was by now in a permanent state of exhaustion, I also became a bit cavalier about places to stay within my budget. In need of a bit of luxury, I booked into a three-star hotel that opened out right onto the beach. Despite the three stars, I had a single room, which was presumably once a broom cupboard before its reincarnation.

That night in the street outside my hotel there was a carnival atmosphere. Chairs were set out around a huge TV screen and people were gathered to watch the match between Italy and Germany. With the view that Germany was the ruler of the EU and was making punitive demands on Italy, which caused their financial difficulties, the match promised to be an exciting one. I bagged my seat straight after my holiday menu meal and, sitting there, just soaked in the night of balmy air, ice creams and flag waving. While waiting for the kick-off I did a bit of Googling about tax collection in European countries and found that, at the last reckoning, Italy was the worst country in the EU for collecting taxes. Their yield was billions of Euros lower than it should be through the existence of an enormous black economy and the failure to collect 36 billion Euros from VAT on an annual basis. Obviously, this must have had a knock-on effect for the tax demands on people and businesses that did pay. Did they have to pay more to make up for lost income, nationally? I bet it was a lot more complicated than this since Italy had the third largest economy in the EU.

I shuffled nervously in my seat while holding this information in my hand. Maybe the people next to me could read English and might see what I was looking up. However much the crowd was cheering Italy and cursing Germany that night, maybe part of the answer to their woes lay closer to home, but this was obviously the wrong time to pull out that particular red card.

It was a fairly even game in terms of shots to goal. Germany's actual goal in the 65th minute deflated the crowd around me like a pricked balloon, but when an equalizing penalty was driven home, 13 minutes later, we let out an enormous cheer, which seemed to inflate the whole town. Instantly, Leonardo Bonucci became the darling of Gabicce Mare. Unfortunately, that was the way it stayed: a 1:1 draw, with Germany having had the lion's share of the possession. A bit like their tax collection, but that was going to remain an elephant in the room, for the time being.

My mind was full of football and unresolved questions about the Italian economy on Saturday 2 July, while the next day it was cluttered with opera (Rossini to be precise) and the fact that I was probably going to surpass my target of 1200 miles (1931.2 km) at some stage of the day. I must have been born a masochist because the majority of the day was going to be spent on the dreaded SS16. I could have chosen the scenic cliff-top route from Gabicce Mare to Pesaro, but that would have added many more miles owing to the number of long hairpin bends. When the cards fall like that, you just have to play them.

In Yorkshire, I play poker with a small group of younger men. I am completely without talent when it comes to card games (or any game for that matter) and so when really up against it, I find that card game analogies shuffle (sic) into my mind.

The entire day was beset by car fumes, the squeal of motorbikes at full throttle, fleets of racing bikes, and battalions of people vying for space on the pavement as I walked through small towns. The only saving grace was that lorries were grounded, it being Sunday. I ate a much needed, but late, large bowl of spaghetti carbonara in Pesaro at about 2.30pm, and then set off for the other side of Fano, which is the next seaside town down the Adriatic coast.

Pesaro was the birthplace of Gioachino Rossini in 1792. Many people might say that they know nothing about this Italian composer until you mention 'The Barber of Seville' and 'William Tell': just two of his 39 operas. Who in my generation does not remember The Lone Ranger and its stirring musical theme? This music accompanied the Lone Ranger and Tonto when they performed their acts of derring-do. We grew up to the William Tell Overture, humming it in the primary school playground as we chased each other around on imaginary horseback. I remember that we used to hit our backsides with the flat of our hand to mimic the noise of the Lone Ranger's hand on the flanks of his stallion.

Beethoven, who was obviously not as mild mannered as you might have imagined, once allegedly explained why Rossini did not rank among the greats: 'Rossini would have been a great composer if his teacher had spanked him enough on the backside.' Whether or not he said that, it had a draconian ring about it, which could have been uttered by someone, like Beethoven, who stormed off the stage immediately a member of the audience spoke. Anyway Rossini, if needs be, could easily have spanked himself like we did, while he was humming to compose the William Tell overture – just a thought.

No wonder that I began humming that overture as I started the afternoon's walk to Fano. I was to be staying at the Borgo del Faro, which was advertised as a small B&B with the possibility of an evening meal. That meal was appealing because I could already predict that I would be too tired to walk to the nearest café or restaurant. Having said that, I never imagined such a fabulous restaurant as the one I found at the Borgo. I sat on the terrace drinking white wine while the sun slipped down the sky like a ripe peach thrown against a wall. I ate oysters in a thick chickpea sauce, drizzled with olive oil. This oozingly sensuous meal easily made up for a gruelling day on the SS16.

The drawback was that I was to follow that particular road for two more days until I reached the regional city of Ancona. At which point, Libby (Kate's cousin from Edinburgh) was going to join me for a one-day walk to Numana. That was an exciting enough prospect to help me banish the rigours of the SS16 from my mind. Libby would then travel on to Santa Vittoria to meet me at the end, always assuming that I could summon up the energy to keep going. That task was getting harder day by day. Mentally, I kept telling myself that I had done the hard work and now I just wanted it to end. Paradoxically, as my stiff resolve dwindled, my tired limbs stiffened.

17: Kate over Ancona

I set off early the next morning after one of those breakfast that had been left out in containers and in a small fridge. It was convenient because I could leave when I wanted to. By 8am I was well on my way to Senigallia, which is another popular seaside town jammed packed with an immense array of European families on holiday. I had reserved a room at The Hotel Europe before the referendum, so I wondered what quips they would make when I checked in at the Reception.

One of the reasons I left early was that Kate's flight into Ancona arrived that day at 8.45am. The approach route taken by the Ryanair jet was over the very road on which I proposed to walk. With a clear sky I should be able to see it coming into land. Usually, it circles out over the Adriatic before thundering over the oil refinery on the north side of the city. At one point near to the allotted time, I thought I heard the roar of a plane's engines throttling back to make its final approach. I rushed from the main road through an underpass towards the beach so as to get a better look, but as I emerged from the underpass I found that the noise I heard was that of the sea crashing, in loud booms, on the rocks below the concrete promenade on which I stood looking forlornly into the sky.

Dispirited at not seeing the plane, I lumbered back onto the SS16 cycle track and looked for a café for an espresso, which I needed urgently. My mood was lifted by being cheered on by a group of cyclists, some of whom shouted 'Buongiorno' in the most embracing of ways; by a field of sunflowers, the scent of oregano and tarragon wafting up from the wayside and clumps of purple toadflax, which gave off a sweet smell that reminded me of being in The Garden of Eden. So what if I had not seen Kate's plane? At least she was here now and going to get things ready for my arrival. However hard I found putting one foot in front of the other, I could not possibly give up now.

I remembered reading 'Walking Home' by Simon Armitage, which is his account of a trek south along The Pennine Way in England. When he got to within a few miles of the end at Marsden, which is where he lived, he gave up. He rationalised stopping the walk there as a statement about having done the slog but not needing the kudos of arriving – all the fanfares and flag waving. At my lowest moments, I thought about ending my walk at Ancona (if not all the other places along the way at which I had felt defeated) but somehow not seeing the plane – but knowing Kate had arrived -smelling the toadflax, spotting the sunflowers, and being cheered by the cyclists, all had an unspoken effect on my sense of determination. I was going to make it. I was going to get to Santa Vittoria on foot, step by step, one boot down and then the other – even if it was the last thing I did!

In the small café in which I bought a second breakfast and the much-needed coffee, I was accosted by a fellow customer who told me proudly that he was a Swiss/Italian by birth. Apparently, he had been educated in a Swiss private school. In 1974, he had an Englishman as a teacher, who pontificated about Britain in a way that seemed to ignore that it had lost its Empire years before.

'I was totally surprised that people wanted to put the "Great" back in "Great Britain", my new friend told me, 'because I could never imagine it having dropped off, in the first place.'

I replied that, at home, there were millions of people who sensed that we had progressively lost our sovereignty by being in the EU. That had gone a long way, in their opinion, to cut off the 'Great' from 'Great Britain.' We needed to reclaim our sovereign status and our national pride.

He quickly dismissed this little homily on behalf of the Leave campaign by saying simply that 'we were shocked when the vote was Leave because we always looked up to Great Britain before that. You gave a perspective that is lost to us now.'

I left the café feeling that I had been told off by the headmaster: sore, resentful and hallowed. So, when I finally arrived at The Hotel Europe I tried to have my say first before I received another GB-bashing conversation. I said, quite humbly, 'I wonder if it is alright for me to stay here since we voted to leave the EU?' The kind receptionist laughed at my rather lame joke and replied: 'don't worry about that. You are not the problem. It is the lazy Africans who come here for handouts that are our problem. They are a heavy weight on our economy and we wish that the EU could help us do something about them instead of insisting that they stay with us and sort it out ourselves. Our unemployment rate is too high anyway. There is not enough work for Italians. How we are expected to find these people jobs? It's crazy.'

Phew! I felt like saying 'I'm sorry to raise your blood pressure, you obviously feel very strongly about this.' But I held my tongue. She treated me very kindly for listening to her rant, showed me to a very cheap but suitable single room, booked me in for the holiday menu, and told me about an aperitivo bar just for residents, all in the space of a few minutes.

It was a glorious evening. I ate my meal alone as usual looking out at the slate-grey sea. The sky was ribboned in streaks of blue, cream and pink, fading into the horizon. The street lamps cast a yellow mist over the sand, which made the collapsed beach umbrellas look like delicate flowers that had folded in on themselves as the sun went down. The beach was peaceful, but the road between the beach and me was rasping with fast cars.

Tomorrow I would be in Ancona to meet Libby and some friends who live there, so perhaps this was my last night alone along the coast. I tried to savour every last drop of seaside life but found it hard to grasp the true essence of what I was seeing. I had planned it all as an adventure through – river, mountain, and coast. Now it was coming to a close, I panicked as if slipping down a steep mountainside on shale. I was not able to grab onto tree roots to steady myself before the impending thud at the bottom.

Over coffee, my thoughts kept returning to what the receptionist had said: the pain and anger in her voice. She wanted her country back. A return to a time that probably never actually existed, when Italy was, in her mind, a place of security and employment: a vision for Italy of which all true Italians could feel proud. While I was trying to grab the roots of my own thoughts, other reflections kept nagging in my brain. Was the plethora of Zimmer frames in Germany an indication of that national wealth and social security had gone too far in their favour? Was the support for the old, for example, so plentiful that they were not encouraged to walk on their own? I could not remember ever seeing a Zimmer frame in Italy. I guess there must be some, but older people here seemed to be far more resilient and independent. Also, in Italy, the barking of small dogs was such a frequent phenomenon. Rarely, did I hear them in Germany or Austria but in

Italy they were ubiquitous. Did the frequent presence of their barking go hand-in-hand with the social discontent? Matteo Salvini and Beppe Grillo of The Five Start Movement were, perhaps, lurking around every corner. I decided to go to bed. My mind was so full I could not think. The walk to Ancona the next day was going to be a long and exhausting one, and I had to be in good shape.

18: Carlo and Giuseppe

In the morning, I walked along quiet beach roads, parallel to the SS16, hugging the shadows given off by beach huts, bushes, avenues of trees and cafes. I stopped to buy water often, because the day dawned the same as all the others: incessantly hot from early morning to dusk. At about 10am along the Lungomare Italia, I saw an eye-catching memorial. The inscription told of an event that happened on the 4 and 5 April 1918 concerning two men: Carlo Grassi and Giuseppe Maganuco who had acted very bravely along this very coastline. I had to reach for a dictionary and search Google to work out the full extent of their exploits. I discovered a fascinating story that altered the course of the naval war in the Adriatic.

By the end of 1917, during World War One, the Italian navy had purchased some motorised torpedo boats (MAS – Motoscafo Armato Silurante). These were moored in the harbour at Ancona and used across the Adriatic to damage or actually sink destroyers belonging to the Austro-Hungarian navy. They proved to be very effective thanks to their size, speed and ability to sneak into enemy territory without raising the alarm.

The MAS each carried a 10-man crew, two torpedoes – that were lowered into the water and fired off from alongside – and machine guns. One of the most significant strikes carried out by the Italians took place in December 1917. Lieutenant Luigi Rizzo and his crew used his MAS to sink the SMS Wien battleship, which was anchored at Trieste, a city that was still part of the Empire. This was a massive success for the Italians and one that, when two more audacious MAS raids were taken into account, warranted a significant reprisal.

On 4 April 1918, in the afternoon, Admiral Miklos Horthy, commander of the Austro-Hungarian navy, wished good luck to a well-trained force of 63 sailors, chosen from 120 volunteers. They set sail in a 140-foot long torpedo boat that was escorted by a large destroyer. They really did send in the 'big guns' as revenge for the strikes by the Italian MAS. Their objective was to land the men very near to Ancona. They would then make their way to the port to bomb the submarine base, steal the Italian torpedo boats and make off in them back to base. The raid, meticulous in the planning, was expected to blind the media with its brilliance and raise the morale of sailors, officers and the general public. What could go wrong?

Apparently, the uniform worn by Austrian sailors was very similar to that worn by the Italians and at night they were very hard to tell apart. What is more, to add authenticity to the raid, there were two Italian speakers in the team: trainee officer cadets from Trieste and Trentino (both areas part of Italy now, but being fought over in World War One).

They planned to row the last two miles, in a landing motorboat, and drop the men at Torrette, which is only 2km from Ancona: about half an hour's walk. The men had bandaged themselves to make it look as though they had been shipwrecked and needed help. Underneath their battledress tunics they concealed pistols, daggers, hand grenades and dynamite. Unfortunately, owing to the strong currents and the fact that they had mistaken the lights of the railway station at Falconara for the one at Torrette, they landed right where I was standing at Marzocca, which is well over 10 miles from Ancona. They were in for a long walk and ironically I was heading the same way. They landed at about 2am and after three hours of walking they had only reached the town of Falconara Marittima.

When I got there it was about 1pm and lunchtime, but they arrived at about 5am, dispirited and tired (and still wrapped in bandages). If it had all gone to plan they would have bombed the port and been speeding away back to their base at Pula (on a headland outside Trieste) two hours before that. Their Lieutenant made a decision to find somewhere to sleep and told the men that the raid would take place the following evening. They found a farmhouse at Barcaglione, which is a small village a few kilometres inland. Despite the inconvenience of having to walk inland to the farm, they were afforded a good view of the coastline and the Ancona harbour. After locking a woman and her children in a bedroom, they settled down to revise their plan and get some sleep, even though the sun was already up. They decided to abandon the destruction of the port and submarines and plant the dynamite at the base hoping to cause as much mayhem as possible. Then they would commandeer the Italian torpedo boats and make off in them firing the torpedoes at the moorings as they left.

As they slept, their landing boats were discovered. The Italian army and the Carabinieri started to search for these enemy sailors, but they looked in all the wrong places never imagining that the Austrians were heading towards Ancona.

I carried on walking near the shore, thinking hard about these exploits. I passed many derelict buildings and a stretch of beach that was littered with sea wrack, just like the first one I saw on this coastline. Then I came to an oil refinery just before the airport perimeter. At that point, I had to join the SS16 again and walk on it until I reached Ancona. Had I been walking this route, in April 1918, I would have bumped into the Austrian sailors coming down from their farmhouse.

What they did in the farmhouse all day on 5 April is not known, but one of the Italian speakers was disguised as a local farmer and sent to reconnoitre the moorings in the harbour. He returned saying that the MAS had been moved from their position next to the submarines to a mooring near to the main gate into the city called Porta Pia. The Austrian knew the layout and the fact that the MAS were previously near the submarines because their Lieutenant had flown over the site and taken photographs only a few days before the raid.

Later that evening they made their way to the port at Ancona. The Italian speakers managed to convince the guards at the harbour barrier to let them pass, but by now there was dissent among the group. On reaching the area around Ancona Station, Mario Casari from Trentino and Giuseppe Pavani from Trieste ran away and gave themselves up to some Carabinieri who were searching nearby. Their surrender, plus two shots fired by Casari, triggered the alarm: the first being sounded when the landing craft was discovered.

Still intent on using the dynamite and grabbing the boats, the rest of the group entered the Mole Vanvitelliana, which is an 18th-century pentagonal fortress built in Ancona harbour on wooden piles, Venice-style. It was being used as a war hospital and warehouse for valuable goods, like sugar, which needed protection from the Finance Police (Guardia Finanza). It was at this fortress that the torpedo boats were now moored. Unfortunately for the raiders, the boats had been sent out on patrol as soon as the first alarm was sounded. One was left behind because it was damaged and not in operation.

I imagined, at this stage, morale among the sailors was as low as it could get. Just then the heroes of this story confronted them: Carlo Grassi and Giuseppe Maganuco, two members of the Guardia Finanza who were protecting the stockpile of sugar stored there. They called out, 'who goes there?' To which the reply came, from one of the remaining Italian speakers who had not deserted: 'We are the crew for the MAS and we are going to take them out on patrol.'

It is hard to imagine how these two Guardia Finanza would have felt. They were not trained fighters, a bit like Dana Mudd. In their task of guarding sugar, they were suddenly confronted by 61 suspicious looking sailors who wanted to go and launch the entire fleet of MAS, not realising that they were already at sea, on patrol, manned by their regular crew.

Carlo and Giuseppe followed them at a distance and watched as one of the Austrians tried to start up the only remaining MAS: predictably, it would not work. Panicked, one of the raiders withdrew a dagger and stabbed Grassi. Maganuco opened fire immediately, which scattered the insurgents who ran straight into the Carabinieri, alerted by the deserters, who were now entering the Mole Vanvitelliana in full force. Not surprisingly, the Austrians surrendered, only after throwing their dynamite and grenades into the sea.

I guess they were mightily relieved that the whole botched episode was over. Since they were wearing uniform, they knew that the worst that could happen was to be detained as prisoners of war. That was not much solace for Carlo who was bleeding from the knife wound in his shoulder.

Then this surreal episode got even stranger. Along came Luigi Rizzo, the commander who had been in charge when the SMS Wien had been sunk, which started this whole episode. He interrogated

Lieutenant (Count) Weith, the 27-year-old officer in charge of the Austrian insurgents, after which he congratulated Weith on the courage shown by him and his men. This I thought was a weird thing to do given the catalogue of self-imposed disasters that had befallen them under Weith's command, including the desertion of two of his team.

As luck would have it, the Italian king, Vittorio Emanuele III, happened to be in Ancona at the time and was inspired to award Grassi and Maganuco with a Silver Medal for military valour. Luckily for Grassi, his stab wound was superficial and he was able to sit up in bed to receive his award. Maganuco received his afterwards.

By this time, I had finished my lunch and was about to risk my life on the fast-moving approach road into Ancona.

I chose the shady side of the road, which was my 11th snowball type of mistake because the traffic came from behind me, but the alternative was to walk in the full glare of the sun. At some points the narrow cycle track became almost non-existent, so I was forced to lean, face down, into the steep-sided rocks and weeds that lined the road. Generally, though, it was the wind, noise of the engines and hoots from their claxons that made me extremely fearful of the lorries. Once more the SS16 became my nemesis.

I knew I was getting close to Ancona when I passed Torrette. I could see how optimistic the Austro-Hungarian sailors would have been had they landed there. At that time in the morning and before the road was widened for the volume of traffic, which ploughs along it now, they would have felt confident in their mission.

A short while before the first Marina, there is a slip road to the right, the Via Mattei, which bends round immediately to cross over the SS16 on a bridge. This leads straight to the embarkation point for the ferries. Somehow, I was forced to take this road along with all the lorries going abroad. Although I did not know it at the time, any minute I would be boarding a ferry to Greece. It was only when I heard an announcement above my head saying: 'Could all drivers have their paperwork and boarding passes ready for inspection?' that I jumped ship by leaping over a wall, crossing a railway line and squeezing my way through a gap in a fence onto a road beside a ships' chandlers workshop. From then on, I followed my nose. I took narrow paths in the direction of the pentagonal fortress. I approached it from the outer-harbour direction and saw the moorings from which the MAS would have been taken out of harm's way in 1918.

It was not easy for the raiding sailors to get near to the Mole Van-vitelliana in 1918 and it was not easy for me that day. Finally, I came alongside it and emerged onto the road not far from the Porta Pia. This 18th-century gate into the city of Ancona was built on the request of Pope Pius V1 and would have been a landmark for the raiders in 1918 to head for on the night of 5 April. I thought of Grassi and Maganuco. I celebrated their bravery, before crossing the road and weaving my way through the city streets to my hotel. Libby would be arriving soon and I had to arrange our meeting. Very soon all thoughts of events at the Mole Vanvitelliana in 1918 had evaporated.

What lingered was the catalogue of failure and missed opportunities amassed by the Italian coastal defences in letting 63 sailors dressed in enemy uniform march around the countryside for two days before two young, brave sugar guardsmen confronted them. What a shambles and what bravery, all in one largely forgotten episode.

19: Ancona friends

Libby was booked into a hotel at Ancona Passetto, which was over the headland at a beach area, facing in the opposite direction to the harbour. I was staying very close to the old town. Since I was exhausted and still shaking from the afternoon's walk, we agreed to meet the next morning to explore the city before we met my friends, Francesca and Stephanie, in the evening for a meal. This was going to be a novel experience for me. That last time I had a meal with anyone I knew was with Mark in the Austrian Alps. That was four weeks ago. In Ancona I was to eat with three others. It felt exciting and daunting at the same time. There could have been one more, but unfortunately Cristiano was on night duty at the oil refinery, which I passed before I got to Torrette.

Kate and I had bumped into Cristiano and Francesca at Peschici, in Puglia. We were sitting in a café talking about the plans for my walk when Cristiano bent forward from the next table and said in good English, 'you know you are mad, don't you?' That was the start of our friendship: a joint appreciation of mad adventures and life in general. Since they lived at Ancona, we were only one and a half hour's drive away from each other or a four-days walk!

Some people only know Ancona for its ferry port. They drive in to the city, stay a night in a hotel and then drive on to a ferry bound for Greece the next morning. When travelling to Croatia, they do not even have to stay a night in a hotel – they just drive through the city and take a night ferry to Split or Zadar. At a quick glance, the city shows all the signs of being an ancient seaport which never really recovered from being badly bombed in World War Two. Ever since the Greeks discovered the strategic value of its safe and secluded harbour, the city had become the envy of, or target for, different peoples. Underneath a topsoil of fishing crawls, boarding ramps and shipping containers there are many things to discover, which can transport you back to ancient times.

Libby and I experienced a tremendous welcome from Francesca and Stephanie and also an insight into the secret marvels of this unsung city. We posed for photographs next to the Fontana del Calamo, which is a row of 13 marble fountains each looked over by its own bronze mask of a mythical creature. We touched the spectacular Arch of Trajan and imagined the crowds cheering the Emperor and his army off to battles across the Adriatic. Not many people, like me, seem to know much about Emperor Trajan, but I liked finding out that this ceremonial arch was built to commemorate his war with a tribe called the Decians who lived in what is now called Transylvania in Romania. The Romans were pushing their empire east but had to fight the Decians, in 106AD, by laying siege to their main town called Sarmizegetusa. Needless to say, the Romans won, but this was considered to be the last great conquest before the Roman Empire went into gradual decline. Trajan must have felt truly triumphant when marching through his arch on his return to Ancona.

The Cathedral of San Ciriaco sits up high above the sea. You can peer down through a glass plate in its floor and see the foundations of the Greek temple that stood there before Christianity. From outside the cathedral, you can look across the harbour and watch the small boats leaving their moorings at the pentagonal fortress and quarantine (the ex-sugar storage), just as if you were watching the MAS torpedo boats go out on patrol after the first alarm was sounded.

On that evening, Wednesday 6 July, Francesca and Stephanie took us out for a meal. The venue was a secret on the proviso that we liked fish. The sky was perfectly clear; only a few jet plumes sullied its blue wash. The evening sun made the buildings near the Arch of Trajan look a deeper yellow than usual. On the way to eat, in the shadows of the harbour walls, we chatted endlessly about my walk, the choirs that Libby, Francesca and Stephanie belonged to and how working at an oil refinery had its disadvantages on a night like this.

When we reached the place that we were going to eat, the surprise was perfect. Sometimes in the summer there is a pop-up restaurant right in the heart of the harbour. We were lucky that it had popped up this week. Plastic tables and chairs were laid out across a massive concrete apron opposite the terminal from which the huge ferries cast off to gather speed before they cleared the harbour walls and cruised off into the Adriatic proper. They came alongside us, passing slowly, as if beckoning for us to jump aboard before it was too late.

Beside us on land, there were fish-frying mobile kitchens, under a fixed canopy, all along one side of the apron, which served every kind of fish, crustaceans and molluscs caught in the local waters: mussels, vongoli, octopus, tiny crabs, white and red fish, squid, shrimps, large prawns, mixed-fish spiedini (skewers) and anchovies – much of which was cooked in a light, delicate, tempura-style batter. These treats were served with portions of fried potato slices and white wine from vineyards around Ancona. Why would I have worried about being back in people's company again? The conversation flowed like the wine. We sat there until the evening-light faded, leaving pink and yellow stains above the rim of the sea.

20: Leaving the Coast

Leaving Ancona early next morning was hard. I had begun what turned out to be a series of goodbyes. Being on the last leg of anything was full of promise but also sadness about what was left behind, unfinished. Long before Ancona, I had given up looking back at the places I had left and was looking forward; but the nearer I got to the finish; the more I wanted to linger in a way that would spin out my time of discovery. How many more tales like that of Grassi and Maganuco could I find if I had longer on the road? I was clutching at straws.

I collected Libby from her hotel at Passetto before the sun was too high. Although we were only walking 14 miles, the forecast was for a very hot day again and she was not used to walking that distance in such demanding temperatures. I had no qualms about her being ready on time as she was, for many years, a Chief Nursing Officer in East Lothian, Scotland. I worked on the basis that if a Matron cannot be on time there is no hope for any of us. We were both going to Numana, which is a seaside town on the other side of Monte Conero. Then she would get a taxi to take her back to her hotel and I would walk on to Loreto Stazione.

Loreto is a famous Italian town about six miles inland. It is perched up on a hill and overlooks the coast from a discreet distance. I was to stay at a B&B at the bottom of the hill near the railway that brings thousands of religious tourists every year to the Cathedral at Loreto. This is a world-famous place of worship, because inside it stands The Holy House where Mary (Jesus' mother) lived in Nazareth. Legend has it that angels flew it over from the Holy Land when times there were turbulent and the house's safety was at risk. After a short stay in Croatia, the house came to Loreto. Numerous tales of miracles surround this house in terms of the curing of illness, for example. Whatever the truth behind the legend, this house has been attracting visitors on pilgrimage since it arrived on 10 December 1294.

To get to Numana we had to climb up and over the highest piece of headland on the whole of the Adriatic coastline from Trieste to Puglia. Monte Conero is designated as a national park for its natural beauty and wildlife. Unlike my journey through the Parco del Delta del Po, we would be walking on roads, but they were fairly quiet in the early morning when we set off.

One theory about why it was called Monte Conero harks back to when the Greeks first developed the harbour and went exploring. They discovered a tree that grew locally on the hillsides, which bore a fruit similar in looks to a strawberry. The Greek word for strawberry sounded a bit like Conero, so it was named after it. Pity then that during the whole day we saw nothing that resembled a strawberry tree, especially since the fruit is edible and tastes succulently sweet. We did, however, see fabulous countryside and spectacular views of the beaches, many hundreds of feet below the cliffs on which we stood. Throughout the day, we saw Aleppo pines, the sap from which is used in Greece to make retsina, the pine nuts for cooking and the actual saplings for clipping to make into what the Japanese call bonsai trees. These pines and the abundance of pastel pink azalea bushes made up for the lack of strawberry trees.

The Aleppo pines were similar to the pines that I saw in Dante's Garden of Eden, but on Monte Conero they seemed a little more irregular in shape: they straggled a bit, compared with the more regular, rounded candelabras in the Parco. Regardless of any local differences, the name made me feel distressed thinking of how Aleppo, once one of Syria's most beautiful cities, is now a bombed-out shell with dust-covered trees. This ancient, rich and fertile land of origin has been crushed into submission.

Just before lunch, we took a wrong turning – one that would lead us down to Portonovo, where an old Napoleon Fort has been turned into a prestigious hotel. It took us about 30 minutes to backtrack uphill, but when we got to the top again, a miracle had happened.

A snack van was there with opened shutters, serving the most delicious rolls stuffed full of porchetta, which is an Italian version of hog roast. In Italy the rolled meat is stuffed with wild fennel, rosemary and thyme, salt, black pepper and a sprinkle of chilli flakes. The crackling before us was cooked to perfection and served in chunks, on request. We sat on the ground beside the van and gorged ourselves on these heavenly parcels of roast pork. If we had not taken a wrong turning we would never have seen this snack van. It was a culinary miracle.

Unbeknown to us at the time we were sitting at a road junction that in times past would have been a major route used by Greek traders, Roman soldiers, Napoleon's armies, British sailors and Austrian soldiers – all heading to and from Ancona. At least we got there in time for porchetta rolls.

After lunch, we had a long, but downhill, walk to Numana. Stopping only for cold drinks and a short rest at a café, we reached the town at just after 2pm. By way of celebration, we sat sunning ourselves in a beach café, drinking a well-deserved glass of white wine, while we decided what to do about finding a taxi.

The spell of being alone had been broken by the magical meal at the harbour and the camaraderie of the walk to Numana with Libby. I was coaxed back into the present gently, but it still felt a bit like a poignant goodbye to solitary reverie. No sooner had that thought appeared from nowhere than the taxi appeared, Libby was waving from the passenger seat, and I was walking down the coast to find the turning for Loreto. There were three more days before I had to emerge into normal life again; the last two days had been a valuable rehearsal; a decompression chamber before the diving bell reached the landing platform.

When I got to a place called Scossicci, I knew it was time to turn inland. I calculated that I had been walking through seaside resorts for 11 days and would never regret taking that busy, noisy, baking-hot route even though sometimes I felt like the odd man out – a wild man of Borneo in a nudist camp. Baez, Dante, Botticelli, Grassi and Maganuco had been the beacons that had lit my way. Coincidently, just as I was looking on the map to make sure of my turning, I passed the Adam and Eve Camping Park and saw a young couple coming out of its gates. They were pushing a baby for a walk. I resisted the temptation to ask whether it was Cain or Abel in the pushchair.

The last three miles that day were through barren fields that led to a grubby underpass below a motorway. Suddenly, I was in dull, quiet streets, away from the coast sitting in a bedroom that overlooked a railway. The only thing for it was to eat a pizza. That had to be after getting out the duct tape and doing some serious binding.

While wandering around Loreto Stazione, I came across the Pasticceria Picchio, which happened, as it turned out, to serve brilliant pizzas. They advertised a deal, called a Giropizza, which meant that you were served nine rectangular slices of pizza that gave you a taster of every topping cooked by the restaurant. They were brought to the table one at a time. With great dedication to the cause, I made it to seven slices, but then I had to hold up the white flag. I was not on the mountains any longer, so my body was probably telling me that I no longer needed a minimum of 3400 calories a day. Whatever the reason, I met my Waterloo after the artichoke, tomato, cheese and onion slice.

I began to add up the number of endings, which I had experienced during the walk. The last being my capacity to consume vast amounts of food and still need to tighten my belt, until the seventh pizza slice that is. I realised that while I was worried what the end of my journey would feel like, there had been many endings and if I could bring them all to mind, it might soften the blow of the final ending. This was the thought that rocked me to sleep, three nights before I reached Santa Vittoria.

21: The Last Push

The last sizeable hill that I climbed was when I left Trento. When I came down from that high point, I gatecrashed a wedding party and was politely told to leave. Walking to Macerata the next morning meant that I had to get used to hill walking all over again. I was heading for the Sybillini Mountains and their foothills now lined up in front of me. The road to Loreto was extremely steep and after that it was up and down all day. Soon the sweat was pouring off my head, which caused the suntan lotion to ooze down my forehead in a salty lava flow. This white magma then seeped into my eyes making them incredibly sore. I spent most of the day mopping my eyes with tissues just to relieve the irritation. I was back to begging for water at farms.

The thing about dogs in Italy is that farmers and smallholders do not always feel obliged to keep them tied up or enclosed in a fenced area. Some do keep their dogs under control, so when a walker hears a bark up ahead they never know whether to feel mildly agitated or very afraid.

At midmorning, I was walking beside a very busy road facing the oncoming traffic and practising my fist-on-heart hand signals, when I heard some frantic barking on the other side of the road coming from the back of a farm building. Feeling assured that I was fairly safe owing to the cars and lorries flashing past me, which were acting as a moving barrier between me and the as-yet-unseen aggressor, I moved forward resolutely. Suddenly, without warning, a large brown dog leaped out from behind the building, raced for the edge of the road and launched itself into the traffic. Cars were hooting loudly and lorries were braking with a whoosh. One car skidded to a halt. Miraculously, the dog was not squashed immediately, nor were any cars piled up. The dog made it to the centre of the road, but it then had to face the vehicles coming the other way.

Terrified for the dog's safety, and my own, I could not stand by any longer. I turned to confront this by now panicked-looking beast and, avoiding the slowing traffic, ran towards it waving my arms, shouting 'Go back you mad fool.'

It got such a shock. The walker that had been the subject of its anger had risen up and was heading its way. With that the dog turned tail and bolted back across the road. It sprinted onto the verge and then straight into its home territory, disappearing around the back of the farmhouse completely out of sight.

Cars started moving again, honking as they went, as I stood transfixed in the middle of the road. I waited for a safe space to cross back with my heart pounding so loudly that I worried that the stents might pop out. I could not get over the fact that I had just saved an aggressive dog from being flattened in front of me. Someone who trembles even at the barking of small dogs had just won the day and saved a dog's life!

My legs wobbled for at least two miles before I found a cafe in which to rest during the hottest part of the day. Alone, I ate a sandwich, while watching gaunt-eyed, retired men gamble their pocket money away on fruit machines in a small roadside café in the middle of nowhere. There was no conversation between the gamblers and I too sat in silence remembering saving a vicious dog from becoming yet another example of roadkill for my journal. That silent lunchtime, the sore eyes, and memories of that panic-struck dog made me feel cut off, adrift and lonely in a way that all the solitude of the journey so far had never managed to do. At least my heart had calmed down while surrounded by the silent gamblers. I left them to it after I had finished a dreadful vacuum-packed Panini and drunk a bottle of fizzy pop containing enough sugar to require two Guardia Finanza to watch over it.

A couple of hours later I was in need of water again. I stopped at what looked like a Farm Supply Merchants. The men in the queue in front of me were buying sacks of seeds, which took some time because there was a lot of conversation about which kind would be best for their particular farms. The woman behind the counter peered round to the back of the queue and asked me what I wanted in case it was an easy request to deal with while the men in front of me continued to deliberate.

I said I wanted water and she asked me what I was doing. I then had 10 minutes of congratulations in Italian that contained the regular repetition of 'porco dio,' which I took to be a term of amazement. I stood among a group of farmers with a counter assistant in the background all of whom were astounded at what I had done and telling me what they had always dreamed of doing. My legs had never felt so weak at the knees so many times in one day.

I followed their directions to a café at which I bought a big bottle of water. On the brow of the next hill I stopped to check my map. A car driven by a man looking slightly older than me stopped to ask if I needed help. He spoke to me in Italian but as soon as he heard my reply, and accent, he swapped to English. He told me that he had lived in Manchester for two years and never saw the sun once but liked it despite that. He asked me what I thought about the referendum in the UK and I told him what I had said to everyone else along the way. 'Don't be worried,' he replied, 'it will be a good ending. You need come back Churchill.'

His final comment about us needing Churchill back stayed with me for some time. For a person like him who had lived through the war, it was the spirit of Churchill that he chose to invoke when he learned of our decision. I only hoped that what happened to Churchill after the war did not happen to the Brexit debate. As long as we had tough clear-sighted leadership throughout the negotiations we would be safe in the future, was what I took him to say. I was keeping my fingers crossed for that, but not holding my breath, as I waved him goodbye.

I had often looked quizzically at people in Italy who stopped their cars for a roadside chat (or even in the middle of the road) and held up the traffic in doing so. Now I had taken part in such a chat, it felt good to have been involved. We both waved at the little group of cars, which was able to get going again now that we had finished. Everyone seemed to understand the situation. There was no hint of road rage.

On the final approach into Macerata, I turned off the main road and began a long uphill slog past a farmhouse, set back about 150 yards. I had time to see two huge dogs, which turned out to be Alsatians, set off at a good speed in my direction. My courage with dogs was at a raised level, owing to my adventure earlier that day, but adrenalin still pumped quickly when I saw these two. Instinctively, I got out both of my folded walking poles and clicked them to a fixed position. I squared off to the two loudly barking creatures and stood my ground, holding the two poles like twin Excaliburs. When the creatures got within about 20 yards of me, suddenly, I started speaking like Ray Winstone in one of his cockney gangster roles, 'Alright, which one of you two want some of these poles first? Come on then, make my day. You started this now come and finish it. You'll wish you had never been born...'

It could have been my very bad cockney accent or just the waving of walking poles, but they stopped dead in their tracks. Still barking, but less ferociously, they backed away a few paces and then turned around and ran back to the farmhouse. A gruff man came out and told them off for running away and then went indoors again. I could hear them barking for at least five minutes more as I walked up a steep hill away from the farm. I gave myself several 'porco dios' for being so brave. I had lived my life in terror of something like that happening and then when it did, Ray came to the rescue just when I needed him. I could almost hear the ring of Bow Bells in the distance.

I stayed at a small hotel, Albergo Arena, tucked in at the back of the wall that ran around the stage area of the open-air Opera House, or Sferisterio, in Macerata. From my bedroom window, I could hear the rehearsals for Norma, an operatic tragedy by Vincenzo Bellini, set in Gaul, about a love affair between a Druidic priestess and a Roman officer, first produced at La Scala in Milan on Boxing Day 1831. The Sferisterio sits 3000 people and is one of the leading open-air opera stages after Verona. I was reading that information from a leaflet in my room because I know very little about opera. We had been to the Sferisterio once to see Nabucco by Verdi and been awestruck by the music and spectacle but disturbed by the wealthy-looking Italian in front of us in the stalls who was talking on his mobile throughout the entire first act. Other people around him seemed to accept this behaviour as normal.

The day had been exhausting, more perhaps than any of the 79 previous days and so sleep was a bounteous gift.

22: Almost there

The destination on my penultimate day had been chosen because it left me only 16 miles to walk on the final day, Sunday 10 July. I wanted to be on time. I had been receiving enigmatic texts for a couple of days from a very friendly Italian man in Santa Vittoria, called Valeriano, hinting at a Festa on the day I arrived. Being the chairman of the Town Band Committee, general music and art lover, and the driving force behind many events in the summer, he was contacting me to make sure that I was on time. That time being 6pm, not any earlier.

I found the insistence on time a bit strange because it was my experience, in Italy, that events never started on time; that was part of the charm and fun of everything. You learned to accept things when they happened.

I had no idea about what kind of accommodation I had booked for the night, only that it was in the vicinity of Loro Piceno. This was to be my last bed and breakfast stop, and I had chosen a place called Gran Bosco for its low price and position. I was going to walk there via Abbadia di Fiastra, which is an ancient Cistercian monastery and abbey, set in enormous grounds that have been turned into a nature reserve.

I felt slightly flat as I walked out of Macerata that morning and it finally dawned on me why that was. I was familiar with the roads and places of interest. It was my home territory even though I had never walked through it before. The excitement about the discovery of new places was fading. It was one of my endings: the loss of new discoveries.

I was soon busy making decisions about which road to take and where to beg for water; I quickly forgot my self-absorption. The mysteries of nature never dulled for me despite the approaching end. At about 10.30am, looking up from the tarmac, I saw a coating of blue mist on the Sybillini Mountains: its morning-sheen was clearing slowing. It being a Saturday, the cicadas seemed to be having a lie-in: they were quiet in the trees, too sleepy to make a noise. Lizards sunned themselves sluggishly at the edge of the road, finding it hard to budge as I went by. When they did move, they rustled in the leaves making them sound like the tinsel being hung from Christmas trees.

At 11.30am precisely, the cicadas began to sing. It was as if someone had switched them on, a bit like the Blackpool Illuminations. Perhaps, the air had suddenly reached a temperature to spark them off. All along the roadside, under the trees and tucked into the leaf litter was a forested carpet of deadly nightshade. I had never seen this poisonous, and somewhat ominous, plant in such profusion.

I took a little side road to get some relief from the incessant thrum of cars, a kind of country lane bypass. A little way along, I saw a man dressed only in a white vest and black trousers standing beside a tree. He looked resigned, a bit vacant as if life had become too much – or too little perhaps? Seeing me, he seemed to brighten up a fraction; he waved for me to stop: he wanted to talk. After we had completed the usual niceties he hugged me. Thinking of what I had just told him, he said that he used to walk a lot when he was young, long distances, but now he didn't go anywhere. He said that he was happy to stay at home, but somehow what he said and what was in his heart seemed in different galaxies. There was a look of yearning in his eyes, as he scanned the distance for an answer. Some small dogs barked behind him as a door to the house opened, to let them out, and he jerked back into the present.

With his hand firmly clasping my arm, he said: 'Coraggio.'

I put my hand on his and gave him a smile. We held our clasp for a moment and then he disappeared back inside the door and I wandered on, down a steep lane lined with overhanging trees. He had used that one word, 'Coraggio', with a kaleidoscope of meaning. Who needed the courage? Him or me? If it was me, did I need courage to tackle what I had done or what I had to do? Which needed greater courage to begin or to end? If he was asking for courage for himself, did he need it to carry on living at his slow pace, in a vest, not going anywhere, or to hang on to the memories of what he was? I carried on weaving permutations for a few miles until I came to the conclusion that I must choose for myself which picture in the kaleidoscope fitted my circumstances the best.

I couldn't stop thinking about that last moment between us – when his eyes seemed to plead with me, almost begging me to realise that to end something needed all the courage I could muster. He knew. He must have been there before and felt the pain, a sense of desolation. That was it, he was warning me to be brave in the adversity of victory. To succeed is only partly a blessing; there must be a side of it that takes you to the cliff's edge, contemplating the fall. I might have been on the familiar road between Macerata and Loro, but these thoughts were freshly forged in an unfamiliar place. He had been a soothsayer waiting for me to pass by; I was convinced of that.

I had waltzed away from Hebden Bridge more than 11 weeks before thinking that the hard bit was both leaving home and the walk ahead, but now he had made me realise that the ending might be even harder. In my conscious mind, I never saw that coming, but in the depths of my soul I already knew the truth lay there. It was waiting there to be experienced.

I reached the Cistercian monastery for a very late lunch. I was in desperate need of food and drink so I set up camp at a café table and ate a couple of Panini and drank Coke Zero until I was entirely sated. The television on the wall stopped my mind from going over, perpetually, the soothsayer's message. It was an Italian Internet station, which is merely a radio studio with a DJ playing music videos: bland yet insistent enough to dull the mind from its constant cicada-style whirring.

From the Abbadia di Fiastra the road to Loro is uphill all of the way. The sun in the late afternoon was not fierce, so I wandered happily alongside the wheat fields, copses and smallholdings that grew vegetables, grapes and olives. This was a kind of rural idyll, so different from the SS16 and its deadly lorries. Nearing Loro Piceno and not being sure of the whereabouts of Gran Bosco, I walked up to an elderly couple sitting out on their veranda, meaning to ask the way.

Our conversation had to be conducted in Italian throughout, but I managed well enough. The husband was quite poorly. He sat with his feet up; his legs bandaged. Even though he wore pyjamas, the extent of the bandaging, right up his legs, could be seen. Not only that, but his whole manner suggested convalescence: his very slow reaction to my questions, his glazed expression and his need for constant support and approval from his wife. He wanted me to sit beside him and chat. Spotting the chance for a little respite, the spritely woman disappeared into the kitchen to do some jobs while I entertained her husband.

He told me, 'I walk a long way every day, I…' His speech petered out at that point. He was trying to catch his thoughts the way some people try to catch their breath, or stop a hiccup, but it was impossible. I never knew what he was trying to say because he repeated what he had already told me as if it was all recorded on a loop tape. I nodded, encouraged and smiled in ways that seemed to please him. His wife returned with something to drink and some little snacks and I tried to ask what help she had in her role as a carer, but my vocabulary let me down, badly. I guessed from her reply that in Italy there is very little in the way of social service assistance. Basically, she was the sole carer and that was that. I was humbled by her resilience; she soldiered on every day in ways that made my walk seem self-indulgent – all the so-called mistakes that I had made into a giant snowball melted in an instant.

It was time to go when I felt my muscles seizing up. Sadly, I had not realised that I needed to walk another two miles. My hostess told me that the Gran Bosco was a farm specialising in breeding horses and providing riding holidays. She shook me warmly by the hand, we kissed on both cheeks, and then she congratulated me on my achievement, more than once, which made me feel not so self-indulgent. The sorrowful look in her eyes, and the slight sideways nod of her head, told me that she wished her husband could have understood what I was doing. I waved back at them, sitting on their veranda, even after I turned a bend in the road.

Gran Bosco was down a long white road in a secluded valley some way from the centre of the village. Momentarily, I felt a sharp pang of regret about staying too long on the veranda, but then I realised that it was all part of my re-acclimatisation into the real world. Resilience in struggling with the commonplace, like she displayed, was a victory as much as any long pilgrimage.

After stumbling down the chalk-white rough track to the farm for what seemed like hours, I came across a blissfully peaceful sanctuary devoted to horses, donkeys, hens, pigs, geese, dogs, cats, a bull and even a parrot. Even before I met the keen young couple that ran the business, I could feel their sense of purpose and love of the countryside: it radiated from everything around me. The young woman, Arianna, was just going out to work as a chef at a local restaurant and leaving me in the capable hands of her partner, Daniele, who was a master horseman. Neither of them spoke any English and we were miles from a restaurant. Later, he and I settled down for a meal together in their inglenook-style farm kitchen in a restored farmhouse, which was surrounded by fields and tangled woodland. It was miles from a road or village. Arianna had prepared the meal before she left for work, which was kind of her and very welcome. Daniele cooked and served it enthusiastically. I had become accustomed to the way that Italians practise the art of serving simple food in a passionate way; I loved being part of that drama.

I could see from photographs around the kitchen that Daniele was a prizewinning horseman who had perfected some ways of the Native American Indians with his steeds. Our conversation was interrupted sporadically by his job of ensuring a whole menagerie of animals got ready for the night. I could not have found a better place to spend the last night before my arrival at Santa Vittoria. In the company of a man and his animals; I felt very close to nature in the same way as I had when staying with Josef and Angelika Jochum at Schröcken in Austria.

23: Going Home

Walking away from Gran Bosco in the morning I felt ready to be part of the world again. Not just a walker passing through it. For that, I thanked the horseman and the chef. Through their passion for the simple life the couple had created an oasis of peacefulness. In the middle of their oasis was a well; they gave you the bucket to pull up your own tranquillity from far below. I walked back up to Loro Piceno along the white road with a light step only just remembering then that this was the last morning of my walk and that by night-time I would be sleeping in my own bed.

I stopped to look around me at the rough track as it sliced its way through a forest of chestnut and beech trees. Suddenly, I felt faint and rudderless. By that Sunday morning in July, I had been on the road since April, for 81 days, and now it was time to stop moving. My boots were worn through at the heels. I had already bound them up with duct tape. They might just last another day, but, all the while, when I put my foot down I continued to hear the sticky, squelching sound of the tape as my foot lifted off the surface of the road.

My friend Ian McCarthy was born in the UK, but since his marriage to Gabriella, more than 25 years ago, has lived in Curetta, which is a village about four miles down the hill from Santa Vittoria. Ian offered to walk with me until lunchtime on the last day, so that he could show me some shortcuts, which would save time and keep me away from noisy traffic. A short way after Loro Piceno, I saw him and Gabriella in their car going the other way. I flagged them down and we all stayed chatting for a while; it was very pleasant to see people I knew who realised exactly how far I had come. Ian and I spent about three hours together walking on minor roads and rough tracks (luckily he was not fazed by dogs) until we got to Servigliano where we took a lunch break at the Re Leone restaurant.

He is a great enthusiast and expert on the history of the World War Two PoW Camp in Servigliano and has collected oral histories from Italian farmers and country folk who hid and looked after escapees from that camp, along with stories from the escapees themselves and their descendants. I was enthralled the whole way because he pointed out actual barns in which soldiers were hidden from the German SS. Occasionally, the Partisans who helped them were taken out and shot by the Germans. This made me remember passing a monument to some brave Partisans who had been shot on 3 July 1944. That was just before the two rampaging alsatians got the wrong end of my Ray Winstone impersonation. The five Partisans who had been shot for their resistance were: Picchio Costantino, Picchio Raoul, Picchio Lino, Cicare Attilo, and Marcolini Giuseppe. It was a very bad time for all three families involved; especially tragic for the Picchio family, who lost three members in one day for helping the escaping soldiers.

While we had been talking about the resistance movement in World War Two, we had ignored the extremely hot sun beating down on our heads. Entering Servigliano, we were both at the end of our energy reserves. The owner of the Bar dello Sport stopped her car and congratulated me on my arrival. She is always so friendly but on that occasion she looked suitably dazed at what her congratulations were actually celebrating. Incredulity and disbelief covered her face. How could someone really walk that far?

By the time we reached Re Leone for a late lunch, not only were we drained of energy, but Ian also became very faint from the sun bashing we had received in the morning. He faded in the middle of our pasta course. The restaurant allowed him to lie down on a sofa until he recovered, while I continued to eat my pasta alone to give me energy for the final push. From Servigliano to Santa Vittoria it is just over five miles, but it is all up hill. I anticipated it taking me a little more than two hours. I waited for Ian to recover but then, bearing in mind that Valeriano was quite insistent that I should not arrive before 6pm, I still had about an hour to kill.

Gabriella collected Ian to take him home for a rest before he came to see me arrive. I understood that Kate and a few friends would be there to welcome me home. My original intention was to walk from one front door to the other. Therefore, I was keen to walk up Via Roma to the top where it doubles back into Via Cisterna. From there I would walk two thirds of the way down Via Mazzini to our front door. Silly I know, but I wanted to touch it like in the primary school playground games we used to play, to demonstrate to all of the others in the game that I had made it home: to our safe place. It would also give me a chance to see Kate on her own to thank her for being my rock in this adventure. Her spectrum of tough love ('Don't even think of coming back home if you give up!') to sympathetic ear ('Tell me, where the pains are?') was a deciding factor in not only me getting to Servigliano, but hopefully all the way.

For the rest of the hour, which I spent waiting to begin the climb up to Santa Vittoria, I rehearsed all my endings so far. There was the beginning, of course, whereby I ended months of planning and training. Then the end of England and the near mugging by a herd of wildebeests, followed by the end of Holland, Germany, Austria (and Switzerland, of course) – all before I arrived in Italy. Geographical endings were accompanied by emotional and spiritual ones, like the end of blaming my father for dying and leaving me alone to face the world without him. Physically, there was the end of worrying so much about having three stents in my heart and on a lesser note the end of blisters and shin splints, which actually caused far more pain than the stents ever did.

At Pforzheim it was the end of my journey with PLF and Nick Hunt; I followed the chimney sweep into Italy but left him on the road to Florence. At Padua it was the end of the anticipation before the EU referendum. After that the Leave EU protagonists backed away and David Cameron resigned. We would have to wait one more day (11 July) after my arrival to find out if the invocation of 'come back Churchill,' had materialised, like the man in the car at Macerata said it should. I somehow doubted it.

I had been lucky to have some of my family come and walk with me on several occasions, but there was also the end of solitary travelling. I had cherished the sense of freedom that walking alone had given me. Now that was ending and I anticipated having to learn to become social again. That education had already begun, taught partly by men in white vests or pyjamas.

Sitting on the steps of the Re Leone, I was so deep in thought about endings that I misjudged the time and had to get my rucksack on in double quick time if I was going to get up the hill by 6pm. The road ahead was very familiar to me, I must have driven up and down it a hundred times at least but walking up it with 1321 miles behind me felt different all together. On a whim, I ripped off the duct tape from around my heels so that I did not arrive looking too much like a tramp. How pathetic, I thought afterwards, to be worried about appearances after the gruelling time through which I had been.

When you leave Servigliano you are very soon surrounded by

fields of sunflowers: iconic symbols of the fertility of Marchigiane organic farming and the longevity of people who live here. Through their customs and traditions, locals show loving loyalty and appreciation for their beloved region, which is why foreigners from around the world want to share in their lifestyle.

My personal appreciation for sunflowers has a lot to do with the patterns made by the seeds in that dinner-plate sized head. When I started teaching in 1970, I remember reading that these patterns correspond to the Fibonacci number sequence. This is a fact, with which, I can send standing people to sleep at parties. Leonardo Fibonacci was born in Pisa in 1170 and became one of the most iconic mathematicians in the world, but obviously not at the parties to which I go. Here I was ruminating on a medieval Italian mathematician while walking up to Santa Vittoria when I should have been rehearsing my little speech of thanks just in case I needed it when I got to the end. I had sat up in bed at Gran Bosco and composed a few lines on my mobile phone, with the help of Google Translate, just to be on the safe side, not really expecting to use it.

Just as I was promising myself to rein in my interest in Fibonacci, I saw up ahead yet another white-vested man. Thinking that I was becoming delusional, I blinked frantically to rid my sight of what was clearly an illusion. But no, he was real and heading straight for me. He was not in pyjamas, not staring vacantly into the distance like a man who was struggling with reality. This man was walking normally downhill, in the opposite direction to me, with the kind of gait that suggested leisurely purpose, an after-lunch good humour, and a light hearted approach to anything that I might say when he launched in with 'Dove stai andando?'

I said 'Santa Vittoria' and then told him my well-rehearsed story and he replied with the by then predictable – 'On foot?' – with walking fingers. He made me repeat where I had started and when I confirmed that I had come from England, on foot, strangely we then both turned to face north and gazed in that direction looking to see beyond the horizon, which made us both laugh sponteanously out loud. We were completely alone. He started to dance. First, he held my hands and danced in front of me and then we both turned together like a dancing couple, pirouetting. One moment we were laughing and whooping and then the next it was over. He had places to go and with a final flourish, a wave and a mock bow, he was gone, continuing downhill.

I stood watching him go, transfixed. I had so many people to thank for that moment of welcome from a man in a vest, whom I had never met before or since. William Gill for giving me my weak heart but also his zest for adventure. Alice Gill, my mother, for having the kind of resilience shown by that woman on the veranda in Loro Piceno: a steely strength to look harsh reality in the face every single day and soldier on. Kate, my wife for her unfailing love and encouragement; Alice, Max, Anna, Mark and Libby all of whom also walked with me and helped me through some rough times, and all the friends and supporters on Facebook, Twitter, WhatsApp and text who sent encouraging messages that provided a boost, just when it was needed.

I snapped out of my meditation, facing north, to realise that I had just voiced a heartfelt tribute to the back of a man in a white vest who was disappearing down the hill, the like of which would have defeated me in Italian. I turned around to face Santa Vittoria again and made my final approach with three miles to go.

That was my ending, my arrival. How fitting to have had a 'vested welcome party' even if it was from a stranger. I knew I had yet to meet Kate at our front door and maybe there might be a gathering at the bar tonight, care of Valeriano, but with that little dance in the road, I had come home – been welcomed back.

24: Ending up arriving

When you get to the last mile before the heart of Santa Vittoria there is a choice of road to take. You can either fork right up a truly steep hill, which takes you in to the town on the Via San Salvatore. This is the shorter route, or you can make it slightly longer, but less steep, by keeping straight on past the only petrol station, and near to the cemetery. I chose the longer route because my legs were feeling progressively weaker and wobblier the closer I got to the end. What is more, the route via the cemetery seemed more fitting.

A little further on, I squinted to see three figures in the road coming towards me. I checked and noted that none of them was wearing a white singlet type vest. It was Cristiano, Francesca and Stephanie from Ancona. After hugs all round, they asked if I minded them walking with me to the end. I was stunned and so pleased to see them. I agreed immediately. From then on, we chatted sporadically in between me forcing back some tears of sheer relief.

After the petrol station, which is always unmanned – with just a radio playing to indicate that the pumps are open for trade – the road swings round to the right up to the sign that officially announces that you have arrived in Santa Vittoria. The sign also tells you that you have climbed 627metres (2057 feet) above sea level to get there.

This was followed by a walk past the home and parlour of the funeral director, Signor Fabio Sagripanti. When his official van is parked in the drive it is always a good sign that everyone in the town, for that moment, is still alive. Luckily, it was there when I walked by. After that the trees bend over the road, darkening the view ahead. This is why I found it hard to focus on what looked a little crowd gathered at the top in the Piazza Della Repubblica.

When I came level with our much-frequented family-run restaurant called the Taverna Vittoria, more locally known as Rosario's, I saw Valeriano walking towards me in his typically bouncy style – full of enthusiasm and energy. Beside him was Fabrizio Vergari our Sindaco (mayor) who was brimming with smiles. After that, the people I met, the hands I shook, the kisses I received all became a blur. That was when the town band struck up and the crowd started cheering. From a dancing man in a singlet vest to a huge crowd with flags and banners headed by Fabrizio and Valeriano: what a transformation in a few miles.

I kept spotting people in the crowd who I then thanked for coming, shook hands with and kissed. Raffi and Luca, the sons of Phil and Wendy who used to live in Hebden Bridge, had painted a 'Well Done Roger' banner with scenes on it from my Facebook posts and a map of Europe, rather like the one on News at Ten, showing the route I took. The town band played on, standing in a prominent position at the top of the Piazza with their backs to the fruit and vegetable shop and one of the many hairdressers in town.

We all listened to their most rousing number and then Valeriano whispered to me that everyone knew that I wanted to go up Via Roma to touch our front door. He told me that they would all be waiting in the Chiostro (Cloisters) behind Bar Centrale when Kate and I were ready to come down. With that, I bowed and waved at the crowd and instead of walking under the medieval clock town of the Torre dell'Abate Odorisio, which would have taken me past the gastronomically renowned Hotel Farfense owned and run by the very talented and friendly Giamperio and Daniela with their daughter Francesca and son Federico (who incidentally cooks the best pizzas in Le Marche), I took a right turn up the Via Roma to more cheering and clapping.

Now I knew why Ian, Libby, Francesca, Stephanie and Kate had all been so reticent about talking about my arrival at Santa Vittoria. I found out later that 6pm was the appointed hour because most of the town band had been on the beach all afternoon and they needed time to get home, change and tune up before I waltzed (actually – plodded) up the road past Rosario's.

On my walk up to our street, at the top of the town, I felt the bumps of the cobbles as never before. I must have been walking with sore feet for weeks, but only now on the final approach would my brain allow the pain to register. I also thought how sad it was that Alice, as a nurse, was on nights and therefore unable to come out and see me finish.

Kate was waiting for me on the steps of our house in Via Mazzini. Having heard the band playing, she knew that I would be coming soon. What she saw was an exhausted traveller with a very rusty weathered face, a bleached straggly beard, a Tarp hat hanging from his belt, and an expression that said 'for goodness sake, let me get this rucksack off. I can't walk another step because I ache all over and my shoulders are killing me.' That was what the expression said, but what I actually said was 'Hello love, remember me?' After a long, big hug, the removal of my deadweight rucksack and the touching of our door – we both had no time to waste. In minutes we were ready to walk down to the centre of the town.

The Chiostro, behind the Bar Centrale, was awash with people. A small band consisting of an accordion, trombone, sax, trumpet, drums and cymbals – just the sort of group to raise the spirits of a weary walker at his welcome party – was playing. I thought 'well done Valeriano.' Then the first of two bombshells were dropped. There tucked behind a pillar of the colonnade were Alice and Max, beaming with the surprise of it all. But then, as I was choking back the tears from seeing them, I was called over for an official welcome from Fabrizio with Ian standing there (fully recovered) waiting to translate. Having been alone for most of my 81 days away, I was now looking out at a large crowd and having a speech addressed to me by our Sindaco. I was trembling inside. That was when the second bombshell was dropped. It had been decided, by the town council, that since I had raised money for two charities on my walk and that I had promoted Italy, Le Marche and Santa Vittoria – I was going to be made an Honorary Citizen of Santa Vittoria. I was stunned. Never did I imagine such an honour would be bestowed on me, which is why my little speech penned at Gran Bosco, before I knew about the award, was read out in such a nervous and faltering way. I said (in Italian and English): 'From the bottom of my heart – a heartfelt thanks, to you all, for the warm welcome you have given me on my arrival into Santa Vittoria. It has taken me a long time to get here: 81 days, six nations, 2,134 km/1326miles, 2,652,000 steps and now I need a new pair of boots! I greatly appreciated the many good wishes I received during the walk. The support of my family and especially of my wife Kate was invaluable. I love Santa Vittoria in Matenano and Le Marche. You are all very dear to me. Thanks again to everyone.'

Then there were three cheers, a spontaneous collection for my charities, glasses of prosecco and beer, cakes and savouries, more music from the band and chats with scores of people who just came up to me to talk, congratulate or just hug. What an ending and no one in a white vest in sight. I thought, as the party continued, that if Franz Kafka really did say the quote that is always attributed to him: 'Paths are made by walking,' then I had just made a path to Santa Vittoria that never existed before. That was my contribution. So, when people asked constantly for the next few weeks: 'Are you going to walk back to Hebden Bridge now?' The answer was always 'No. I would love to but maybe not just yet, or even in this lifetime.'

Selected Bibliography

Alighieri, Dante., The Divine Comedy (1472)

Burns, Robbie., To a Mouse, (1786)

Dylan, Thomas., The Force That through the Green Fuse, (1934), The Dylan Thomas Omnibus, Orion, 2024

Elliot, T.S., The Hollow Men, 1925

Fermor, Patrick Leigh., A Time of Gifts, John Murray, 1977

Hartmann, Kathrin., We must stay outside, Random House, 2012

Heine, Heinrich., Die Lorelei, 1824

Hesse, Hermann., Siddhartha, (1922), Penguin Essentials, 2011

Hesse, Hermann., Steppenwolf (1927), Penguin Essentials, 2011

Hunt, Nick., Walking the Woods and the Water, Nicholas Brearley, 2014

Kempis, Thomas à., The Imitation of Christ, (1420-27), Penguin Classics, 2013

Kepler, Johannes., Astronomia Nova, 1609

Ovid., Metamorphoses, (8AD), Penguin Classics, 2016

Seabrook, W.B., An Adventure in Arabia, Harrap and Co, 1927

The Hiker & Camper' magazine, August 1933

Traditional, German., (about 1200) The Song of the Nibelungs, Penguin Classics, 2018

Acknowledgements

When I first conceived of walking to Italy from England I felt a mixture of boyish excitement and dread at the prospect. I might have parked it as a 'good idea' if Kate (my long suffering wife) had not encouraged, supported and cajoled me into believing that I could do it. In the end, my obsession with the project grew its own wings and I let the warm air of optimism buoy me up above the rocky obstacles that littered the ground below me.

Like Patrick Leigh Fermor, I looked forward to writing about my adventures. Unlike him, I was lucky to have several family members who were keen to join me on what amounted to six - out of the 81 - days: Kate in Holland and Germany; Anna (sister-in-law) in Germany; Alice and Max (daughter and son-in-law) in Germany, Mark (nephew) in Austria and Libby (cousin) in Italy. I am truly indebted to their unfailing energy, friendship and passion for the journey.

I discovered that my hosts (Couchsurfing, Airbnb and campsites) were a great source of support, particularly at the end of a long day when I was ready to curl up in a ball and hibernate. Thanks to everyone who helped me get to Italy by providing warmth, food, drink, shelter and laughs, especially those who did it by dipping into their own pockets.

Jane Schaffer, Alan McGlynn and everyone else at Seven Arches Publishing have been great colleagues and friends with whom to work. Jane proved to be a marvellous publisher whose encouragement was invaluable, especially when deadlines loomed. Many thanks to Sara Valentin-Byers and Gaynor Greenwood who proofread the manuscript with eagle eyes, but in the end any mistakes that remain are mine alone.

I am grateful to my daughters for suggesting the two charities for which I fund raised through JustGiving: The British Kidney Patients' Association and Creating Adventures for Adults with Complex Learning Difficulties.

Thank you for the help and support from the British Heart Foundation.

Kickstarter Contributors

Door to Door in 81 Days was partly funded through a Kickstarter campaign. The author, Roger Gill and everyone at Seven Arches Publishing would like to express their sincere gratitude to all those who supported our campaign so generously:

Sally

Georgina Schaffer

Tim Sargent

Max

Kate Gill

Michael Troke

Nick Wigmore

Joanna Low

Brenda Brown

David Atherton

Margaret McGowan

Peter Wilson

Christopher Reason

George Mandis

Muthoni Garland

Mark Pinto

Jenna Port

Mark Dean

Ian Hocking

Jan Knai

Trevor Sunderland

Ann McDonnell

Gregor Donnelly

Wallace Garland

Vladislav Bukerova

Christano Ubaldi

Anthea Wilton

Mike Whitehead

Yvonne Weatherhead

Sara Hayton

Guy Mayger

Julie Yates

D Guardascione

Annette Calver

Madeleine

Avril Emmerson

Margaret Nivison

Pete

Hannah Nunn

Linda Green

Emma Ferguson

Michelle Hayes

Guest 1168750064

Libby Campbell

E Kellett

Guest 57748239

Amy Ruth McEwen

Tina Freeman

Richard Wilmshurst

Guest 2079614877

Guest 1369107789

Guest 237224946

Guest 27143380